Baptists and War

McMaster General Studies Series, vol. 5
Canadian Baptist Historical Society Series, vol. 2

Baptists and War
Essays on Baptists and Military Conflict, 1640s–1990s

edited by
Gordon L. Heath
and
Michael A. G. Haykin

☙PICKWICK *Publications* • Eugene, Oregon

BAPTISTS AND WAR
Essays on Baptists and Military Conflict, 1640s–1990s

Copyright © 2015 Wipf and Stock Publishers. All rights reserved. Except for brief quotations in critical publications or reviews, no part of this book may be reproduced in any manner without prior written permission from the publisher. Write: Permissions. Wipf and Stock Publishers, 199 W. 8th Ave., Suite 3, Eugene, OR 97401.

McMaster Divinity College Press
1280 Main Street West
Hamilton, Ontario, Canada
L8S4K1

Pickwick Publications
An Imprint of Wipf and Stock Publishers
199 W. 8th Ave., Suite 3
Eugene, OR 97401

www.wipfandstock.com

ISBN 13: 978-1-62564-674-3

Cataloguing-in-Publication Data

Baptists and War: Essays on Baptists and Military Conflict, 1640s–1990s / edited by Gordon L. Heath and Michael A. G. Haykin

xii + 234 p. ; 23 cm. Includes bibliographical references.

ISBN 13: 978-1-62564-674-3

1. 2. 3. I.

CALL NUMBER 2014

Manufactured in the U.S.A.   03/09/2015

Scripture quotations marked NASB are taken from the New American Standard Bible® copyright © 1960, 1962, 1963, 1968, 1971, 1972, 1973, 1975, 1977, 1995 by The Lockman Foundation. Used by permission (www.Lockman.org).

Table of Contents

List of Contributors | vii

Introduction—Michael A. G. Haykin and Gordon L. Heath | xi

1 Baptists, Peace, and War: The Seventeenth-Century British Foundations—Anthony R. Cross | 1

2 Andrew Fuller and the War against Napoleon —Paul L. Brewster, Sr. | 32

3 A House Uniting: Americans, Baptists, and the War of 1812 —James Tyler Robertson | 58

4 The Nile Expedition, New Imperialism and Canadian Baptists, 1884–1885—Gordon L. Heath | 98

5 The Call to Arms: The Reverend Thomas Todhunter Shields, World War One and the Shaping of a Militant Fundamentalist —Doug Adams | 115

6 Reluctant Warriors: Australian Baptists in World War Two —Robert D. Linder | 150

7 Soviet Baptists and the Cold War—Maurice Dowling | 169

8 Baptists and the War in Vietnam: Responses to "America's Longest War"—Nathan A. Finn | 203

Author Index | 231

Subject Index | 233

List of Contributors

EDITORS

GORDON L. HEATH (PhD, St. Michael's College) is Associate Professor of Christian History at McMaster Divinity College, and serves as Director of the Canadian Baptist Archives. His recent appointment to the Centenary Chair in World Christianity at the college reflects his growing interest in how Christian communities around the world have been eliminated. His publications include *A War with a Silver Lining: Canadian Protestant Churches and the South African War, 1899–1902* (MQUP, 2009), and *Doing Church History: A User-friendly Introduction to Researching the History of Christianity* (Clements, 2008). He has also recently edited *Canadian Churches and the First World War* (Pickwick, 2014), and co-edited *Canadian Baptists and Public Life* (Pickwick, 2012), and *Baptism: Historical, Theological and Pastoral Perspectives* (Pickwick, 2011).

MICHAEL A. G. HAYKIN was born in England of Irish and Kurdish parents. He is currently Professor of Church History at the Southern Baptist Theological Seminary, Louisville, Kentucky. Dr. Haykin is the author of a number of books dealing with Patristic and Baptist studies and is also the general editor of a forthcoming 16-volume edition of the works of Andrew Fuller (Walter de Gruyter). Dr. Haykin and his wife Alison live in Dundas, Ontario.

OTHER CONTRIBUTORS

DOUG ADAMS is currently pursuing a PhD in history at the University of Western Ontario. His father was a loyal supporter of Shields and in time became the principal of Toronto Baptist Seminary. Doug studied at the seminary and graduated in 1977 with a Master of Divinity degree. He went on to serve as an assistant pastor in Briscoe Street Baptist Church and later as Pastor of East Williams Baptist Church, a position he occupied for twenty years. During that time, Doug also pursued further education at the University of Western Ontario and by the mid-1990s achieved his Master of Arts degree. Doug also served as the Professor of Church History at Toronto Baptist Seminary for nearly twenty years. Involvement in both Shields's school and his church gives Doug unique opportunities to study the life of Dr. Shields. Jarvis Street Baptist church has graciously granted him access to their extensive archives, which contain most of the Shields papers. Doug is currently writing his dissertation on Shields as something of a revisionist biographical account of Shields's life and ministry.

PAUL BREWSTER is the pastor of Ryker's Ridge Baptist Church, Madison, Indiana. He is also an Assistant Professor of Religion at Liberty University and a fellow of the Andrew Fuller Center for Baptist Studies at the Southern Baptist Theological Seminary, Louisville, KY. He has been in the pastoral ministry for almost twenty-five years, serving congregations in Arkansas, North Carolina, and Indiana. He was educated at the University of Arkansas (BA 1986), New Orleans Baptist Theological Seminary (MDiv 1989), and Southeastern Baptist Theological Seminary (PhD 2007). He is the author of *Andrew Fuller: Model Pastor-Theologian* (Broadman & Holman, 2010) and several articles on Baptist history and theology. Pastor Brewster and his wife Debbie have four grown children.

ANTHONY R. CROSS is a Member of the Faculty of Theology and Religion, University of Oxford, and in the fall of 2013 was Scholar in Residence in the Department of Dogmatics and Ecumenical Theology, Vrije Universiteit, Amsterdam. Among his most recent work is *Recovering the Evangelical Sacrament: Baptisma Semper Reformandum* (Wipf & Stock, 2013); with Pieter J. Lalleman and Peter J. Morden, editor of *Grounded in Grace: Essays in Honour of Ian M. Randall* (Spurgeon's College and The Baptist Historical Society, 2013); with John H. Y. Briggs, editor of *Freedom and the Powers: Perspectives from Baptist History* (Didcot: The Baptist Historical Society, 2014), and, forthcoming, an historical and theological volume on the importance of a theologically educated Baptist ministry, *Able and Evangelical* (Wipf & Stock, 2015), and a volume on *Baptism and the Origins of the Baptists* (Wipf & Stock).

List of Contributors

MAURICE DOWLING comes originally from Liverpool. He majored in Russian language, literature, and history at the University of Cambridge (BA 1969), obtained the BD from London University in 1973, and completed his MTh (1982) and PhD (1987) in Patristics at Queen's University, Belfast. For over 40 years Maurice taught at the Irish Baptist College in Northern Ireland, mainly in the areas of church history, historical theology and Hebrew. He was a Recognized Teacher in the theology department at Queen's University, and subsequently also in theology departments at the Universities of Wales and of Chester. Since his retirement in 2012 he has continued to teach and to supervise research on a part-time basis. For over 20 years Maurice travelled regularly to the former Soviet Union, teaching short-term courses at seminaries and Bible colleges and ministering in many (mainly Baptist) churches and speaking at conferences. For nearly 30 years he has been an elder in a Baptist fellowship in Belfast. Maurice is married to Brenda and they have four children.

NATHAN A. FINN serves as Associate Professor of Historical Theology and Baptist Studies at Southeastern Baptist Theological Seminary in Wake Forest, North Carolina. He has contributed over two-dozen essays to scholarly books and journals and is co-author of a forthcoming Baptist history textbook. He also serves as an associate editor of the multi-volume *The Complete Works of Andrew Fuller* (Walter de Gruyter, forthcoming) to which he is contributing the volume on Sandemanianism. Nathan is married with four children and serves as one of the elders of the First Baptist Church of Durham, North Carolina.

ROBERT D. LINDER is University Distinguished Professor of History at Kansas State University in Manhattan, Kansas. He earned his BS degree in history and political science at Emporia State University and his MA and PhD in history from the University of Iowa. He taught at the University of Iowa as a Graduate Teaching Assistant and as a full-time faculty member at William Jewell College in Missouri before joining the faculty at KSU in 1965. He also has done postgraduate work at the University of Oxford and has been a visiting professor of history at the University of Wollongong and at Macquarie University in Australia. Linder is the author and/or editor of seventeen books and of scores of articles in professional journals and books. His main research interests lie in American, European, and Australian religious, and political and social history from the Reformation to the present. He spent eight years on the Manhattan

City Commission and was twice Mayor of his city. He served in the United States Army Reserve from 1959 to 1967, two years of which was on active duty. His forthcoming books include *The Age of Anxiety: Australian Evangelical Christians and the Inter-War Years* and *New Light on the Southern Cross: Essays on Australian Religious and Political History*.

JAMES TYLER ROBERTSON received his PhD in 2013 from McMaster Divinity College. He is currently editing his book *A Good Fight: The Religious War of 1812*. He has published journal articles and book chapters on a variety of subjects related to the War of 1812, Canadian history, missionaries, the crusades, British imperial history, and Baptist, Anglican, and Methodist histories. He currently works in the history department of Tyndale Seminary as well as pastoring two rural Baptist churches in southern Ontario. A frequent speaker at popular and academic societies, Robertson has presented on British identity in Northern Ireland, imperial history in England, and throughout America on the topic of Christianity in the early republic, military morality, and the religious implications of Francis Scott Key's "The Defence of Fort M'Henry" which became the American national anthem. He resides in Hamilton, Ontario.

Introduction

THE ESSAYS IN THIS volume were originally papers given at the fifth annual conference of The Andrew Fuller Center for Baptist Studies, co-sponsored by the Canadian Baptist Historical Society, which took place at The Southern Baptist Theological Seminary in Louisville, Kentucky. This annual conference is normally stretched over a two-day period with a variety of plenary sessions and some smaller parallel papers. All but three of the papers given at the plenary sessions on 26 and 27 September 2011—the three being those of Larry Kreitzer, Keith Harper, and George Rable—are contained in this volume.

While Baptists have generally not shunned military involvement, there has been a Baptist stream of pacifism, which the first paper by Anthony Cross seeks to ground in the Anabaptist witness in the sixteenth and seventeenth centuries, and which he sees represented in the thought of John Smyth. Cross's paper contrasts Smyth's view with that of Thomas Helwys, a forerunner of English Baptist engagement in the political and military turmoil of the mid-seventeenth century. Paul Brewster's paper then looks at the thought of the eighteenth-century author and preacher Andrew Fuller about war during the British Empire's struggle against Napoleon. Fuller recognized that there was a place for patriotism in the Christian life and thus the military defense of one's homeland against the aggression of a foreign power. Yet, he was quite adamant that loyalty to Christ superseded this natural duty. James Robertson's chapter reflects on the oft-forgotten (though not by Canadians) War of 1812 and Baptist response to it within the American republic. Gordon Heath's essay explores the exuberant support of Canadian Baptists for the fight of the mother country (the British Isles) in Egyptian Sudan and Abyssinia during the 1880s. Heath sees this support as a forerunner of the way Canadian Baptists would react when they were called to greater sacrifice during the South African War at the turn of the century.

Introduction

Four essays look at Baptist response to war in the twentieth century, possibly the bloodiest century on record. Doug Adams details the impact of World War I upon the life and ministry of T. T. Shields, and sees it as a key turning-point in that influential Baptist's thinking. Doug's essay is the only one in this volume not actually given at the conference. Robert Linder examines the way Australian Baptists approached participation in World War II and, upon the whole, finds them "reluctant warriors." The seventh paper draws upon Maurice Dowling's extensive knowledge of and involvement with Russian Baptists, and provides a fascinating look at their perspective on the Cold War of the 1950s and 1960s. The final paper in this book is a fresh examination by Nathan Finn of the way that American Baptists profoundly disagreed among themselves about how to regard the Vietnam War—in this they reflected the larger culture of the United States.

Preparing these papers for publication has been a strong reminder for the editors of two things in particular: while Baptists in their history have been certain that, as the saying has it, "war is hell," they have not been able to agree about how to respond to it. In our day, it is imperative that serious thought be given to the way Baptist followers of the Prince of Peace should live in a world increasingly filled with violence and war and rumors of war. That this book might in some small way aid in that process of thinking is the ardent wish of its editors.

Michael A. G. Haykin and Gordon L. Heath

July 2014

1

Baptists, Peace, and War: The Seventeenth-Century British Foundations

Anthony R. Cross

INTRODUCTION

As a tradition we should rightly be proud of the fact that there have been two[1] Baptist Nobel Peace Prize winners—Martin Luther King, Jr., in 1964,[2] and Jimmy Carter in 2002.[3] That said, however, we have had comparatively little to say on the issue of peace, and, all too often, have been all but silent at times when a prophetic voice has been required. None of this is to our credit.

H. F. Lorkin's 1969 booklet examining Baptists and the issues of war and peace opens with the question, "What do Baptists teach about war?" The author's answer is that this is "impossible to answer" because Baptists do not have a denominational structure that works out answers to moral

---

1. See "50 Nobel Laureates and Other Great Scientists Who Believe in God" (http://www.adherents.com/people/100_Nobel.html); accessed 18 February 2014.

2. See "Martin Luther King Jr.—Biographical," online: http://nobelprize.org/nobel_prizes/peace/laureates/1964/king-bio.html (accessed 18 February 2014); and "Martin Luther King Jr.—Nobel Lecture," online: http://nobelprize.org/nobel_prizes/peace/laureates/1964/king-lecture.html (accessed 18 February 2014).

3. See "The Nobel Peace Prize 2002," online: http://nobelprize.org/nobel_prizes/peace/laureates/2002/#, (accessed 18 February 2014); and Jimmy Carter, "Nobel Lecture," http://nobelprize.org/nobel_prizes/peace/laureates/2002/carter-lecture.html (accessed 18 February 2014).

questions for its members. Rather, "we are expected to find the answers for ourselves," and he ties this in with the Baptist principle of liberty of conscience,[4] a note that Timothy George also strikes in his 1984 article, "Between Pacifism and Coercion: The English Baptist Doctrine of Religious Toleration."[5] Lorkin maintains that:

> One of the consequences of such liberty is the variety of individual views on the same matter of Christian concern, even though the Scriptures are the same for all. Baptist views on war are a notable example of this. On the one hand, Baptist chaplains, officers and men have served with distinction in the armed forces since the days of the Civil War. On the other hand, in the last two centuries Baptists have been imprisoned as conscientious objectors, following a pacifist tradition which can be traced at intervals since the sixteenth century. And in between these extremes, there have been many who have preferred to have no pronounced views on the subject, but to withdraw from such controversial matters, to pray and practise simple virtue. These varied views have existed side by side, and only very occasionally have they been openly and publicly debated.

What is needed, then, is dialogue, and Lorkin offers his booklet "in support of such dialogue, on a matter increasingly vital to the world and to the Christian, a matter in which the agonies of personal choice are linked with a complex pattern of racial and international relations."[6] Written at the height of the Cold War and the Vietnam War, his words read as strikingly contemporary, not least when he speaks of "high explosives, remote-control weapons and the mushroom cloud of nuclear bombs," though now the conflicts are the Second Gulf War, the war on terror, and a time of revolutions in the Middle East and North and West Africa, and when talk is not just of conventional warfare, but also dirty bombs and biological weapons.

Twenty-four years after Lorkin, Paul Dekar published his *For the Healing of the Nations: Baptist Peacemakers*, which offers a helpful Baptist discussion of the various nuances of the word "peace," and he bases his book around three concepts. First, there is "negative peace," which he understands "as opposition to war." Second, there is "positive peace," which is the "effort to eliminate the causes of war." Third, there is "prophecy,"

---

4. Lorkin, *Baptist Views*, 3.
5. George, "Between Pacifism and Coercion."
6. Lorkin, *Baptist Views*, 4.

which is a "critique of religion and wider society based on a biblical vision of a better world."[7] He then draws two further helpful distinctions.

First, there is "pacifism," for which he adopts as his working definition "principled opposition to all war,"[8] while recognizing that it can mean different things to different people:

> It can mean conscientious objection, or refusal to bear arms and, in some cases, to pay for the preparation of war. It can refer to love of enemy. Some pacifists withdraw from society. Others engage in active politics. Some devote themselves to "life service for the enthronement of love in personal, social, commercial and national life." Others pledge to resist war. Some equate pacifism with weakness or appeasement. Others identify pacifism with nonviolent struggle. Some regard pacifism as a faith. Others see it as ideology. Many pacifists eschew use of the word altogether. Others think they ought to.[9]

Second, a cognate to pacifism is "pacificism," "the advocacy of peaceful processes such as arbitration and conciliation."[10] All these nuances have found expression in Baptist life and thought. The present chapter does not set out to distinguish these different understandings or their expression by individual Baptists and by various Baptist bodies, because they are not mutually exclusive; rather they often overlap in the thought of various Baptists as they have sought to respond to changing circumstances.

What is particularly useful is Lorkin's classification of three views held by Baptists throughout their 400-year history. First, there is the pietistic view. This recognizes that the world is gripped by evil, and those adopting this position "contract out" and separate themselves from the evil world. They do not bear arms, take oaths, appeal to the law, or engage in politics, for these are all worldly; rather their focus is on the spiritual.[11] Second, there is the patriotic view where obedience to the monarch or government is seen as a Christian duty.[12] Third, there is what Lorkin calls the pacifist view in which Baptist pacifists try to express their beliefs in

---

7. Dekar, *For the Healing of the Nations*, 14.
8. Ibid., 12.
9. Ibid., 11.
10. Ibid., 12.
11. Lorkin, *Baptist Views*, 5–7.
12. Ibid., 7–9.

positive service and also in their refusal to fight and kill.[13] This framework is particularly useful as the founding fathers of the Baptist movement, John Smyth and Thomas Helwys, exemplify the pietist and patriotic positions respectively, while the pacifist view is closely associated with the pietist one. That said, I am unconvinced that these three positions can be as sharply distinguished as Lorkin suggests.

The aim of this chapter is modest. It does not attempt to set Baptist views of peace and war within a broader ecclesiastical and/or social context, but merely to illustrate the variety of Baptist views in the formative years of their existence in Britain during the seventeenth century. And what we see is that in their differences of opinion, Smyth and Helwys raised many of the issues that reappear throughout 400 years of Baptists trying to deal with issues of peace and war.

JOHN SMYTH AND THE BAPTIST PIETIST VIEW

While I believe that the Baptist movement developed out of English Puritanism and Separatism in 1609,[14] within less than a year the majority of the first Baptists followed John Smyth's lead in seeking union with the local Anabaptists, a company of Waterlander Mennonites under the leadership of Hans de Ries. During this year, 1609–10, it is clear that the nascent Baptists and local Mennonites had considerable contact, so much so that the split between Smyth and Helwys was interpreted by Helwys as due to Smyth's adoption of four positions that closely allied him with the Waterlanders' beliefs, and these comprised the four sections of Helwys's 1611 *An Advertisement or Admonition*—on Christ's flesh, on keeping the Sabbath, the issue of successionism, and on the role of the magistracy.[15] The Anabaptists, then, most certainly did influence the development of the pietist position among the first Baptists; therefore it is important that we briefly sketch the Anabaptist views of peace and war in order better to understand the adoption by some Baptists of the pietist viewpoint.

---

13. Ibid., 10–12.

14. Cross, "Adoption," 14–16. See also, e.g., Kliever, "General Baptists Origins"; White, *English Separatist Tradition, passim*; and Manley, "Origins of the Baptists."

15. Helwys, *Advertisement or Admonition*. However, at the end of his life, Smyth, *Last Booke*, 758, denied that it was succession that motivated his approach to join the Waterlanders; rather it was out of a desire for unity with them, desiring not to break "the bond of love and Brotherhood in churches."

The Anabaptists' formative statement of faith is *The Schleitheim Confession* (1527). Article 6 declares,

> The sword is ordained of God outside the perfection of Christ. It punishes and puts to death the wicked, and guards and protects the good. In the Law the sword was ordained for the punishment of the wicked and for their death, and the same [sword] is [now] ordained to be used by the worldly magistrates.

This contrasts sharply with "the perfection of Christ" where "only the ban is used for a warning and for the excommunication of the one who has sinned, without putting the flesh to death." In answer to whether a Christian should be a magistrate, believers should follow Christ and "not walk in darkness." The Anabaptists held a dualistic view of the worldly and spiritual realms, what they termed darkness and light. The government magistracy "is according to the flesh," while the Christian's is not of this world; their citizenship is "in this world," the Christian's "is in heaven"; "the weapons of their conflict and war are carnal and against the flesh only, but the Christian's weapons are spiritual, against the fortification of the devil. The worldlings are armed with steel and iron, but the Christian is armed with the armor of God, with truth, righteousness, peace, faith, salvation, and the Word of God."[16]

In his Hutterite *Confession of Faith* (1540–42), Peter Riedemann states, "One should therefore be obedient to rulers as to those who are appointed by God to protect us, as long as they do not attack the conscience or demand what is against God."[17] Since the office of government is appointed and instituted by God, it is both right and good, even if the positions are held by godless men. An earthly king was given to Israel because they rejected God and his reign over them, so the authority of government, Riedemann argues, comes from God's wrath.[18] Therefore, God's people "are not to use the worldly sword or rule with it"; instead "they should be led and ruled by the spirit of Christ alone." This illustrates well the dichotomy between the kingdom of this world and Christ's kingdom in Anabaptist—and later some Baptist—thought, for "as the old order

---

16. *The Schleitheim Confession*, Article 6. See also Stayer, *Anabaptists*, who shows that not all sixteenth-century Anabaptists were non-resistants, contending that the reality was far more diverse, and that there were militants among them. For a critical summary and discussion of Stayer's work, see Wright, "'The Sword': An Example of Anabaptist Diversity."

17. Friesen, *Riedemann's Hutterite Confession of Faith*, 130.

18. Ibid., 131.

was to punish evil, so the new is to recompense it with good. As the old way was to hate the enemy, so the new way commands us to love him," for Christ wants "his servants to submit themselves to [his kingdom] and become like him."[19] He continues:

> Therefore, all that was given in wrath must come to an end in Christ. It has no place in Christ. Governmental authority was given in wrath, so it cannot find a place in Christ or be a part of him. No Christian is a ruler, and no ruler is a Christian, for the child of blessing cannot be the servant of wrath. In Christ, temporal weapons are not used.[20]

As Riedemann expresses it later, "Christians should not take part in war, nor should they use force for purposes of vengeance,"[21] because vengeance belongs to God and so it is to be left to him and not practiced by his disciples. Jesus could have repaid evil with evil, and could have protected himself against his enemies, but he did not, and he would not let anyone else do so for him. Anabaptist pacifism comes out when Riedemann declares, "it is clear that Christians cannot take part in war or avenge themselves. Whoever does so forsakes and denies Christ and is untrue to Christ's nature."[22]

Many of these themes appear in the writings of other Anabaptists. Menno Simons, writing in 1535, contrasts the kingship of Christ and the pretensions of John of Leiden, who led the bloody debacle of Münster. For example, in the middle of summarizing the teaching of Jesus and Paul on the sword and repaying evil with evil, Simons asks, "How can Christians fight with the implements of war?" and states unequivocally, "It is forbidden to us to fight with physical weapons."[23]

For Pilgram Marpeck, "Even though we walk in the flesh, yet we do not fight with physical means," for "our victory is not won with our own power and might, nor is it done with earthly or physical power and sword."[24] Like Simons, Marpeck condemns the recourse to violence of the

---

19. Ibid., 132 and 133 respectively.

20. Ibid., 133. In the same way that a Christian cannot be a ruler, neither can they "go to court or be a judge." See the discussion in ibid. on "Whether a Christian Can Go to Court or Sit in Judgment," 139–40 (p. 140).

21. Ibid., 134–35.

22. Ibid., 135.

23. Simons, "Blasphemy," 45.

24. Marpeck, "Admonition," 165.

Münsterites in 1534–35, as well as the use of the sword by Luther during the Peasants' Revolt in 1525, and Zwingli's involvement in the two battles of Kappel, during the second of which in 1531 he was killed. Of these three, Marpeck writes,

> All of these Satan raised up in order to confuse and disrupt the true baptism of Christ, which, through patience in faith and love alone, can do good to friend and enemy alike by fighting with the sword of the Spirit in the Word of truth . . . [N]o true Christian needs to occupy or defend either city, land, or people, as earthly lords do, nor to carry on with violence, for such belongs to the earthly and temporal rulers and not at all to true Christians, who show forth the faith in Christ . . . Those who are truly and correctly baptized in Christ are baptized with Christ in patience under tribulation. Committed to suffer even unto their physical death, every Christian who is baptized with Christ is a participant in His tribulation.[25]

Passages such as these could be multiplied many times over from the writings of other Anabaptists, among them leaders such as Hans Denck and Balthasar Hubmaier,[26] and are also to be found in the writings of the Waterlander Mennonites in Amsterdam,[27] the city in which the soon-to-be first Baptists settled in 1608.

The two leaders of the first Baptists were John Smyth and Thomas Helwys. Smyth's theological pilgrimage took him from being an Anglican/Puritan, through Separatist views to being a Baptist, and finally holding Mennonite convictions.[28] Timothy George notes that while Smyth's rejection of Calvinist understandings of original sin and predestination coinciding with his move towards the Mennonites in 1610 have been the focus of most scholars' work, less attention has been given "to the equally

---

25. Ibid., 209–10 (the original is italicized).

26. A useful collection of extracts from Anabaptist writers on both government and non-resistance is to be found in Klaassen, *Anabaptism in Outline*, 244–81; see also the brief bibliographies supplied at the end of each chapter.

27. De Ries's "A Statement of Faith Presented to the Town Council of Middelburg by Hans de Ries in 1578, while in Prison," quoted by Dyck, "Middelburg Confession"; see especially what de Ries says on peace, war, and the sword in Article VIII, "The Church", 152, Article XI, "On Government," and Article XII, "On War," 153–54. On 147 n. 1, Dyck describes de Ries as "a recognized leader and pioneer of unity and peace" in the Waterlander Mennonite group, and refers to his dissertation, "Hans de Ries." See the other articles by Dyck below.

28. See Burgess, *John Smith*; Coggins, *Congregation*; Lee, *Theology*; and Wright, *Early English Baptists*, 13–44.

significant shift . . . on the question of coercive jurisdiction of the magistrate and the proper Christian response to force and violence."[29] This is clearly important, because the difference of opinion on the magistracy was an important matter that contributed to the parting of the ways between Smyth and Helwys in 1610–11.

While the Anabaptists' discussions relating to peace revolve around the language of the magistracy *and* the sword, Smyth's and Helwys's language focuses on the magistracy and the means they employ to sanction those who contravene the laws of the land. In 1605, while still a Puritan in Anglican orders, Smyth maintained that the magistrate was to enforce the commandments when "the Commandments concerning justice and equitie is transgressed," that is, in the earthly realm, but also when those matters pertain to the kingdom of God, that is, the spiritual realm.[30] His acceptance of a hierarchical structure in society is reflected in his belief that the devil wished to abolish the magistracy and that the Anabaptists' egalitarianism did away with all rule and authority. This would remove the fear of punishment and the hope of reward. "[I]t is better," he says, "to have a Tyrant than no King," even though "a Tyrant might doe and suffer much impietie and iniquitie, yet some good must needes proceed from him," for it is better to have tyranny than anarchy as there is "some order in the one, and none in the other."[31] For Smyth at this time, religious toleration would result in the kingdom of God being pushed out by the devil's kingdom, for the devil would subtly take advantage of human inclination to false doctrine and worship, and thousands would follow strange religions. Therefore, "the Magistrates should cause all men to worship the true God, or else punish them with imprisonment, confiscation of goods, or death as the qualitie of the cause requireth."[32]

By 1606, Smyth had become a Separatist and one of the leaders of the Scrooby-Gainsborough congregation in the East Midlands, and two years later led his congregation to Amsterdam. When, in 1609, Smyth baptized himself, then Helwys and the rest of the Separatist congregation, thereby founding the first Baptist church,[33] he still acknowledged that magistrates were ordained by God "that every soule ought to be subject

---

29. George, "Between Pacifism and Coercion," 32.
30. Smyth, *Paterne*, 165.
31. Ibid., 165–66.
32. Ibid., 166.
33. See Cross, "Adoption."

unto them" for "they are the ministers of God for our wealth: that we ought to be subject unto them for conscience sake: that they are the ministers of God to take vengeance on them that do evil." However, when magistrates were converted to the true faith and added to the true church by baptism Smyth admitted he did not know what to tell them to do; he simply expressed the hope that the Lord would show them what to do.[34]

Timothy George suggests that Smyth's reluctance to make a definitive break on the question of the role of the magistrate probably reflects a tension within the young Baptist church that would eventually lead to its split. The minority led by Helwys refused to join Smyth and the majority's application to join the Mennonites. They believed that Smyth's re-baptism and the baptism of the whole congregation had indeed been valid and required no validation from the Anabaptists whom Smyth had come to recognize as also a true church after their baptism, and one that antedated their own.[35]

In 1577 Hans de Ries and four others had written the first Waterlander confession of faith,[36] and, while the earliest extant edition is that of 1618,[37] the first version is believed to have been revised in 1610[38] for the discussions between the Baptists and the Waterlanders.[39] Article 37 on "Government" recognizes the secular authority as ordained by God as necessary for maintaining public life and orderly citizenship, and for the protection of the good and punishment of the evil, and says that believers are to obey magistrates so long as they do not contravene God's word. But this office was not for members of Christ's church. Rather disciples "are called to lead a nonresistant life" and nothing is further from the call to follow in the Master's footsteps "than to rule this world with the sword." While in maintaining their position de Ries declares, "we in no way seek to despise honest government," nevertheless "the waging of war, the destroying of life

---

34. Smyth, *Character*, 572, "The Epistle to the Reader."

35. George, "Between Pacifism and Coercion," 34. Details of the events and communications between Smyth's and Helwys's groups and the Waterlanders are discussed by Cross, "Adoption," 24–26.

36. Dyck, "First Waterlandian," reproduces the confession on 8–13. See also Lumpkin, *Baptist Confessions*, 44–66, and his introduction, 41–43.

37. Dyck, "Short Confession," reproduces the confession on 11–19.

38. See Coggins, *Congregation*, 84–94; Coggins, "A Short Confession of Hans de Ries."

39. In the 1618 Confession's preface (see Coggins, *Congregation*, 85 n. 82, citing Cate, *Geschiedenis*, 1:386), de Ries states that he wrote it "for the use of some Englishmen, who had fled from England for their conscience' sake."

and property of the enemy, etc., which things do not harmonize with the new life in Christ—lead us to avoid these offices and service."[40]

Smyth and his group signed de Ries's confession,[41] and at some point Smyth wrote in Latin a *Defense of de Ries's Confession* (1610).[42] Also in support of their application to join the local Waterlanders, Smyth wrote first a *Short Confession of Faith in XX Articles by John Smyth* (probably late 1609, Latin title, *Corde credimus*),[43] followed by a 38-article confession entitled *A Short Confession of Faith* (1610).[44] While the *Confession in . . . XX Articles* has nothing relevant to our subject, in Article 35 of the *Short Confession*, Smyth echoes much of de Ries's confession in that the magistracy is a "necessary ordinance of God," necessary "for the preservation of the common estate," "for the reward of the good and punishing of the evil," and believers are to obey the magistrates, but it is not an office for them to hold. Rather, disciples are commanded to follow Christ's "unarmed and unweaponed life, and of his cross-bearing footsteps." Wars and the hurting of enemies' bodies or goods do not belong to Christ's way, so it "beseemeth not Christians to administer these offices."[45] In his *Defense of de Ries's Confession*, Article 10, Smyth also denies that a Christian can be a magistrate, because the two kingdoms preclude it. Christ is a spiritual king and his kingdom is spiritual, and its weapons, laws, punishments, rewards, soldiers, and warfare are all spiritual; therefore "I do not see how the church of Christ can administer that external and fleshly commonwealth." A little later he declares, "when Christ bade us to love our enemies, I wonder how the Christian magistrate can take revenge of his foes?"[46] At the end of his defense of de Ries's Article 37,

---

40. Dyck, "Short Confession," 18–19. All quotations from 19.

41. See Coggins, *Congregation*, 89, for a reproduction of their signatures.

42. For the Latin, see Whitley, *Works*, 2:685–709. The English translation is by Coggins, *Congregation*, 172–94.

43. Smyth, *Corde credimus*, in Whitley, *Works*, 2:682–84; "Short Confession of Faith in XX Articles by John Smyth (1609)," in Lumpkin, *Baptist Confessions*, 100–101.

44. Smyth, "Short Confession," in Lumpkin, *Baptist Confessions*, 102–13.

45. Ibid., Article 35, 111–12. The text around the discussion of wars and Christ's enemies is unclear in several places, but the above conveys the apparent meaning of this article.

46. Smyth, *Defense of de Ries's Confession*, Article 10, in Coggins, *Congregation*, 182.

Smyth categorically states, "neither Christ nor the apostles nor that first and pure church recognized the office of magistrate or the use of the civil sword."[47]

After Smyth's death in August 1612, his congregation published his *Propositions and Conclusions*, which comprised 100 articles,[48] and, as his last confession, it sets out his final position on the magistracy. As George notes, it "reflects the extent of his move toward the Anabaptist view of the state."[49] Article 83 recognizes that the magistrate "is a disposition or permissive ordinance of God, for the good of mankinde: that one man like the bruite beasts devoure not another . . . and that justice and civilitie may be preserved amonge men," who must please God by doing what is righteous and just in God's eyes. Article 84 adds that despite his office the magistrate is not "to meddle with religion, or matters of conscience, to force and compell men to this or that form of religion, or doctrine: but to leave Christian religion free, to every mans conscience, and to handle onely civil transgressions . . . injuries and wronges of men against man." But, Article 85 declares, should the magistrate become a disciple

> he must deny himself, take up his crosse, and follow Christ: he must love his enemies and not kill them, he must pray for them, and not punish them, he must feed them and give them drink, not imprison them: banish them: dismember them: and spoyle their Goods: he must suffer persecution and affliction with Christ, and be slaundered, reviled, blasphemed, scourged, buffeted, spit upon, imprisoned and killed with Christ: and that by the authoritie of magistrates, which things he cannot possiblie doe, and reteyne the revendge of the sword.[50]

George's summary of Smyth's position is succinct:

> By the end of his life, then, Smyth had embraced an apolitical, radically pacifist view of the state. In good agreement with the Schleitheim Confession, Smyth believed that the sword was ordained by God outside the perfection of Christ. But it was a "permissive ordinance" only, playing no positive role within the church. The office of magistrate, with its penchant for violence,

---

47. Ibid., Article 37, 193.

48. Smyth, *Propositions*, in Whitley, *Works*, 2:733–50; and in Lumpkin, *Baptist Confessions*, 124–42.

49. George, "Between Pacifism and Coercion," 35.

50. Smyth, *Propositions*, 748.

war, and capital punishment, was fundamentally at odds with the Christian commitment to noncoercion.[51]

THOMAS HELWYS AND THE BAPTIST PATRIOTIC VIEW

More widespread among Baptists than the pietistic view of war and peace has been the patriotic view, first articulated by Thomas Helwys. In the 1611 *Declaration of Faith*, Helwys contrasts Smyth's denial that Christians could be magistrates[52] with his own view, expressed in Article 24:

> That Magistracie is a Holie ordinance off GOD, that everie soule ought to bee subject to it not for feare onelie, but for conscience sake. Magistraets are the ministers off GOD for our wealth, they beare not the sword for nought. They are the ministers off GOD to take vengance on them that doe evil . . . And therefore they may bee members off the Church off CHRIST, reteining their Magistracie, for no Holie Ordinance off GOD debarreth anie from being a member off CHRISTS Church. They beare the sword off GOD, which sword in all Lawfull administracions is to bee defended and supported by the servants off GOD that are under their Government.[53]

In *An Advertisement or Admonition*, also published in 1611, Helwys wrote "Of Magistracie," which shows that this had become a key issue between the two former friends and their respective congregations. This section opens with the statement that the king, princes, and magistrates, "ruleing & governing by the power of god, with the sword of Justice, may be members of the church of Christ reteyning their Magistracie," and that anyone who resists their power resists God's ordinance.[54]

> They are further called. The ministers of god, and their administration is set downe. To take vengance of them that do evill, and to praise them that do well. And the instrument wherewith they are to punish evilldoers, is the sword. And in all this they are the ministers of god for good & for the good of gods children especially . . . Thus is their power (being of god) holie & good: and

---

51. George, "Between Pacifism and Coercion," 36.
52. Helwys, *Short Declaration*, B2r.
53. Ibid., A6 v.
54. Helwys, *Advertisement or Admonition*, 55–56.

their office & administration holie, & good being . . . appointed of god for good . . .⁵⁵

This was not, however, to cede a free hand to magistrates, for they "are comaunded of god to judg righteous judgment."⁵⁶

But what about Christians and the sword? According to Helwys, "the thing that misleads you all"—and here I think he is addressing not just Smyth and his congregation, but the Waterlander Mennonites as well, as they had influenced Smyth's change of mind—is that "you can see no sword" other than the sword of the Spirit, the Bible, "and no armor but spirituall armor in the kingdome of Christ: and therefore the disciples of that kingdome (say you) must have no other weapons, nor put on no other armor, and then can there be no putting to death, nor anie warr neither ought to be, but all spirituall."⁵⁷ It is unclear from this passage whether Helwys is permitting here, presumably in circumstances that might be described loosely as a "just war," the Christian's use of the sword, or whether this is solely the prerogative of the magistrate, Christian or otherwise. The latter is suggested by the way the argument in the paragraph ends with the discussion specifically revolving around the magistracy, though, that said, Helwys is directing his argument not only against Smyth and his congregation, and probably the Waterlanders as well, but also magistrates, some of whom he envisions can be Christians. In support of this interpretation, it is significant how he continues his discussion immediately after we left it, in which he references the Christian's treasure, bags, buildings, clothing, and food:

> If then you will cast a[way] all weapons and armor but su[c]h as the disciples of Christ use in his kingdome, so must you [also] c[a]st away all your baggs and treasure, and all your buyldings and houses, and you must weare no apparell, but spirituall apparel[, eate] no meate but spirituall meate. If to all this it be answered, that in the new Testament the lawfull [us]e of al these things be all[owe]d, wee [answer] eve[n] so is the lawfull use of Magistrac[ie] [with] the sword to punish evill doers allowed and approved in the new Testament, as is proved from Rom. 13. which no man with anie good conscience shall ever be able to gainsay.⁵⁸

55. Ibid., 56.
56. Ibid., 68.
57. Ibid., 72.
58. Ibid., 72–73.

This is in no way to suggest that war is anything other than a terrible thing. Helwys rhetorically asks, "what holie hart will not easilie be brought to thinke, that warr is an unchristianlike thinge, where there is so much slaughter and blood shedd, and which is accompanied with so manie calamities and mi[series], and which is followed & m[aint]eyned by so great force and violence by the arme of flesh: so likewise is it a lamentable thing that men should be executed and put to death by sen[te]nce of l[aw] for o[ff]ences."[59] Nevertheless, it is a "great sinne of ingratitude and unthankfulnes" to "disaprove of Magistrats, and of their punishing of evill doers by the sword," for if this did not happen then he believes that "all the Godlie on earth should be destroyed and the most Godly first."[60]

What is more, "who are fitter to support and mainteyne the holy ordinance of god then they that professe to be the children of god, and who are fitter to feight just and good battells then good and just men."[61] In the early seventeenth century the king could call his subjects to arms, and this is something Helwys and company could obey in all good conscience: "Our lord the king hath power to take our sonnes & our danhters [sic] to do all his services of warr, and of peace, yea all his servile service whatsoever,"[62] and he and later Baptists saw this as one of the legitimate claims of the monarch on his subjects.[63]

Smyth's congregation was finally accepted into fellowship with the Waterlanders in 1615,[64] three years after Smyth's death, and two years after Helwys and his smaller congregation had returned to London. During the 1620s the five English Baptist churches (in London, Tiverton, Sarum [Salisbury], Coventry, and Lincoln) with 150 members[65] were in

59. Ibid., 69.
60. Ibid., 75–76.
61. Ibid., 76.
62. Helwys, *Short Declaration*, 39–40.
63. Cf. Busher, *Religions*, 27, who says of king and Parliament, "we ought to give (by the law of God) al earthly honor feare and reverence, and willingly to pay tribute and custom, tax and tol, so much and so often as it shal please his Majesty and parliam: to appoint and gather by any officer or officers whatsoever. For whom also, and for the whole common wealth of al his kingdoms, we ought to be diligent and ready to hazard and lay downe, not onely our goods, but also our lives at al tymes and occasions."
64. Smyth's congregation was finally and completely assimilated into the Waterlander Mennonite church when the last services in English ended in 1640. See Coggins, *Congregation*, 107–14.
65. Letter by Cornelius C. Aresto (according to Burrage, *Dissenters*, 1:xiii, "Cornelius Claesz. Anslo[o]"; see Burrage's Dutch transcription of this letter, 239–41) to Hans

correspondence with the Waterlander Mennonites.[66] In early 1624, Elias Tookey and seventeen others separated from John Murton, who had succeeded Helwys as pastor on his death in 1615, and the London congregation he now led. In a letter dated 17 March 1525, Tookey discussed Christology, the taking of oaths, and war, as these were three areas over which they disagreed with the Waterlanders. On war they agreed with the Murton congregation that Christians can participate in a just war,

> as we must use spiritual weapons in a spiritual war, it follows simply that it is allowed to Christians to use worldly weapons in a worldly warfare for a righteous matter . . . Indeed, we think that it is now not less allowed to Christians to use worldly weapons or arms in a just war, with which they must protect themselves, as it has been before, and even to perform all other exercises, on condition only that they govern their warfare by justice . . . We are also of opinion that, if the enemies who carry on an unjust war are killed in that war, their blood will be on their heads, while the defenders are innocent.[67]

Smyth and his congregation had adopted the Mennonite position on the magistracy when applying to join with the Waterlanders, but Tookey and his group maintained the position we have already seen advocated by Helwys. In a letter dated 18 November 1526, Tookey suggested that the difference they had with the Waterlanders was not over the office of the magistracy but its "manner of execution," specifically, "whether the magistrature may use the sword which is given her by God to the protection of the right of the good subjects of this world against all invasions, wrongs, and similar crimes, and with which she punishes murderers."[68] For him, the office of the magistracy concerned worldly not ecclesiastical affairs, but he did not separate them, for "worldly ordinations" are also "from God, and are good." He therefore asked the Waterlanders, "Can those things which are good be an obstacle that one can be a disciple of Christ, or that he may be a Christian? Or are men hindered by the church to do those things which are good? . . . If magistracy impedes us from Christianity, then it must be considered as sin and evil," in which case

---

de Ries, dated 13 November 1626, in Evans, *Early Baptists*, 2:24–25 (25).

66. Some of this correspondence is reproduced by Burrage, *Dissenters*, 2:222–59; and Evans, *Early Baptists*, 2:21–44. The fuller correspondence is housed in the Municipal Archives, Amsterdam, MS#B 1367–MS#B 1378.

67. Evans, *Early Baptists*, 2:37–40 (40).

68. Ibid., 2:26–30 (28).

Christians are to desire its ruin and not pray for it, nor thank God for it. "But it is no evil and no sin," and Christians are to pray and thank God for it "as a good ordinance established by him . . . and, therefore, it cannot hinder one to be a Christian."[69]

Tookey develops this: as a good ordinance God has given the sword into the hands of the magistrates, who, as we have seen, he believed could be Christians, and God has done so "to revenge on him who commits evil, and to protect him who acts rightly." To take away the sword, then, would be to take away the magistracy's authority, for to do so would mean that the wicked would not "esteem their command, if they have not the power to compel one to the things that are right by the sword." The magistrates, therefore, need the sword to prevent those who would take life. But all this pertains to the worldly realm, in which the disciples can participate as magistrates: "arms are good, and the possession of them right among the disciples just as all other worldly things." But God does not allow their use "to protect his spiritual kingdom" because "the arms of the host of his kingdom are not carnal, but spiritual."[70]

If the interpretation put forward here of what Helwys was saying, which was carried on by Tookey, is valid—that there are occasions when it is their patriotic duty for Baptists to employ violence in defense of their country—then it set a precedent for both General and Particular Baptists fighting in the civil wars of the 1640s, their serving as army chaplains,[71] and, by extension, for Baptist service in the armed forces in later conflicts. But it must be underscored that these conflicts were not religious, for Baptists have almost always eschewed[72] the resort to violence to impose Christianity on anyone. That this has in fact been the case can now be illustrated.

The Particular Baptist First London Confession of 1644 was an apologetic work, seeking to answer unjust charges and misunderstandings of who they were. Articles 48 to 51 all deal with the civil magistracy, which,

---

69. Ibid., 2:28–29.

70. Ibid., 2:29.

71. See Laurence, *Parliamentary Army Chaplains*. E.g., the General Baptist James Brown served in Edinburgh (see Hannen, "Browne (or Brown), James [1615–c.1685]), while John Pendarves, Baptist and Fifth Monarchist, served as a chaplain in Cromwell's New Model Army, probably between 1645 and 1647. See Kreitzer, "Fifth Monarchist."

72. There have been exceptions, including some of those millenarians/millennialists in the seventeenth century who, spurred on by the times and the apocalyptic imagery of the Bible, sought to establish the kingdom of God by violent means. See below.

according to Article 48, is an ordinance of God "for the punishment of evill doers, and for the praise of them that doe well," and to whom subjection is to be given in the Lord; Article 49 says the supreme magistracy is the king and Parliament, and draws the distinction between civil laws that are to be obeyed, and some ecclesiastical laws that are not binding when they contravene Christians' consciences. "[Y]et are we bound to yeeld our persons to their pleasures" (cf. Article 51).[73] In *The Faith and Practise of Thirty Congregations* of 1651, Midland General Baptists note that in order that righteousness may reign and vice be overthrown, "we do own a Magistratical power for the governing of this our English Nation, to be determined in a just Parliamentary way."[74]

However, much of the attitude of Baptists during this period of civil and political revolution has to be deduced from their actions and reactions to events. Many General and Particular Baptists became embroiled in the social and ecclesiastical turmoil, upheaval, and ferment that marked the English revolutionary period (1638–60),[75] which provides the context for these two confessions. The machinery of ecclesiastical repression so closely allied to the system of episcopacy began to be dismantled by the Long Parliament, which began in November 1640, and these and other challenges to the monarchy's authority led to the outbreak of civil war in 1642. Along with Presbyterians and Independents (Congregationalists), Baptists actively fought on the Parliamentarians' side during the two phases of the English civil wars (1642–46 and 1648–49). General and Particular Baptists fought in the wars, not only in Cromwell's Parliamentary Army; they were also well-represented among the many radical sects that sprang up throughout the revolutionary period, up to the restoration of the monarchy.[76]

Both General and Particular Baptists served in Cromwell's Parliamentary Army, being "prepared to fight for a just cause and serve in the armies of a godly regime," and while "they shared the sectarian principle of the Anabaptists that the national church was unchristian, they also held to the Puritan ideal that reformation of society and its institutions

---

73. *Confession of Faith, of those Churches which are commonly (though falsly) called Anabaptists*, C3r–C4 r, quotation from C3v.

74. *Faith and Practice of Thirty Congregations*, Postscript, 30.

75. See Bell, *Apocalypse How?*

76. See, e.g., Hill, *World Turned Upside Down*; Watts, *Dissenters*, 117–42, on the Levellers and Fifth Monarchists; Dow, *Radicalism*; Underdown, *Revel, Riot and Rebellion*; McGregor and Reay, *Radical Religion*.

was possible through the action of godly men."[77] Among the many that could be mentioned who rose to high positions were Edmund Ludlow, Lieutenant-General in Ireland;[78] Colonel Henry Danvers, for a time Governor of Stafford;[79] Colonel John Hutchinson, made Governor of Nottingham Castle in 1643; and Captain Edmund Chillenden, who later became a Fifth Monarchist. Others rose to high office in the state, among them Henry Lawrence of Huntingdonshire, Commissioner of Plantations, Commissioner for Ireland, and from 1654–59 Lord President of the Council of State of the Protectorate; William Steele was Recorder of London, Chief Baron of the Exchequer and Lord Chancellor of Ireland; Colonel John Fiennes was Commissioner of the Great Seal in the restored Upper House, which included Henry Lawrence, and Colonels John Jones, Philip Jones, and John Disbrowe. Among the thirty-eight central Triers in 1654 were John Tombes, Henry Jessey, and Daniel Dike (Dyke).[80] Others, however, are worthy of note. In early 1650, the Particular Baptist Thomas Patient joined the invasion of Ireland, using this as an opportunity to plant Baptist congregations along the way.[81] Paul Hobson, the evangelist who on a tour in Suffolk introduced Lawrence Clarkson, the later Ranter, to Baptist convictions, became an army officer as early as the spring of 1644, and rose to be Deputy-Governor of Newcastle and a Lieutenant-Colonel.[82]

Many Baptists became caught up in the Leveller movement,[83] whose heyday was in the 1640s and which arose among those who were increasingly skeptical of Parliament's ability to achieve its aims. Since many of them were soldiers, there was always the threat of violence, perceived or real. Thomas Lambe[84] was for a while a chaplain in Cromwell's army, and

---

77. McGregor, "Baptists," 31 and 49.

78. Ludlow, *Voyage*.

79. Greaves, "Gentleman Revolutionary."

80. For those listed in this paragraph, see Underwood, *History*, 74–81; and Whitley, *History*, 81–84.

81. See White, "Thomas Patient."

82. Whitley, "Paul Hobson"; Greaves, "One of the Most Dangerous Fellows."

83. These are to be distinguished from the Diggers, who were thoroughgoing egalitarians who wanted to equally redistribute the country's wealth and abolish property rights. The Levellers advocated religious toleration, legal reforms, an extended franchise, and free trade enshrined in a written constitution in a government truly answerable to the people, unlike the monarchy of the existing Parliament.

84. See White, *English Baptists*, 28.

Samuel Oates disseminated the Leveller manifesto, *The Agreement of the People* of 1647, in December of that year. For this he was arrested, but escaped, then rearrested and though the court proceedings against him collapsed, he was again in trouble the following May for seditious and treasonable speeches against the monarchy.[85] Later in the 1650s Oates served as a chaplain in Colonel Pride's regiment in Scotland, and during 1654–55 became involved with more radical officers who wanted greater democracy and the abolition of tithes, which were to be used to support a state-financed ministry.[86] Yet another General Baptist evangelist and pastor, Henry Denne, from Fenstanton near Cambridge, joined the army, though not as a chaplain, sometime between June 1646 and May 1649. In May 1649, Denne narrowly missed execution after the Leveller-led army mutiny at Burford, and in his explanation of his participation claimed that he had become entangled in what he felt at the time and in all good conscience was the right thing to do, though afterwards he was ashamed of his involvement.[87] That said, he does offer an insight in what he had hoped to achieve in the army: "The Service we granted both very honourable, and also necessary, for the prevention of War, and setling of Peace in this Nation."[88] However, with the establishment of the Commonwealth, the Levellers, who had had an increasing presence in the New Model Army from 1647 onwards, came into conflict with both Cromwell and Lord General Fairfax and the Council of State. Following several mutinies, the movement was efficiently put down, effectively ending it by the end of 1649.

Unlike other millenarian groups, the Fifth Monarchists believed Christ's second coming would be preceded by the rule of the saints, a godly kingdom in which England was both pivotal and central, and that the two civil wars and execution of the king were precursors.[89] Originating in 1651, it drew many of its supporters from former members of the army. With the dissolution of the Barebone's Parliament in December 1653 and the establishment of Cromwell's Protectorate, many, militant Baptists among them, felt that Cromwell had usurped the place that

---

85. See Betteridge, "Early Baptists," 206–11.
86. White, *English Baptists*, 34, 82.
87. Denne, *Levellers*, 3–4. See also White, *English Baptists*, 35–36.
88. Denne, *Levellers*, 3.
89. See, e.g., Farrer, "Fifth Monarchy Movement"; and Farrer, "Fifth Monarchy Men, 1654"; Brown, *Political Activities*; Rogers, *Fifth Monarchy Men*; and Capp, *Fifth Monarchy Men*; also Capp, "Millenarianism."

could only belong to King Jesus.[90] Inspired by the signs of the times, and fuelled by apocalyptic imagery and millenarian zeal, not least from the book of Daniel, the Fifth Monarchy movement attracted prominent Baptists, including Henry Jessey, Nathaniel Strange, Thomas Tillam, and the Welsh Baptist leader Vavasor Powell.[91]

After the establishment of the Protectorate, the General Baptists met in London to repudiate false accusations against them and reasserted their loyalty to the magistracy and government.[92] They rejected the position of the Fifth Monarchists that the rule and government should be in their hands now rather than waiting for Christ's return when

> the Kingdoms of this world, shal become the Kingdoms of the Lord and of his Christ, and that then the Kingdom, and Dominion, and the greatness of the Kingdom under the whole Heaven, shal be given to the people of the saints of the most High; but till then they rather expect it as their portion, patiently to suffer from the world, as the Scriptures direct them, and as the saints usually have done, then any wise to attain the Rule and Government thereof.[93]

But, significantly, before that statement they came close to articulating what later came to be called passive resistance. They acknowledged that, obliged by God's rules, they were "to be subject to the Higher Powers, to obey the Magistrates, and submit to every Ordinance of man for the Lords sake," and should the civil powers impose on the Baptists anything that they could not in all conscience obey before God they recognized that they would need "patiently to suffer, or humbly to intreat favour."[94] While this is not exactly what later came to be called passive resistance, namely the peaceful exercise of civil disobedience, this, I contend, is a precursor to passive resistance, that is, the withholding of compliance to the law and acceptance of whatever punishment the state imposes on them for doing so. A similar position was adopted the following year at the sixth

---

90. During the course of his trial in 1655, John Carew (who became a Baptist in 1658), accused Cromwell that he had taken "the crown from the head of Christ, and put it on his own." See Clouse, "Carew, John (1622–1660)," 125.

91. On these and other Baptists, see Capp, *Fifth Monarchy Men*. On Powell, see Bassett, *Welsh Baptists*, 30, 47; Capp, *Fifth Monarchy Men*; and Capp, "Millenarianism," 174, 176.

92. *Humble Representation*, 1–2.

93. Ibid., 3.

94. Ibid., 2.

meeting of the Midland Particular Baptist Association at Tewkesbury in Gloucestershire.[95] As J. F. McGregor has put it, "In general the Baptist movement rejected the hazardous prospect of reform through militant action for the tangible benefits of toleration under the protectorate."[96] A key figure in all of this was the Particular Baptist leader from London, William Kiffen, who, with other leaders, sought to moderate the excesses of some.[97] In 1649 Kiffen opposed the Leveller pamphlet, *The second part of Englands new Chains discovered* (1649),[98] which had been read in several London congregations on 25 March 1649 with a view to enlisting subscribers to the movement. Kiffen disavowed the work, insisting that "our meetings are not at all to intermeddle with the ordering or altering Civil Government (which we humbly and submissively leave unto the supream Powers) but solely for the advancement of the Gospel. It being our grief that our meetings should be perverted to any sinister ends, or earthly respects whatsoever."[99]

Following Oliver Cromwell's death in September 1658 and the failure of his son Richard's attempts to maintain the Protectorate, London Baptists published their repudiation of five misrepresentations of their views.[100] The first was that they opposed the magistracy, the last that they were intent on murdering and destroying those who differed from them in religious matters. With regard to the former they acknowledged that they could not speak for all Baptists, nevertheless "it hath been our profession, and is our real practise, to be obedient to Magistracy in all things Civil, and willing to live peaceably, under whatever Government is, and shall be established in this Nation: for we do believe, and declare, Magistracy to be an Ordinance of God, and ought to be obeyed in all lawful things." To the latter charge, "We do not only abhor and detest it

---

95. White, *Association Records*, "The Sixth General Meeting, 15 October 1656," 29–31 (30).

96. McGregor, "Baptists," 54.

97. See ibid., 54–55. White, *English Baptists*, 72, suggests John Spilsbury as one of those sharing Kiffen's moderate political position and loyalty to Cromwell. On Kiffen, see the first three of a projected six-volume reassessment of Kiffen, drawing on documents previously never used by Baptist historians: Kreitzer, *William Kiffen and His World (Parts 1–3)*; and also Haykin, *Kiffin, Knollys and Keach*, 42–52.

98. See Lilburn, *Englands New Chains*; Lilburn et al., *Second Part*.

99 *Humble Petition*, 5.

100. McGregor, "Baptists," 55, says this was the first time the two wings of the Baptists, General and Particular, collaborated in such a manner.

[murder], as a cursed practice; but we hope, have approved ourselves, both in this City and the Nation, to the contrary."[101]

Following the restoration of the monarchy in 1660, and despite their many protestations to the contrary, Baptists were still held under suspicion and were actively persecuted. In the minds of ordinary people and authorities alike they were "Anabaptists" and tied to the Münster debacle, which itself, like so many of the events tied to radical groups of the revolutionary era, had been fuelled by apocalyptic millenarianism.[102] Further, Baptists were implicated in the Venner Revolt in London in January 1661. Venner's supporters were killed (thirteen of them including Venner), or imprisoned, or fled, and, though vague, their sympathies seem to have been Fifth Monarchist. Though Thomas Venner was not a Baptist, Dissenters were arrested in the uprising's wake, Baptists, Independents, and Quakers among them.[103] By the end of January both Baptist groups—led by Henry Denne for the Generals, and William Kiffen, as well as Thomas Lambe and John Spilsbury, for the Particulars—repudiated Venner and his followers, highlighting the fact that to the best of their knowledge all but one of his followers were paedobaptists, that the Baptists had themselves been attacked by the rebels for their support of the magistracy and submission to civil authorities, and they yet again distanced themselves from the continental Anabaptists.[104]

However, as Barrie White remarks, Baptists *had been* involved in the violence of the civil wars and the attempts to remove the monarchy.[105] Some Baptists had been among those involved in Charles I's execution. The regicides can be divided into two different categories. There were those who actually signed Charles I's death warrant,[106] and then there were those implicated in the king's execution. Among the former were John Okey, Thomas Harrison, John Hewson, Richard Deane, Edmund

---

101. *Declaration Of several of the People called Anabaptists*, broadsheet.

102. See, e.g., Cohn, *Pursuit of the Millennium*, 252–80; and Horst, *Radical Brethren*, 66–78.

103. See Underhill, *Tracts*, 313, citing Kennet's *Register* (details of which are not given), 352, in his "Introductory Notice" to Sturgion, *A Plea*.

104. See *Humble Apology*; and what is now called *The Standard Confession*.

105. White, *English Baptists*, 102.

106. "Death Warrant of King Charles I", Parliamentary Archives, HL/PO/JO/10/1/297A, which was signed by fifty-nine of the commissioners who judged him. It is dated 29 January 1648 (o.s., 1649 n.s.).

Ludlow, Robert Lilburne, John Carew, and Daniel Axtell,[107] whose regiment provided the guard for the trial; among the latter, was Richard Rumbold,[108] who was one of Charles I's guards at his execution,[109] and Henry Lawrence.[110] Following the restoration, retribution against the regicides was swift, with "An Act of Free and Generall Pardon Indemnity and Oblivion" being passed in 1660, article 34 dealing with "Persons excepted by Name who were concerned in the Murder of King Charles I."[111] Those Baptists named were Harrison, Ludlow, Lilburne, Okey, Hewson, Carew, and Axtell, of whom Carew, Harrison, and Axtell were all executed in October 1660.[112]

Baptists, as well as many Fifth Monarchists, were also involved in the failed Yorkshire Plot of 1663, which was infiltrated by agents. One hundred of its leaders were arrested the day before the planned attack on York. Among them were John Wigan, Nathaniel Strange, John Hutchinson, and Paul Hobson.[113] Strange was also implicated in the planned uprising accredited to Henry Danvers and Clement Ireton in 1665, though Danvers evaded capture.[114]

In 1683 several Baptists were implicated in the Rye House Plot, information about which was given to the government by a Baptist informer,

---

107. Axtell was known for his cruelty and, as Governor of Kilkenny, believed that in his suppression of the Irish he was doing God's will. He many times said, "Give her blood to drink, for she is worthy." See Underwood, "Axtell," 30; and Thomson, "Axtell."

108. Southern, *Forlorn Hope*, 147–66. See also Clifton, "Rumbold."

109. Not all of these are accepted as Baptists, or they were at some point Baptist, but, like so many, their ecclesiastical allegiance changed over time. E.g., White, "Harrison," 64, notes that Harrison and his wife, Carew, and Hugh Courtney were dipped (immersed), or re-baptized, but he does not believe (*English Baptists*, 82) that this is the same Thomas Harrison who, with Abraham Holmes, was a member of the Hexham church; Richard Deane the regicide was not the Particular Baptist of the same name, as Underwood, *English Baptists*, 77, mistakenly assumes. For the Baptist Deane, see Greaves, "Deane"; Howell, "Ludlow," 204, says Ludlow "did not fully embrace the ideas of the Baptists or the Levellers."

110. White, *English Baptists*, 25, suggests Henry Lawrence was a regicide, but since he did not sign the king's death warrant, he was, presumably, a regicide in the second sense noted above.

111. "An Act."

112. White, *English Baptists*, 102.

113. See Capp, *Fifth Monarchy Men*, 209–11. Hutchinson's wife, Lucy, published an account of her husband's confinement in the Tower of London and wrote a plea on his behalf. See Hutchinson, *Memoirs*. On the plot, see Gee, "Derwentdale Plot."

114. See Capp, *Fifth Monarchy Men*, 211.

Josiah Keeling. Thomas Walcott, a former officer in Cromwell's army, was responsible for planning the attack on the king's guard as they passed the Rye House, owned by Richard Rumbold. Another Baptist involved was Abraham Holmes, another former Cromwellian officer, who was also involved in the 1685 Monmouth Rebellion. Sampson Clarke, minister of the Particular Baptist church in Lyme, was executed as a result of his involvement in the Monmouth uprising, as were Abraham Holmes and William Kiffen's two grandsons, Benjamin and William Hewling. Andrew Gifford, minister of the Pithay Baptist Church in Bristol, and benefactor of the Bristol Baptist Academy, encouraged the rebellion, raising money and gathering ammunition for the rebels. Happily for Gifford, his involvement was not discovered until later, while, after many years of involvement in such revolutionary movements, Henry Danvers[115] eventually fled to Holland where he died a few years later.[116] Barrie White notes that the Venner uprising and the violence of the eleven-year interregnum (1649–60), made it clear "that any kind of Fifth Monarchy views were regarded as politically dangerous and that the authorities did not attempt to make any distinction between those who were relatively harmless Bible students and those who were potential or actual revolutionaries."[117]

By the end of the seventeenth century, then, the Baptist positions on peace and war had been clearly defined, though it would be the end of the nineteenth and into the twentieth century before the pacifist position would receive viable and concrete expression in national and international peace societies[118] and advocates such as Martin Luther King, Jr. In recent decades, Baptist pacifism has received renewed inspiration from the Anabaptist tradition,[119] bringing us, as it were, almost full circle.

CONCLUSION

Lorkin concludes his short work under the heading "What now?" when he writes,

---

115. See Greaves, "Gentleman Revolutionary"; Greaves, "Tangled Careers"; Nuttall, "Danvers," 217–19.

116. For this paragraph, see White, *English Baptists*, 123 and 159–60.

117. Ibid., 102.

118. E.g., the Baptist Peace Fellowship in Britain was founded in 1932. See Dekar, *For the Healing of the Nations*, 246–54.

119. See, e.g., Randall, "Baptist-Anabaptist Identity."

> The dilemma remains. It is a paradox as well as a dilemma . . . All over the world, Christians feel quite sure that war is against the mind of Christ, but the instinct to defend home and country against evil and violence prevents them from becoming declared pacifists. The world desires, longs for, prays for peace. Yet in fear it continues to arm.[120]

Should Christians, then, "wait upon events, improvising attitudes in the light of changing circumstances?" Or "should we accept at the hands of our Lord the call to think again?"[121] This collection of essays is one response to that call, and I hope it will not be the last.

---

120. Lorkin, *Baptist Views*, 14.
121. Ibid., 14–15.

Bibliography

Primary Sources

"An Act of Free and Generall Pardon Indemnity and Oblivion." Online: http://www.british-history.ac.uk/report.aspx?compid=47259. Accessed 29 April 2011.

Busher, Leonard. *Religions Peace Or A reconciliation, between princes & Peoples, & Nations.* Amsterdam, 1614.

The Confession of Faith, Of those Churches which are commonly (though falsly) called Anabaptists. London, 1644.

A Declaration of Faith of English People remaining at Amsterdam in Holland. n.p., 1611.

Declaration Of several of the People called Anabaptists, In and about the City of London. London: Livewel Chapman, 1659.

Denne, Henry. *The Levellers Designe Discovered: Or the Anatomie of the Late Unhappie Mutinie.* London: Francis Tyton, 1649.

The Faith and Practise of Thirty Congregations, Gathered according to the Primitive Pattern. London: Will. Larnar, 1651.

Friesen, John J., ed. *Peter Riedemann's Hutterite Confession of Faith: Translation of the 1665 German Edition of Confession of Our Religion, Teaching, and Faith By the Brothers Who Are Known as the Hutterites.* Classics of the Radical Reformation 9. Scottdale, PA: Herald, 1999.

Helwys, Thomas. *An Advertisement or admonition, unto the Congregations, which men call the New Fryelers, in the lowe Countries, written in Dutche. And Published in Englis.* n.p., 1611.

———. *A Short Declaration of the mistery of iniquity.* n.p., 1612.

The Humble Apology Of some commonly called Anabaptists, In behalf of themselves and others of the same Judgement with them: With their Protestation against the late wicked and most horrid treasonable Insurrection and Rebellion acted in the City of London. Together with an Apology formerly presented to the Kings most Excellent Majesty. London: Printed by Henry Hills, 1660.

The Humble Petition and Representation of Several Churches of God in London, commonly (though falsly) called Anabaptists. London: Francis Tyton & John Playford, 1649.

The Humble Representation and Vindication of many of the Messengers, Elders, and Brethren, belonging to several of the BAPTIZED CHURCHES in this Nation, of and concerning their Opinions and Resolutions touching the CIVIL GOVERNMENT of these Nations, and of their Deportment under the same. London: Francis Smith, 1655.

Hutchinson, Lucy. *Memoirs of the Life of Colonel Hutchinson, written by His Widow Lucy.* London: Kegan Paul Trench Trubner, 1904.

Klaassen, Walter, ed. *Anabaptism in Outline: Selected Primary Sources*. Classics of the Radical Reformation 3. Scottdale, PA: Herald, 1981.

Lilburn, John. *Englands New Chains Discovered*. n.p., 1648.

Lilburn, John, Richard Overton, and Tho. Prince. *The Second Part of Englands New-Chaines Discovered*. London, 1648.

Marpeck, Pilgram. "The Admonition of 1542." In *The Writings of Pilgram Marpeck*, edited by William Klassen and Walter Klassen, 160–302. Classics of the Radical Reformation 2. Eugene, OR: Wipf & Stock, 1978.

Simons, Menno. "The Blasphemy of John of Leiden (1535)." In *The Complete Writings of Menno Simons c. 1496-1561*, edited by Leonard Verduin, J. C. Wenger, and Harold S. Bender, 33–50. 2nd ed. Scottdale, PA: Herald, 1984.

Smyth, John. *The Character of the Beast or The False Constitution of the Church*. 1609. Reprint in W. T. Whitley, ed., *The Works of John Smyth, Fellow of Christ's College, 1594-8*, 2:563–680. 2 vols. Cambridge: Cambridge University Press, 1915.

———. *Corde credimus, et ore confitemur*. Reprint in W. T. Whitley, ed., *The Works of John Smyth, Fellow of Christ's College, 1594-8*, 2:682–84. 2 vols. Cambridge: Cambridge University Press, 1915.

———. *Defense of de Ries's Confession*, c.1610. Reprinted in W. T. Whitley, ed., *The Works of John Smyth, Fellow of Christ's College, 1594-8*, 2:685–709. 2 vols. Cambridge: Cambridge University Press, 1915.

———. *The Last Booke of Iohn Smith Called the Retractation of His Errours, and the Confirmation of the Truth*. Reprint in W. T. Whitley, ed., *The Works of John Smyth, Fellow of Christ's College, 1594-8*, 2:751–60. 2 vols. Cambridge: Cambridge University Press, 1915.

———. *A Paterne of True Prayer*. London: Felix Kyngston for Thomas Man, 1605. Reprint in W. T. Whitley, ed., *The Works of John Smyth, Fellow of Christ's College, 1594-8*, 1:67–247. 2 vols. Cambridge: Cambridge University Press, 1915.

———. *Propositions and conclusions, concerning true Christian religion, conteyning a confession of faith of certaine English people, living at Amsterdam*. N.p., c.1612–14. Reprint in W. T. Whitley, ed., *The Works of John Smyth, Fellow of Christ's College, 1594-8*, 2:733–50. 2 vols. Cambridge: Cambridge University Press, 1915.

The Schleitheim Confession: Brotherly Union of a Number of Children of God Concerning Seven Articles. In *Confessions and Catechisms of the Reformation* edited by Mark A. Noll, 50–58. Leicester: Apollos, 1991.

The Standard Confession, A brief Confession or Declaration of Faith: Set forth by many of us, who are (falsely) called Ana-Baptists, to inform all Men (in these dayes of scandal and reproach) of our innocent Belief and Practise; for which we are not only resolved to suffer Persecution, to the loss of our Goods, but also Life it self, rather than to decline the same. London: Printed by G. D. for F. Smith, 1660.

Sturgion, John. *A Plea for Toleration of Opinions and Persuasions in Matters of Religion, differing from the Church of England*. London: Printed by S. Dover for Francis Smith, 1661.

Underhill, E. B. *Tracts on Liberty of Conscience and Persecution 1614-1661*. 1846. Repr. Research Source Works Series 189/Philosophy Monographs 11. New York: Burt Franklin, 1966 [1846].

White, B. R. *Association Records of the Particular Baptists of England, Wales, and Ireland to 1660: Part 1. South Wales and the Midlands*. London: The Baptist Historical Society, 1971.

Whitley, W. T., ed. *The Works of John Smyth, Fellow of Christ's College, 1594-8.* 2 vols. Cambridge: Cambridge University Press, 1915.

Secondary Sources

Bassett, T. M. *The Welsh Baptists.* Swansea: Ilston House, 1977.
Bell, Mark R. *Apocalypse How? Baptist Movements during the English Revolution.* Macon, GA: Mercer University Press, 2000.
Betteridge, Alan. "Early Baptists in Leicestershire and Rutland (i)." *Baptist Quarterly* 25, no. 5 (1974) 204–11.
Brown, Louise Fargo. *The Political Activities of the Baptists and Fifth Monarchy Men in England during the Interregnum.* Burt Franklin Research & Source Works Series 97. New York: Burt Franklin, 1911.
Burgess, Walter H. *John Smith the Se-Baptist, Thomas Helwys and the First Baptist Church in England, with Fresh Light upon the Pilgrim Fathers' Church.* London: James Clarke, 1911.
Burrage, Champlin. *The Early English Dissenters in the Light of Recent Research (1550-1641).* 2 vols. New York: Russell & Russell, 1967.
Capp, Bernard S. "The Fifth Monarchists and Popular Millenarianism." In *Radical Religion in the English Revolution,* edited by J. F. McGregor and B. Reay, 165–89. Oxford: Oxford University Press, 1986.
———. *The Fifth Monarchy Men: A Study in Seventeenth-Century English Millenarianism.* London: Faber & Faber, 1972.
Clouse, R.G. "Carew, John (1622–1660)." In *Biographical Dictionary of British Radicals in the Seventeenth Century,* edited by Richard L. Greaves and Robert Zaller, 1:125-26. 3 vols. Brighton: Harvester, 1982–84.
Coggins, James R. "A Short Confession of Hans de Ries: Union and Separation in Early Seventeenth-Century Holland." *Mennonite Quarterly Review* 60 no. 2 (April 1986) 128–38.
———. *John Smyth's Congregation: English Separatism, Mennonite Influence, and the Elect Nation.* Studies in Anabaptist and Mennonite History 32. Scottsdale, PA: Herald, 1991.
Cohn, Norman. *The Pursuit of the Millennium: Revolutionary Millenarians and Mystical Anarchists of the Middle Ages.* Rev. ed. London: Pimlico, 1970.
Cross, Anthony R. "The Adoption of Believer's Baptism and Baptist Beginnings." In *Exploring Baptist Origins,* edited by Anthony R. Cross and Nicholas J. Wood, 1–32. Centre for Baptist History and Heritage Studies 1. Oxford: Regent's Park College, 2010.
Dekar, Paul R. *For the Healing of the Nations: Baptist Peacemakers.* Macon, GA: Smyth & Helwys, 1993.
Dow, F. D. *Radicalism in the English Revolution 1640–1660.* Historical Association Studies. Oxford: Basil Blackwell, 1985.
Dyck, Cornelius J. "The First Waterlandian Confession of Faith." *Mennonite Quarterly Review* 36 (1962) 5–13.
———. "Hans de Ries: Theologian and Churchman. A Study in Second Generation Dutch Anabaptism." PhD diss., University of Chicago Divinity School, 1962.

———. "The Middelburg Confession of Hans de Ries." *Mennonite Quarterly Review* 36 (1962) 147–54 and 161.

———. "A Short Confession of Faith by Hans de Ries." *Mennonite Quarterly Review* 38 (1964) 5–19.

Evans, B. *The Early English Baptists*. 2 vols. London: J. Heaton & Son, 1862–64.

Farrer, A. J. D. "Fifth Monarchy Men, 1654." *Transactions of the Baptist Historical Society* 3, no. 2 (1912–13) 129–53.

———. "The Fifth Monarchy Movement." *Transactions of the Baptist Historical Society* 2, no. 3 (1910–11) 166–81.

Gee, Henry. "The Derwentdale Plot, 1663." *Transactions of the Royal Historical Society* 3rd series 11 (1917) 125–42.

George, Timothy. "Between Pacifism and Coercion: The English Baptist Doctrine of Religious Toleration." *Mennonite Quarterly Review* 58 (1984) 29–49.

Greaves, R. L. "Deane, Richard (fl.1647–1696)." In *Biographical Dictionary of British Radicals in the Seventeenth Century*, edited by Richard L. Greaves and Robert Zaller, 1:218–19. 3 vols. Brighton: Harvester, 1982–84.

———. "Gentleman Revolutionary: Henry Danvers and the Radical Underground." In *Saints and Rebels: Seven Nonconformists in Stuart England*, by Richard L. Greaves, 157–77. Macon, GA: Mercer University Press, 1985.

———. "'One of the Most Dangerous Fellows in the North': Paul Hobson and the Quest for Godly Government." In *Saints and Rebels: Seven Nonconformists in Stuart England*, by Richard L. Greaves, 133–56. Macon, GA: Mercer University Press, 1985.

———. "The Tangled Careers of Two Stuart Radicals: Henry and Robert Danvers." *Baptist Quarterly* 29, no. 1 (1981) 32-43.

Hannen, R. B. "Browne (or Brown), James (1615–c.1685)." In *Biographical Dictionary of British Radicals in the Seventeenth Century*, edited by Richard L. Greaves and Robert Zaller, 1:102–3. 3 vols. Brighton: Harvester, 1982–84.

Haykin, Michael A. G. *Kiffin, Knollys and Keach: Rediscovering Our English Baptist Heritage*. Leeds: Reformation Today Trust, 1996.

Hill, Christopher. *The World Turned Upside Down: Radical Ideas during the English Revolution*. 2nd ed. London: Penguin, 1975.

Horst, Irvin Buckwalter. *The Radical Brethren: Anabaptism and the English Reformation to 1558*. Bibliotheca, Humanistica & Reformatorica 2. Nieuwkoop: B. de Graaf, 1972.

Howell, R. "Ludlow, Edmund (c.1617–1692)." In *Biographical Dictionary of British Radicals in the Seventeenth Century*, edited by Richard L. Greaves and Robert Zaller, 2:204–5. 3 vols. Brighton: Harvester, 1982–84.

Kliever, Lonnie D. "General Baptist Origins: The Question of Anabaptist Influence." *Mennonite Quarterly Review* 36 (1962) 291–321.

Kreitzer, Larry J. "The Fifth Monarchist John Pendarves: Chaplain to Colonel Thomas Rainborowe's Regiment of Foot (1645–7)." *Baptist Quarterly* 43, no. 2 (2009) 112–22.

———. *William Kiffen and His World (Part 1)*. Centre for Baptist History and Heritage Studies, Re-sourcing Baptist History: Seventeenth Century Series 1. Oxford: Regent's Park College, 2011.

———. *William Kiffen and His World (Part 2)*. Centre for Baptist History and Heritage Studies, Re-sourcing Baptist History: Seventeenth Century Series 2. Oxford: Regent's Park College, 2012.

———. *William Kiffen and His World (Part 3)*. Centre for Baptist History and Heritage Studies, Re-sourcing Baptist History: Seventeenth Century Series 3. Oxford: Regent's Park College, 2013.

Laurence, Anne. *Parliamentary Army Chaplains 1642–1651*. Royal Historical Society Studies in History 59. Woodbridge: Boydell, 1990.

Lee, Jason K. *The Theology of John Smith: Puritan, Separatist, Baptist, Mennonite*. Macon, GA: Mercer University Press, 2003.

Lorkin, H. F. *Baptist Views on War and Peace*. Living Issues Booklets. London: The Baptist Union of Great Britain and Ireland, 1969.

Ludlow, Edmund. *A Voyage from the Watch Tower: Part Five: 1660–1662*. Camden 4th Series 21. London: Royal Historical Society, 1978.

Lumpkin, William L. *Baptist Confessions of Faith*. Rev. ed. Valley Forge, PA: Judson, 1969.

Manley, Kenneth Ross. "Origins of the Baptists: The Case for Development from Puritanism-Separatism." *Baptist History and Heritage* 22, no. 4 (1987) 34–46.

McGregor, J. F. "The Baptists: Fount of All Heresy." In *Radical Religion in the English Revolution*, edited by J. F. McGregor and B. Reay, 23–63. Oxford: Oxford University Press, 1986.

McGregor, J. F., and B. Reay, eds. *Radical Religion in the English Revolution*. Oxford: Oxford University Press, 1986.

Noll Mark A., ed. *Confessions and Catechisms of the Reformation*. Leicester: Apollos, 1991.

Nuttall, Geoffrey F. "Henry Danvers, His Wife and the 'Heavenly Line.'" *Baptist Quarterly* 29, no. 5 (1982) 217–19.

Randall, Ian M. "Baptist-Anabaptist Identity among European Baptists since the 1950s." In *Baptists and the World: Renewing the Vision. Papers from the Baptist Historical Society Conference, Prague, Czech Republic, July 2008*, edited by John H. Y. Briggs and Anthony R. Cross, 133–51. Centre for Baptist History and Thought Studies 8. Oxford: Regent's Park College, 2011.

Rogers, P. G. *The Fifth Monarchy Men*. London: Oxford University Press, 1966.

Southern, Antonia. *Forlorn Hope: Soldier Radicals of the Seventeenth Century*. Lewes: The Book Guild, 2001.

Stayer, James M. *Anabaptists and the Sword*. 2nd ed. Eugene, OR: Wipf & Stock, 2002.

Cate, S. Blaupot ten. *Geschiedenis der Doopsgezinden in Holland, Zeeland, Utrecht en Gelderland*. Amsterdam: P. N. van Kampen, 1847.

Thomson, Alan. "Axtell, Daniel (*bap.* 1622, *d.* 1660)." In *Oxford Dictionary of National Biography*, edited by H. C. G. Matthew and Brian Harrison. Oxford: OUP, 2004. Online ed., edited by Lawrence Goldman, January 2008: http://ezproxy.ouls.ox.ac.uk:2204/view/article/928 (accessed 28 April 2011).

Underdown, David. *Revel, Riot and Rebellion: Popular Politics and Culture in England 1603–1660*. Oxford: Oxford University Press, 1985.

Underwood, A. C. *A History of the English Baptists*. London: Kingsgate, 1947.

Underwood, T. L. "Axtell (or Axtel), Daniel (d.1660)." In *Biographical Dictionary of British Radicals in the Seventeenth Century*, edited by Richard L. Greaves and Robert Zaller, 1:30. 3 vols. Brighton: Harvester, 1982–84.

Watts, Michael R. *The Dissenters*. Vol. 1, *From the Reformation to the French Revolution*. Oxford: Clarendon, 1978.

White, B. R. *The English Baptists of the Seventeenth Century*. A History of the English Baptists 1. 2nd ed. Didcot, UK: Baptist Historical Society, 1996.

———. *The English Separatist Tradition: From the Marian Martyrs to the Pilgrim Fathers*. Oxford: Oxford University Press, 1971.

———. "Harrison, Thomas (1616-1660)." In *Biographical Dictionary of British Radicals in the Seventeenth Century*, edited by Richard L. Greaves and Robert Zaller, 2:61-65. 3 vols. Brighton: Harvester, 1982-84.

———. "Thomas Patient in England and Ireland." *Irish Baptist Historical Society Journal* 2 (1969-70) 36-48.

Whitley, W. T. *A History of British Baptists*. 2nd ed. London: Kingsgate, 1932.

———. "The Reverend Colonel Paul Hobson, Fellow of Eton." *Baptist Quarterly* 9, no. 5 (1939) 307-10.

Wright, Nigel G. "'The Sword': An Example of Anabaptist Diversity." *Baptist Quarterly* 36, no. 6 (1996) 264-79.

Wright, Stephen. *The Early English Baptists, 1603-1649*. Woodbridge, UK: Boydell, 2006.

2

Andrew Fuller and the War against Napoleon

Paul L. Brewster, Sr.

HISTORICAL BACKGROUND

The era of the Napoleonic Wars was one of the true watershed epochs in the history of Western civilization. As such, it transformed many facets and institutions of European society, including church, state, and the military. Beyond the institutional changes spawned by more than two decades of conflict, the prevailing attitudes of western Europeans also underwent a radical transformation. As nationalism took root, patriotism grew and flowered. In traditionally Christian countries like Britain, patriotism and piety became closely linked. One measure of the attitudes of British Baptists to war during this pivotal time can be formed by looking at the writings of Andrew Fuller (1754–1815).[1] Fuller was at the peak of his influence among Baptists at exactly the same time that Britain was engaged in her death duel with Napoleon. As such, his sermons, his published writings, and his unpublished correspondence are important sources that reflect Baptist responses to war in early nineteenth-century England.

---

1. Andrew Fuller was considered the leading Baptist theologian of his day. For a time, interest in him seemed to wane, but it has definitely been on the increase in recent years. For older biographies, see Ryland, *Work of Faith*, and Morris, *Memoirs*. Both went through several editions in Britain and the United States. Two recent studies of Fuller are Morden, *Offering Christ to the World*, and Brewster, *Fuller*.

Revolutionary France

Revolutionaries in France discovered that toppling the *ancien régime* was considerably easier than administering a new republic. On top of the difficulties inherent in a complete upheaval of French society, they soon had to face the backlash of the joint military ventures of the great monarchical powers—who saw the seeds of their own demise writ large in the collapse of the French monarchy. As the situation in the young French republic grew more and more desperate societally, economically, and militarily, an ambitious young Corsican, Napoleon Bonaparte (1769–1821), seemed able to exploit every new crisis to his advantage. For a time, he maintained the veneer of a republic, taking on himself the title of First Consul and ruling under the auspices of a new constitution. But by 1804, France had a new supreme monarch, as Napoleon famously crowned himself Emperor Napoleon I in a ceremony at Notre Dame that rivaled all the pomp and ceremony that the house of Bourbon could have mustered.[2]

From 1792 to Napoleon's final defeat in 1815, a kaleidoscope of coalitions battled him militarily in the field, fought France for economic control of Europe, and waged ideological war for the hearts and minds of men. While other nations in these coalitions changed like the seasons, the one constant enemy throughout this time was Great Britain. She remained in open warfare with France for all these years, with the brief exception of about fourteen months during which the Treaty of Amiens was ostensibly in effect.[3] More than two decades of war—during which Great Britain was under more or less constant threat—gave rise to a new national solidarity in England.

The World Is Watching

Though British society in the late eighteenth and early nineteenth centuries was still mostly rural and agricultural, many of her citizens had access

---

2. Following the French Revolution, control of the country had been seized by a broad group of revolutionaries known as the Directory. As a governing body, it was largely ineffective. The Consulate was a thinly veiled attempt to posture Napoleon as a democratically installed ruler, limited by the new Constitution of Year VIII. In actual practice, the First Consul ruled as a supreme monarch, which was made formal with the declaration of a new French Empire.

3. This treaty created an uneasy peace and was in effect from March 1802 until May 1803. Napoleon's obvious thirst for continual expansion led to Britain's decision to renew hostilities.

to news of the world. This meant that political and military developments were increasingly something that they needed to process through the lens of their Christian faith. Although he lived and ministered in the relative obscurity of the market town of Kettering, Northamptonshire, Andrew Fuller was a careful student of the newspapers. Consider the following examples, which illustrate the degree to which he was interested and informed about world affairs:

> Publick affairs wear a dark aspect to a political eye; but to the eye of faith it is otherwise. In France the Mountain (or Marats) party are uppermost, and have Guillotined almost all the rest. Brissot and his party were 21 of them Guillotined together last October . . . The mountain party are desperate men; but perhaps none but such men could carry things through. Their arms last Summer & Winter have been almost every where victorious. I reckon there will be no more Campaigns, worth the name. The combined powers are about done over. Old Catherine is a baggage. She talked all along but never meant to do any thing. She looked on while Prussia & Austria & England were weakening themselves and has reserved her strength to obtain the Turkish Empire, (without interruption from them) at which her mouth has been watering for years, and against which she is now on the eve of declaring war. Prussia has had enough with France, & it is s[ai]d has declared off. We have sent our fleets to take Domingo & [?]French West India Islands.
>
> A dark cloud hangs over us. We expect the French will shortly attempt to invade us. They have been making great preparations for it for several months. Great numbers are going to America. Dr. Priestly & 80 or 90 families are going this month.[4]

A few years later, Fuller clearly did not think that the scene had brightened much:

> Things at present look dark with us as a nation. Perhaps that saying may be verified with respect to those who have declined Missions thro' fear, & you who have engaged in them. "He that saveth his life shall lose it and he that loseth his life for my sake shall find it." The French have now made peace with all Europe but us; and have subdued almost all Europe to their will. They are threatening us with an invasion in the most violent and

---

4. Andrew Fuller to William Carey et al., 25 March 1794–25 May 1794. Unless noted otherwise, citations from Fuller's correspondence are from "The Letters of Andrew Fuller."

> outrageous language. I can compare them to nothing but a raving mad bull, on the other side of a river . . . [I] believe that the French Government from the fall of Robespiere till about six months ago was as good as ought to be expected on this subject. But from that time, another Robespierean faction has gained the ascendancy. It was pretended that a plot was in agitation to restore royalty, and that Pichegru was at the head of it. All of a sudden that General & 60 or 70 members of the legislature, and two out of the five Directors, were seized, & banished without trial; I believed at the time & now more firmly believe that the plot was a pretence—that the whole originated in Buonaparte's jealousy of Pichegru, and every other popular General in France, and a determination to ruin them, lest they should stand in the way of his designs.[5]

The newspaper had brought the affairs of the world to the attention of average men. Pastors like Fuller now found it necessary to help their people apply the Scripture to the many questions that this explosion of information raised, including how they should think about war.

The Threat of Invasion

In both 1794 and 1797 the threat of a French invasion of Britain was uppermost in Fuller's mind. It was no doubt on the mind of his congregants as well, for this topic frequently found its way into British newspapers. Sensationalism in these reports was stock-in-trade, complete with fanciful pen and ink drawings of all sorts of French secret weapons, from aerial invasion by balloons to enormous warships to an imaginary Channel Tunnel. The threat, however, was real enough. France unsuccessfully attempted to land expeditionary forces in Ireland in late 1796. In 1797, a French Legion composed mostly of convicts did manage to establish a beachhead on the coast of Wales—and hung on for three days before being forced to surrender. Those efforts were mostly designed to harass and stir up trouble for the British at home by playing upon the animosities of annexed peoples. Instead, they tended to galvanize British support for the increasingly costly war against France.[6]

After Horatio Nelson (1758–1805) and the British navy devastated the French fleet at the Battle of the Nile (1798), effectively stranding

---

5. Andrew Fuller to William Carey, 18 January, 1797.
6. Emsley, *British Society*, 57.

Napoleon's army in Egypt, the First Consul began to lay plans for a serious invasion effort. Napoleon created an army of up to 200,000 men that was to be single-mindedly dedicated to the task, known as the Army of the Ocean Coasts or the Army of England. He garrisoned his troops near the English Channel and spent years training and supplying them for an invasion that would never come. However, their proximity to the English coast meant that their presence would be prominent in the mind of the English populace. This palpable threat to homeland security further fanned the flames of patriotism in England.[7]

The British responded to Napoleon's threats by strengthening their coastal defenses and by an all-out mobilization of their citizens. At the heart of the coastal defenses was a series of fortresses, the Martello Towers, which sprang up like mushrooms along the Channel rim. Their presence stood as a constant reminder to coastal residents of the pressing French danger. Even more disruptive to the local populace, coastal land was flooded to create quagmires for the French legions, should they dare a landing. And most distressing of all, recruits for the British armed forces were demanded in unheard-of numbers from every county and town. The French had pioneered mobilization by *levée en masse*, and those nations that sought to oppose Napoleon's aggression had to resort to much broader means of recruiting than ever before. Of course, as the ranks of British soldiers and sailors swelled, so did the costs to the crown for their training, equipping, and deployment. Every British citizen was reminded that their nation was in a state of war as they struggled to pay the numerous taxes and fees that became increasingly burdensome as the war continued with no end in sight.

The New Reality of Total War

The upshot of the preparations was that Britain was very much on a total-war footing during the Napoleonic era, especially after the collapse of the Treaty of Amiens. By contrast, the dispute in the New World with the rebellious American colonies had seemed neither threatening nor urgent to most Britons. In fact, the War of the American Revolution was decidedly unpopular in the motherland. British Baptists, in particular, had been surprisingly outspoken in their opposition to the war. John Rippon (1751–1836), the Baptist pastor and chronicler from London, offered this

---

7. Ibid., 112–19.

informal analysis of the lack of support: "I believe that all our Baptist ministers in town [London] except two, and most of the brethren in the country, were on the side of the Americans in the late dispute."[8]

A colorful account of British Baptist sentiment on the American War has been preserved. As it happens, it traces back to men intimately connected with Andrew Fuller and the environs of his ministry, Robert Hall, Sr. (1728–91) and John Ryland, Sr. (1723–92). This story illustrates that a patriotic outpouring of support for the wars of one's homeland was not always a part of Baptist piety. It was told by Robert Hall, Jr. (1764–1831):

> Sir, that war [the American Revolution] was very unpopular, and considered to be very unrighteous by men of true liberty principles. My father, sir, warmly advocated the American cause. When I was a little boy he took me to the school of Mr. Ryland at Northampton, the father of Dr. Ryland, of Bristol: this Mr. Ryland was very eccentric, and a violent partizan [sic] of the Americans; it was in the hottest period of the war, sir, and many persons were indignant at the conduct of the English government. That war, sir, was considered a crusade against the liberty of the subject and the rights of man. The first night we arrived at Northampton from Arnsby, sir, the two old gentlemen (my father and Mr. Ryland) talked over American politics until they both became heated on the same side of the question. At length, Mr. Ryland burst forth in this manner: "Brother Hall, I will tell you what I would do if I were General Washington." "Well," said my father, "what would you do?" "Why, Brother Hall, if I were General Washington, I would summon all the American officers: they would form a circle around me, and I would address them, and we would offer a libation with our own blood, and I would order one of them to bring a lancet and a punch-bowl; and he should bleed us all, one by one, into this punch-bowl; and I would be the first to bare my arm: and, when the punch-bowl was full, and we had all been bled, I would call upon every man to consecrate himself to the work, by dipping his sword into the bowl, and entering into a solemn covenant agreement, by oath, one to another, and we should swear by Him that sits upon the throne, and liveth for ever and ever, that we would never sheath our swords while there was an English soldier in arms remaining in America; that is what I would do, Brother Hall."[9]

---

8. Cited in Robison, "Particular Baptists," 414.

9. Green, *Reminiscences*, 93–94. Fuller considered the elder Hall his mentor in

As Hall indicated, Ryland was noted as an eccentric, and he no doubt blustered in this exchange more than he himself might really have felt. But his outburst does underscore the fact that patriotism among Baptists in the eighteenth century did not necessarily translate into support for all Britain's wars.

ANDREW FULLER ON CHRISTIAN PATRIOTISM

The war against Napoleon was different. France's naked aggression, coupled with the breathtaking success of Napoleon's infantry all across Europe, solidified Baptist support for what eventually came to be seen as a just war of defense. In 1803, during a time when a French invasion seemed imminent, Andrew Fuller delivered an evening sermon to the Baptist Church at Kettering entitled "Christian Patriotism."[10] An analysis of this sermon will help reconstruct what likely was a typical Baptist perspective on war during this era.

Christian Duty in Times of War

Fuller began his sermon by acknowledging that how a Christian views his position in a time of war is a difficult issue that requires careful thought:

> In the course of human events, cases may be expected to occur in which a serious mind may be at a loss with respect to the path of duty. Presuming, my brethren, that such may be the situation of some of you, at this momentous crisis—a crisis in which your country, menaced by an unprincipled, powerful, and malignant foe, calls upon to arm in its defence—I take the liberty of freely imparting to you my sentiments on the subject.[11]

As a long-tenured pastor at Kettering, whose opinions were deeply valued in contemporary Particular Baptist circles, Fuller commanded a position of respect from which to help his people think through the biblical implications of their responsibilities in time of war.[12]

---

ministry.

10. Fuller, "Christian Patriotism." This sermon will be cited from the most accessible edition of it included in Fuller, *Complete Works*. The original was published by J. W. Morris, Clipstone, in 1803.

11. Fuller, "Christian Patriotism," 202.

12. Fuller had accepted the pastorate at Kettering in 1782, having over twenty

Fuller directed the attention of his hearers to a text in Jeremiah. This text, he explained, was given "when a part of the Jewish people were carried captives to Babylon, ten years, or thereabouts, before the entire ruin of the city and temple, they must have felt much a loss in determining upon what was duty."[13] Through Jeremiah, the Lord provided extensive and importance guidance:

> Thus saith the Lord of hosts, the God of Israel, unto all that are carried away captives, whom I have caused to be carried away from Jerusalem unto Babylon; Build ye houses, and dwell in them; and plant gardens, and eat the fruit of them; Take ye wives, and beget sons and daughters; and take wives for your sons, and give your daughters to husbands, that they may bear sons and daughters; that they may be increased there, and do not be diminished; And seek the peace of the city whither I have caused you to be carried away captives, and pray unto the Lord for it; for in the peace thereof shall ye have peace.[14]

Granting there were differences between the original setting and the current national crisis, Fuller reasoned that this text had a heightened applicability to British citizens facing Napoleon's threat:

> I do not suppose that the case of these people corresponds exactly with ours; but the difference is of such a nature as to heighten our obligations. They were in a foreign land; a land where there was nothing to excite their attachment, but every thing to provoke their dislike. They had enjoyed all the advantages of freedom and independence, but now they were reduced to a state of slavery.[15]

Fuller went on to enumerate some of the privileges they enjoyed as British citizens that only compounded their obligations to seek their country's welfare in all things:

> Now if such was the duty of men in their circumstances can there be any doubt with respect to ours? Ought we not to seek

---

years' tenure by the time of this crisis. Morris, *Memoirs*, 92, described his enormous influence thus, "He had a bishopric, without any of its titles and emoluments . . . in every case of difficulty, his assistance was required." One of the negative aspects of the dramatically shortened pastoral tenures of the present era is that pastors no longer stay in one place long enough to develop this kind of weighty influence.

13. Fuller, "Christian Patriotism," 202.
14. Jeremiah 29:4–7, AV.
15. Fuller, "Christian Patriotism," 203.

the good of our native land; the land of our fathers' sepulchres; a land where we are protected by mild and wholesome laws, administered under a paternal prince; a land where civil and religious freedom are enjoyed in a higher degree than in any country in Europe; a land where God has been known for many centuries as a refuge; a land, in fine, where there are greater opportunities for propagating the gospel, both at home and abroad, than in any other nation under heaven? Need I add to this, that the invader [Cyrus] was to them a deliverer; but to us, beyond all doubt, would be a destroyer?[16]

With that introduction, Fuller proceeded to his first point, which was to "inquire into the duty of religious people towards their country."[17] He noted that though Christians had been instructed to beware of conforming to the world, it was also a matter of revelation that they have various obligations in the world to which they must attend. Husbands, for example, had certain obligations toward their wives and children and slaves were called to serve their masters with diligence. When it came to matters of civil society, Fuller was on firm scriptural ground when he summed up, "If we were rulers, our country would have a serious claim on us as rulers; and, as we are subjects, it has a serious claim upon us as subjects. The manner in which we discharge these relative duties contributes not a little to the formation of our character, both in the sight of God and man."[18] How a Christian met his obligations to government, then, was seen as an important component of the sanctification process.

Seek the Peace of the City

Hearkening back to his text from Jeremiah 29, Fuller identified two scriptural injunctions that summed up a Christian's duty to government. They were to be constantly "seeking the peace of the city" and "praying to the Lord for it." Taking up the first injunction, Fuller rightly noted that the Hebrew word *shalom* was very comprehensive. It connoted more than an absence of war, but "prosperity in general" and meant that the captive exiles were to "seek the good or welfare" of Babylon in the broadest of

---

16. Ibid.
17. Ibid.
18. Ibid.

terms. Applying that principle to the Christian era, Fuller concluded that "we ought to be patriots, or lovers of our country."[19]

Lest that be interpreted to mean that one's country had to be supported in all events, Fuller was quick to add an important qualification:

> To prevent mistakes, however, it is proper to observe that the patriotism required of us is not that love of our country which clashes with universal benevolence, or which seeks its prosperity at the expense of the general happiness of mankind. Such was the patriotism of Greece or Rome; and such is that of all others where Christian principle is not allowed to direct it . . . The prosperity which we are directed to seek in behalf of our country involves no ill to any one, except to those who shall attempt its overthrow.[20]

Not content to ignore the elephant in the room, Fuller went ahead and clearly made an application of this stance to the pressing moral issue of his day: "Such, I am ashamed to say, is that with which some have advocated the cause of *negro slavery*. It is necessary, forsooth, to the wealth of this country! No; if my country cannot prosper but at the expense of justice, humanity, and the happiness of mankind, let it be unprosperous!"[21] Fuller, however, entertained no doubts that Britain could still prosper without slavery. Echoing Proverbs 14:34, he argued that "righteousness will be found to exalt a nation, and so to be true wisdom."[22]

This qualified patriotism involved God's people in no conflict of conscience. There were times when Fuller believed that a citizen could not be supportive of his or her country. Fuller carefully staked out the position he wished for his congregation to embrace: "Our concern is to cultivate that patriotism which harmonizes with good-will toward men."[23] When Christians found their country pursuing a course that ran roughshod over the rights of others, he advocated Christians remember that their first loyalty must remain with God: "O my country, I will

---

19. Ibid., 204.

20. Ibid.

21. Ibid. An act abolishing slavery in the British Empire would not garner the votes for passage until 1833. Most British Baptists were, like Fuller, stalwart advocates of abolition.

22. Ibid. The full text of Proverbs 14:34 reads, "Righteousness exalteth a nation: but sin is a reproach to any people."

23. Ibid.

lament thy faults! Yet, with all thy faults, I will seek thy good; not only as a Briton, but as a Christian."[24]

In expounding how Christians are obligated to seek the peace of their country, Fuller reminded his hearers that "we shall certainly do nothing, and join in nothing, that tends to disturb its peace, or hinder its welfare."[25] That would obviously preclude Christian involvement in plots to overthrow the government, but Fuller reached much further in his conclusions. He also applied this principle to a Christian's speech toward the government:

> Whoever deals in inflammatory speeches, or in any manner sows the seeds of discontent and disaffection, we shall not. Whoever labours to depreciate its governors, supreme or subordinate, in a manner tending to bring government itself into contempt, we shall not . . . He that can employ his wit in degrading magistrates is not their friend, but their enemy; and he that is an enemy to magistrates is not far from being an enemy to magistracy, and, of course, to his country.[26]

Fuller did allow that sometimes a Christian could not stand silently by as his country pursued a path that troubled his conscience. But in that event he should choose to express "disapprobation with respect and regret" for "a dutiful son may see a fault in his father; but he will take no pleasure in exposing him."[27]

Having concluded that seeking the peace of one's country implied that there were some things that Christians should not do, he now turned his attention to the positive implications of this command. Fuller put forward a position that recognized the inherent difficulty of supporting government when party loyalties were in play:

> It becomes Christians to bear positive good-will to their country, and to its government, considered *as government*, irrespective of the political party which may have the ascendancy. We may have our preferences, and that without blame; but they

---

24. Ibid. Notice the similarity here between Fuller's position and that expressed in the popular American hymn "America the Beautiful," written by Katharine Lee Bates in 1893. The second stanza runs: "America! America! / God mend thine every flaw / Confirm thy soul in self-control / Thy liberty in Law!

25. Fuller, "Christian Patriotism," 204.

26. Ibid. One might wish that this attitude might catch on during American electioneering.

27. Ibid.

ought never to prevent a cheerful obedience to the laws, a respectful demeanor towards those who frame and execute them, or a ready co-operation in every measure which the being or well-being of the nation may require. The civil power, whatever political party is uppermost, while it maintains the great ends of government, ought, at all times, to be able to reckon upon religious people as its cordial friends; and if such we be, we shall be willing, in times of difficulty, to sacrifice private interest to public good; shall contribute of our substance without murmuring; and in cases of imminent danger, shall be willing to expose *even our lives* in its defence.[28]

Christian citizenship required that the well-being of the country never be sacrificed to party interests. When it came to matters of national policy affecting decisions like the pursuit of war, Fuller recognized that party rhetoric could easily mislead. Thus, he warned his people to be on guard against it. That warning out of the way, Fuller had now arrived at the heart of the matter he intended to address in this sermon: was it permissible for Christians to participate in military service? In light of the possible invasion and the increasing demands that the crown was making on all communities and counties for conscripts, this question was an urgent one for his congregation. Fuller saw that part of his pastoral responsibility lay in helping his people think biblically about the issue.

CAN CHRISTIANS BEAR ARMS?

Fuller developed his sermon by expounding the grounds upon which he believed military service could be construed as an obligation of Christian citizenship. The first observation Fuller made in this regard was to remind his hearers of the example of Abraham. When the patriarch received word that Lot and his family had been plundered and kidnapped into slavery, he did not hesitate in launching a military reprisal. The text of Genesis in no way casts this action in a negative light. In fact, it highlights Abraham's military skill and bravery. Moreover, Melchizedek seems to speak for God when he blesses Abraham at the conclusion of hostilities, going so far as to attribute the patriarch's success to the hand of God: "Blessed be Abram of the most high God, possessor of heaven and earth: And blessed be the most high God, which hath delivered thine enemies into thy hand!" (Genesis 14:19–20, AV)

---

28. Ibid., 204–5.

Fuller anticipated that some critics might complain that his chosen example was from the Old Testament and that it had somehow been superseded by Jesus' instruction not to resist evil. He put forth the strongest case for non-resistance to evil he could imagine by recounting that awful night in Gethsemane on which Jesus was arrested. Jesus rebuked Peter's aggression on that occasion by telling him to sheath his sword and by speaking the memorable words, "For all they that take the sword shall perish with the sword" (Matthew 26:52, AV). How then can Christians justify armed resistance? Fuller argued that a single event in Scripture does not always translate into a universal principle to guide our actions:

> Christianity, I allow, is a religion of peace; and whenever it universally prevails, in the spirit and power of it, wars will be unknown. But so will every other species of injustice; yet, while the world is as it is, some kind of resistance to injustice is necessary, though it may at some future time become unnecessary. If our Saviour's command that we resist not evil be taken literally and universally, it must have been wrong for Paul to have remonstrated against the magistrates at Philippi; and he himself would not have reproved the person who smote him at the judgment-seat.[29]

It appears that the illustrations Fuller selected are less than apt, for in neither instance mentioned does the Apostle Paul resort to armed resistance. However, his broader hermeneutical conclusion appears sound: Jesus' rebuke of Peter's actions in Gethsemane seems to be a slender thread from which to suspend a thoroughgoing policy of pacifism and nonresistance.

Fuller takes pains to distinguish between what a Christian might do when acting in an individual capacity and what he might do when acting as a member of civil society. Though Peter had been forbidden to use the sword to defend his master, Fuller accepted that there may be extreme cases when even an individual has a right to use deadly force in resistance to evil: "I allow that the sword is the last weapon to which we should have recourse. As *individuals*, it may be lawful, by this instrument, to defend ourselves or our families against the attacks of an assassin; but, perhaps, this is the only case in which it is so; and even there, if it were possible

---

29. Ibid., 205.

to disarm and confine the party, it were much to be chosen than in that manner to take away his life."[30]

Lest he be misunderstood, Fuller clarified that this possible justification for an individual to use force was extremely limited in scope. For example, it did not warrant Christians using force to defend their supposedly offended sense of honor. Such activities (e.g., dueling) might be considered honorable in that strata of society that Fuller called the "high life," but they "are certainly in direct opposition to the laws of Christ."[31] Even more restricting, Fuller also did not believe that Christians, when acting as individuals, had a biblical justification for "defending themselves against persecution for the gospel's sake. No weapon is admissible in this warfare but *truth*, whatever the consequence."[32]

Fuller was aware that this limitation could have dire repercussions for the faithful in certain circumstances. Indeed, he reminded his hearers of the bloody trail of persecution that was traceable almost up to his own time. But he defended the premise that "when Christians have resorted to the sword in order to resist persecution for the gospel's sake, as did the Albigenses, the Bohemians, the French protestants, and some others, within the last six hundred years, the issue commonly has been, that they have *perished* by it."[33] By contrast, "In cases where their only weapons have been 'the blood of the Lamb, and the word of their testimony, loving not their lives unto death,' they have overcome. Like Israel in Egypt, the more they have been afflicted, the more they have increased."[34]

But Fuller went on to explain that the restrictions that should rightly restrain the individual Christian from embracing armed resistance, or even from groups of Christians seeking to protect their churches or people, did not apply to matters of civil defense: "But none of these things prove it unlawful to take up arms *as members of civil society, when called upon to do so for the defence of our country*."[35] Fuller believed that although Matthew 26:52 was sometimes used to argue Christians should always opt for non-resistance, when rightly set in its context, it could

---

30. Ibid. Fuller offers no scriptural support for this conclusion. He apparently thought it self-evident.
31. Ibid.
32. Ibid.
33. Ibid., 206.
34. Ibid. The New Testament allusion is to Revelation 12:11.
35. Ibid.

properly be interpreted as providing a positive rationale for the qualified use of force:

> The ground on which our Saviour refused to let his servants *fight* for him, that he should not be delivered into the hands of the Jews, was, that his was a kingdom "not of this world"; plainly intimating that if his kingdom had been of the world, a contrary line of conduct had been proper. Now this is what every other kingdom is: it is right, therefore, according to our Lord's reasoning, that the subjects of all civil states should, *as such*, when required, fight in defence of them.[36]

Fuller linked a series of biblical statements into a chain that he believed clinched his argument that there were times when the path of duty compelled a Christian to take up arms. Appealing to Paul's argument in Romans 13, Fuller reasoned by asking a series of rhetorical questions:

> Has not Christianity, I ask, in the most decided manner recognized civil government, by requiring Christians to be subject to it? Has it not expressly authorized the legal use of the sword? Christians are warned that the magistrate "beareth not the sword in vain" [Rom 13:1]; and that he is "the minister of God, a revenger, to execute wrath upon him that doeth evil" [Rom 13:4]. But if it be right for the magistrate to bear the sword, and to use it upon evil-doers within the realm, it cannot be wrong to use it in repelling invaders from without; and if it be right on the part of the magistrate, it is right that the subject should assist him in it; for otherwise, his power would be merely nominal, and he would indeed "bear the sword in vain."[37]

The final point Fuller offered to bolster his argument was an observation that the general tenor of the New Testament towards soldiering as a profession was neutral, or even positive: "If the use of arms were, of itself, and in all cases, inconsistent with Christianity, *it were a sin to be a soldier*: but nothing like this is held out to us in the New Testament. On the contrary, we there read of two believing *centurions*; and neither of them was reproved on account of his office, or required to relinquish

---

36. Ibid. Fuller cited but a portion of John 18:36, which he believed set the issue of non-resistance in its proper context: "Jesus answered, My kingdom is not of this world: if my kingdom were of this world, then would my servants fight, that I should not be delivered to the Jews: but now is my kingdom not from thence" (AV).

37. Ibid.

it."[38] Fuller also considered the exchange between John the Baptist and some soldiers, who came to him asking how their profession impacted the repentance that the Prophet had said was necessary to prepare for the advent of God's Kingdom. This would have provided the perfect place for Scripture to have indicated that the military profession was incompatible with Christian discipleship. Fuller directed his hearers to consider Luke 3:14, "Some soldiers were questioning him, saying, 'And what about us, what shall we do?' And he said to them, 'Do not take money from anyone by force, or accuse anyone falsely, and be content with your wages'" (NASB). While soldiers, like the tax collectors who asked a similar question at the same time, were "warned against the abuses of their respective employments . . . the employments themselves are tacitly acknowledged to be lawful."[39] Even though this constituted an argument from silence, Fuller felt it had great force: "If either of these occupations [soldiering or tax-collecting] had been in itself sinful, or inconsistent with that kingdom which it was John's grand object to announce, and into the faith of which his disciples were baptized, he ought, on this occasion, to have said so, or, at least, not to have said that which implies the contrary."[40]

What of Conscientious Objection?

In the heart of his sermon, Fuller believed he had demonstrated that the biblical injunction to "seek the peace of the city" of which Christians were a part implied it was a positive duty for Christians to render military service when called upon to do so by their country. At the same time, he clearly was concerned that he not be seen as giving a blanket endorsement to Christian participation in the armed services. He sought to stake out a position that advocated the compatibility of military service with those causes that could be considered just. Fuller anticipated that some might object that no war could ever be truly just, for the motivations of the governing powers are almost never completely pure. Against such an objection, the Baptist theologian argued that weighing the motivations of leaders—which might include elements of revenge, greed, national prejudice, or cruelty—was no part of the evaluation process Christians should undergo. Rather, he instructed that "in ascertaining the justice

---

38. Ibid.
39. Ibid.
40. Ibid., 206–7.

or injustice of war, we have nothing to do with the *motives* of those who engage in it. The question is, Whether it be *in itself* unjust?"[41]

Motivations aside, Fuller also anticipated that many in his congregation might feel inadequate to judge aright the justice of a particular cause. Starting with an everyday situation that his hearers could grasp, Fuller reasoned to the weightier situation of international conflicts:

> If a difference arise only between two families, or two individuals, though every person in the neighbourhood may be talking and giving his opinion upon it; yet it is easy to perceive that no one of them is competent to pronounce upon the justice or injustice of either side, till he has acquainted himself with all the circumstances of the case, by patiently hearing it on both sides. How much less, then, are we able to judge the differences of nations, which are generally not a little complex, both in their origins and bearings; and of which we know but little, but through the channel of newspapers and vague reports![42]

Fuller exhibited a broad willingness to defer to the decisions of the governing authorities in these matters: "Where those who are constitutionally appointed to judge in such matters have decided in favour of war, however painful it may be to my feelings, as a friend of mankind, I consider it my duty to submit, and to think well of their decision, till, by a careful and impartial examination of the grounds of the contest, I am compelled to think otherwise."[43]

He did not, however, completely subordinate the individual's conscience to the desires of the state. Fuller reserved a very important right of private judgment to the individual believer. If asked to participate in a war that one felt to be unjust, Fuller advised that the Christian "stand

---

41. Ibid., 207.
42. Ibid.
43. Ibid. Fuller frequently and publicly allowed that his general sentiments favored the Whig party, though he always maintained an arm's length distance between himself and any party. He had an insight into political discourse that we do well to keep in mind: "Government may have done wrong in pursuing certain measures, but it is not from their being accused of it by interested men that we ought to believe it. Those who are now in power were lately in opposition, and then they were patriots and everything was going to ruin. There never was a period in British history when, in the opinion of what is called the opposition, let that opposition be on which side it might, the nation was not going to ruin; and when its humble adherents did not think so" (Fuller, "Thoughts on Civil Polity," 672).

aloof from it as far as possible."[44] Though he did not use the term, it seems he was advocating for the possibility of a "conscientious objector" status. He did not pursue the ramifications that might be expected to follow such a decision. Presumably, he would have advocated a passive acceptance of any civil consequences that might befall the conscientious objector.

Fuller concluded this first major section of his sermon by applying his reasoning to the scenario then facing England:

> After all, there may be cases in which injustice may wear so prominent a feature, that every thinking and impartial mind shall be capable of perceiving it; and where it does so, the public sense of it will and ought to be expressed. In the *present instance*, however, there seems to be no ground of hesitation. In arming to resist a threatened invasion, we merely act on the defensive; and not to resist an enemy, whose ambition, under the pretence of *liberating mankind*, has carried desolation wherever he has gone, were to prove ourselves unworthy of the blessing we enjoy. Without taking upon me to decide on the original grounds of the difference, the question at issue with us is, *Is it right that any one nation should seek absolutely to ruin another, and that other not be warranted, and even obliged, to resist it?* That such is the object of the enemy, at this time, cannot be reasonably doubted.[45]

Fuller thus sounded a clear note to his congregants that they could fight Napoleon and maintain a good conscience before God and man at the same time. Put another way, patriotism and piety were compatible.

Pray for the City

In Jeremiah 29:7, the prophet had given a second biblical injunction. God's people were instructed not only to seek the welfare of their city, which Fuller had interpreted in broad terms to include defending her militarily when called upon to do so, but also to "pray unto the Lord for it" (Jeremiah 29:7, AV). Whereas Fuller had taken six pages to cover the implications of seeking the peace of the city, he had to content himself

---

44. Fuller, "Christian Patriotism," 207.

45. Ibid. Even in 1797, when the more democratic longings of the French Revolution seemed paramount, Fuller had no trust in Napoleon. He perceptively commented, "It appears plain to me that Buonaparte wishes to be another Caesar" (Andrew Fuller to William Carey, 18 January 1797).

with less than a page for the present section.⁴⁶ He made two brief but important points.

First, he reminded his congregation of the folly of trusting in military strength and not God:

> You are aware that all our dependence, as a nation, is upon God; and, therefore, should importune his assistance. After all the struggles for power, you know that in his sight all the inhabitants of the world are reputed as nothing: he doth according to his will in the army of heaven, and among the inhabitants of earth; and none can stay his hand, or say unto him, What doest thou? Indeed this has been acknowledged, and at times sensibly felt, by irreligious characters; but in general the great body of the nation, it is to be feared, think but little about it. Their dependence is upon an arm of flesh.⁴⁷

In particular, the temptation to rely on military prowess was the Achilles' heel of the great men who commanded armies and navies in Fuller's day: "It may be said, without uncharitableness, of many of our commanders, both by sea and land, as was said of Cyrus, *God hath girded them, though they have not known him.*"⁴⁸ Fuller made application that our awareness of this misplaced confidence should spur God's people to prayer all the more: "But by how much you perceive a want of prayer and dependence on God in your countrymen, by so much more should you be concerned, as much as in you lies, to supply the defect."⁴⁹

Second, Fuller believed that nations needed to stand in fear of the judgment of God for their misdeeds. The awareness of that truth, he thought, should be a constant prod to God's people to be interceding for their country: "You are also aware, in some measure, of the load of guilt that lies upon your country; and should therefore supplicate mercy on its behalf."⁵⁰ It was not France that England had to fear, but God. Napo-

---

46. Fuller tended to preach extemporaneously from minimal notes. J.W. Morris, who printed many of his works, including the sermon "Christian Patriotism," noted that "Mr. Fuller's sketches for the pulpit consisted only of a few brief outlines, committed to memory, and enlarged at the time of preaching. He never filled up any written discourse, except when it was intended for the press, and after it had been delivered" (Morris, *Memoirs*, 84). It was possibly from a shorthand transcription of this sermon by his wife that a text was secured and published.

47. Fuller, "Christian Patriotism," 208.

48. Ibid.

49. Ibid.

50. Ibid.

leon was only a "vain man" with "boasting menaces." His "schemes and devices" could be expected to "come to nothing"—unless "our iniquities provoke the Lord . . . to deliver us into his hand."[51] One national sin was of uppermost concern for Fuller in terms of incurring guilt before God: slavery. He lamented to his people, "When I think, among other things, of the detestable traffic before alluded to, in which we have taken so conspicuous a part, and have shed so much innocent blood, I tremble! When we [his congregation] have fasted and prayed, I have seemed to hear the voice of God saying unto us, "loose the bands of wickedness, undo the heavy burdens, let the oppressed go free, and break every yoke!"[52] Hearkening back to the exchange between God and Abram for the fate of Sodom, Fuller held out hope for God's deliverance: "Yet, peradventure, for his own name's sake, or from a regard to his own cause, which is here singularly protected, the Lord may hearken to our prayers, and save us from deserved ruin. We know that Sodom itself would have been saved if *ten* righteous men could have been found in her."[53]

Motivations to Civic Duties

Following the main verbs in Jeremiah 29:7—seeking and praying—Fuller had expounded the duties he felt a Christian owed to his nation. Very briefly, he turned next to touch upon "the motive by which these duties are enforced."[54] He had time only for two brief thoughts.

First, self-interest demands resistance. He noted that God had "wisely and mercifully interwoven the interests of mankind as to furnish motives to innumerable acts of justice."[55] What Fuller meant was that when a Christian acted out of self-interest merely to protect his own life and property, he was also fulfilling his duty to seek the good of his city. Some British citizens who chafed under the increasingly heavy demands the crown made upon the populace for money and men had questioned whether these sacrifices were only for the benefit of the wealthy class-

---

51. Ibid.

52. Ibid.

53. Ibid. Not long after this sermon, the King called for a national day of fasting. Robert Hall preached a celebrated sermon on that day that greatly expanded on the theme Fuller here introduced (Hall, "Sentiments").

54. Fuller, "Christian Patriotism," 208.

55. Ibid.

es.[56] Yet Fuller saw that the interests of his own common people were inextricably linked with the fate of England:

> Yes, if men of opulence lose their property, you will lose your employment. You have also a cottage, and perhaps a wife and family, with whom, amidst all your hardships, you live in love; and would it be nothing to you to see your wife and daughters abused, and you yourself unable to protect them, or even to remonstrate, but at the hazard of being thrust through with the bayonet? If no other considerations induce us to protect our country, and pray to the Lord for it, our own individual and domestic comfort might suffice.[57]

Second, religious liberty is worthy of protection. Fuller believed that England's religious freedom would be jeopardized if the French were able to subdue them. He reasoned, "So long have we enjoyed religious liberty in this country, that I fear we have become too insensible of its value. At present we worship God without interruption. What we might be permitted to do under a government which manifestly hates Christianity, and tolerates it at home only as a matter of policy, we know not."[58] Fuller shared, with many of his contemporaries, a deep loathing for the Jacobins. He characterized them as "unprincipled men . . . who have been labouring to overturn [Britain's] constitution . . . [and] have a deep-rooted enmity to the religion of Jesus."[59] He prayed, "May the Lord preserve us, and every part of the united kingdom, from their machinations!"[60]

---

56. Some Britons maintained an undercurrent of sympathy for the supposed emancipating goals of the French Revolution, particularly those set forth by the Jacobins. Such sympathies waned as things unfolded in France.

57. Fuller, "Christian Patriotism," 209.

58. Ibid.

59. Ibid. The Jacobin party in France had been rabidly anti-Christian, especially during the early days of the French Revolution. Napoleon had moved far away from many of their extreme positions, even reaching an agreement with the papacy in 1801 that restored much of the Catholic influence in France. Baptists like Fuller were hardly reassured by a French-papal alliance.

60. Fuller, "Christian Patriotism," 209.

Fuller's Closing Thoughts

Fuller had time for only a few tidbits of application. Recognizing that some of his young men were contemplating volunteering for service, Fuller assured them of congregational support should they choose that path:

> I know that it is the intention of several whom I now address freely to offer their services at this important period. Should you, dear young people, be called forth in the arduous contest, you will expect an interest in our prayers. Yes, and you will have it. Every one of us, every parent, wife, or Christian friend, if they can pray for anything, will importune the Lord of hosts to cover your heads in the day of battle![61]

Then Fuller's sermon provides an insight into the priority with which Baptists set apart the Lord's Day for religious purposes in the early nineteenth century. Fuller was concerned that those from his congregation who did join the armed services take advantage of their right to reserve the Lord's Day for worship. His last word was addressed to that issue:

> Finally, it affords satisfaction to my mind to be persuaded that you will avail yourselves of the liberty granted to you of *declining to learn your exercise on the Lord's day*. Were you called to resist *the landing of the enemy* on that day, or any other work of *necessity*, you would not object to it; but, in other cases, I trust, you will 'Render to Caesar the things that are Caesar's, and unto God the things that are God's.'[62]

In summary, Fuller believed that there were times when a Christian was justified in taking up arms in defense of his country. He stands squarely in the long Christian tradition of support for a "just war." In cases when a believer was not convinced that the cause was just, Fuller seems to have advocated allowing for the status of a conscientious objector. The overall impression Fuller leaves is that of nuanced—even reluctant—support for the Christian's participation in the armed services. Though not addressed in this sermon, one factor that may have colored his thinking in this regard is the corrupting tendencies he thought were inherent in military service. This area of his thought can best be explored against the backdrop of his experiences with a wayward son who died a member of the Royal Marines.

---

61. Ibid.

62. Ibid. In 1803, under pressure from the Methodists, Parliament granted an exemption to Christian soldiers from training on the Lord's Day.

THE CORRUPTING TENDENCIES OF MILITARY SERVICE

Fuller's eldest son was named Robert (1782–1809). Though he showed some early inclinations toward the ministry, he never made a public profession of his faith. Thus, at age fourteen, he was apprenticed to a businessman (and friend of Fuller) in London. Almost immediately, Robert began to exhibit symptoms of instability and a penchant for choosing the wrong company. Though his father tried numerous things to reclaim him to a path of stability and morality, Robert increasingly turned to a dissolute lifestyle, unable to stay long in any employment. In a letter to a friend, Fuller revealed his fears that Robert would turn to the army, which he characterized as "that sink of immorality."[63]

Fuller's fears were realized when Robert, at age sixteen, did join the army. He served on and off again in the army and the Royal Marines for the rest of his short life. His career there was as checkered and unstable as had been his civilian life. Among other things, he received the incredible sentence of 350 lashes for desertion. More than once he begged his father to raise the necessary funds to purchase his release from his term of service; each time, Fuller complied and tried unsuccessfully to reclaim his son to civilian occupations. From 1798, when Robert first enlisted, until 1809, when he died of illness on board a ship, Andrew Fuller's life was filled with the unique and painful sorrow that only a wayward child can inflict.[64] His prophecy that the army would only mire Robert in sin had been fulfilled beyond his worst imagination. Thus, Fuller had an added reason to caution his congregants about the potential dangers of military service for their spiritual life.[65]

---

63. Morris, *Memoirs*, 53. Years later, in another letter to his son, Fuller further revealed the low opinion he held of the company of soldiers: "My dear son, you had advantages in early life, but, being continually in profligate company, you must be debased in mind and in a manner reduced to a state of heathenism" (Andrew Fuller to Robert Fuller, December 1808, in Haykin, *Armies*, 221).

64. The story of Robert Fuller is summarized in Haykin, *Armies*, 283–88. There is reason to hope that Andrew Fuller's efforts to reach Robert with the gospel were not in vain. He appears to have been converted in the last year of his life after having written his father in repentance and with a foreboding sense that he would not return from his next voyage. Robert begged his father to send him a letter proclaiming again the gospel he had long spurned. According to the testimony of one of his shipmates, he was indeed converted.

65. It should also be added that Fuller may have softened these negative views on the military toward the end of his life. As conscription pressed more and more

CONCLUSION

Andrew Fuller never had to make the choice, but it is clear he would have made a reluctant warrior. He recognized that God had ordained the use of force as a necessary means for checking the otherwise unlimited progress of evil in a fallen world. Thus, as members of civil society, Christian people must sometimes bear arms and otherwise assist their country in the horrible scourge of war. True patriotism did not consist of unthinking allegiance or blindness to the faults of one's native land, but in fervent prayer for an outpouring of God's mercy on a guilty people.

Fuller recognized that war and politics stood in very close relationship. What he said about politics, then, also describes his attitude toward war: "The political world is a tumultuous ocean; let those who launch deeply into it take heed lest they be drowned in it . . . Time is short. Jesus spent his in accomplishing a moral revolution in the hearts of men."[66] For Fuller, God's people owed ultimate allegiance to "the armies of the Lamb."[67]

---

rank and file Britons into military service, Fuller thought he could see a positive influence taking hold. Seven years after he preached the sermon "Christian Patriotism," he wrote: "Look at our fleets and armies: did we ever before hear of so many lovely groups of Christian people among them?" (Andrew Fuller, "Expository Discourses on the Book of Genesis," 306).

66. Andrew Fuller to William Carey, 18 January 1797.

67. Fuller, "Promise of the Spirit," 359.

Bibliography

Primary Sources

Fuller, Andrew. "Christian Patriotism, or, The Duty of Religious People towards Their Country: A Discourse Delivered at the Baptist Meeting-House in Kettering on Lord's Day Evening, Aug. 14, 1803." In *The Complete Works of the Rev. Andrew Fuller with a Memoir of His Life by Andrew Gunton Fuller*, edited by Joseph Belcher, 1:202–9. 3 vols. Philadelphia: American Baptist Publication Society, 1845; reprint, Harrisonburg, VA: Sprinkle, 1988.

———. "Expository Discourses on the Book of Genesis." In *The Complete Works of the Rev. Andrew Fuller with a Memoir of His Life by Andrew Gunton Fuller*, edited by Joseph Belcher, 3:1–200. 3 vols. Philadelphia: American Baptist Publication Society, 1845; reprint, Harrisonburg, VA: Sprinkle, 1988.

———. "The Letters of Andrew Fuller—Copied from Various Sources, by Miss Joyce A. Booth, Gathered by the Rev. Earnest A. Payne." Scanned to disc from the original by Nigel Wheeler, 13 January, 2005. The original is at the Angus Library, Regent's Park College, Oxford.

———. "The Promise of the Spirit the Grand Encouragement in Promoting the Gospel." In *The Complete Works of the Rev. Andrew Fuller with a Memoir of His Life by Andrew Gunton Fuller*, edited by Joseph Belcher, 3:359–63. 3 vols. Philadelphia: American Baptist Publication Society, 1845; reprint, Harrisonburg, VA: Sprinkle, 1988.

———. "Thoughts on Civil Polity." In *The Complete Works of the Rev. Andrew Fuller with a Memoir of His Life by Andrew Gunton Fuller*, edited by Joseph Belcher, 3:670–74. 3 vols. Philadelphia: American Baptist Publication Society, 1845; reprint, Harrisonburg, VA: Sprinkle, 1988.

Green, John. *Reminiscences of the Rev. Robert Hall, A.M.* 2nd ed. London: Frederick Westley & A. H. Davis, 1834.

Hall, Robert. "The Sentiments Proper to the Present Crisis." In *The Works of the Rev. Robert Hall, A.M.*, edited by Olinthus Gregory, 1:79–111. 4 vols. New York: Harper & Brothers, 1854.

Morris, J. W., ed. *Memoirs of the Life and Writings of the Rev. Andrew Fuller*. 2nd ed. London: Wightman & Cramp, 1826.

Secondary Sources

Brewster, Paul L. *Andrew Fuller: Model Pastor-Theologian*. Studies in Baptist Life and Thought. Nashville: B & H, 2010.

Emsley, Clive. *British Society and the French Wars, 1793–1815*. Totowa, NJ: Rowman & Littlefield, 1979.

Haykin, Michael A. G. *The Armies of the Lamb: The Spirituality of Andrew Fuller*. Dundas, ON: Joshua, 2001.

Morden, Peter J. *Offering Christ to the World: Andrew Fuller and the Revival of Eighteenth Century Particular Baptist Life*. Studies in Baptist History and Thought 8. Carlisle, UK: Paternoster, 2003.

Robison, O. C. "The Particular Baptists in England: 1760–1820." DPhil diss., Regent's Park College, Oxford, 1986.

Ryland, John. *The Work of Faith, the Labour of Love, and the Patience of Hope, Illustrated; in the Life and Death of the Rev. Andrew Fuller*. 2nd ed. Charleston: Samuel Etheridge, 1818.

3

A House Uniting: Americans, Baptists, and the War of 1812

James Tyler Robertson

WHEN PRESIDENT JAMES MADISON declared war against Britain on 18 June 1812, America was plunged into its second violent contest with the Imperial superpower in less than thirty years. Citing maritime rights, crippling trade embargos, the impressments of American sailors into service on British vessels under the often dubious charge of desertion, commercial restrictions, the use of natives to destabilize the western frontier lands, and—most critically for the scope of this chapter—national disrespect, Madison rhetorically posed the question, "whether the United States shall continue passive under these progressive usurpations and these accumulating wrongs." In such a statement two things were taking place. First, the "progressive usurpations" allowed for an opening military strategy of invasion while still claiming a defensive—therefore just—position.[1] Second, the term "United States" must not be overlooked, for at the time of Madison's declaration, political schisms, financial threats, questions of national identity, concerns over democratic governance, and

---

1. "In Massachusetts the Federalist-controlled legislature voted overwhelming against an 'offensive war' . . . The Kentucky legislature railed against both Great Britain and France . . . [and the South Carolina legislature called for] a 'triangular war' against both Great Britain and France" (Borneman, *1812*, 48). Due to the fact that there was vocal opposition to the war by both political and religious leaders, the President was forced to explain his actions in ways that could calm criticism and show that his actions were not contrary to the will of God or the ideals of the citizenry.

rumors that some states were considering secession from the Union made the individual states seem anything but united. However, even under the aforementioned circumstances, Madison had declared war and thus concluded his war speech by stoically pronouncing, "[We] shall commit a just cause into the hands of the Almighty Disposer of Events."[2]

While numerous books have been written about the various political and social dynamics in play before and during the struggle on both macro and micro levels, this chapter will restrict its focus to examining the official teachings of Baptist church associations and personal writings of Baptist people spread throughout the young nation.[3] It will begin by challenging the denial that such a person as an "American Baptist" even existed and that, in the early decades of the nineteenth century, the term is, at best, a misnomer and, at worst, a gross oversimplification of a very nuanced and regionally influenced and isolated collection of like-minded individuals and churches. The crisis of the war brought urgency to the motif of unity throughout the nation and even provided a backdrop through which disparate churches could unite under common theological and ministerial themes. This chapter will defend two separate, yet intertwined, ideas that need to be developed and understood in order to come to a fuller understanding of how the war impacted the churches. The first idea is that an American citizen was a definable entity and it was the impinging on that identity that helped start the war in the first place. The second is that while this chapter argues against the existence of American Baptists as a denomination, it will assert that "Baptist American" was a recognizable identity and that the term "American" was just as important a moniker as the term "Baptist." It is by studying early colonial writings about politics, the nation, and social culture alongside the Baptist sources that the cross-pollination (to borrow an agricultural

2. A series of Madison's speeches can be found at http://www.famousquotes.me.uk/speeches/presidential-speeches/presidential-speech-james-madison.htm. Accessed 28 August 2011.

3. Due to space limits, a proper literature review is not possible, but see Hickey, "War of 1812." This article references an assortment of academic articles and books dealing with the War of 1812 from a variety of interpretive paradigms. While Hickey's work is fairly complete, he admits, "even though we know more about the War of 1812 than we did ten or fifteen years ago, there are still plenty of opportunities for those interested in pursuing research on the 'forgotten conflict'" (Hickey, "War of 1812," 769). My essay hopefully answers this challenge in a small way. Heath's "Ontario Baptists" also contains an overview of relevant scholarship on the topic. While beyond the scope of this chapter, Heath's article is of special interest due to his concentration on Upper Canadian Baptists during the war.

term) between the burgeoning American nationalism and printed Baptist ideologies can be recognized.

These Baptists are an important segment of the early Republic's religious landscape to examine because their story shares certain similarities with the nation itself. Whereas the United States had rebelled against the imperial might of Great Britain's government, the Baptists had traditionally balked at government-sponsored establishment churches like that found in Anglicanism. Both the nation and the Baptists residing in that nation experienced the pitfalls and jubilation that came with the freedom from British institutions. Both struggled with common themes such as how to unify diverse and independent regions under a common banner without reenacting the autocracy that both of them had fought so long and hard against. Just as the government of James Madison[4] wrestled to insure success in the war without the taxes or mandate to build a national army of regulars, so, too, the Baptists struggled with the monumental task of overseas missions and combined ecclesiastical initiatives without the benefit of an overarching governing body. Both the nation of America and the American Baptists were coming to a deeper understanding in that first generation after the Revolutionary War that freedom, whether civil or religious, had a price. Both the nation and the churches had to struggle with the core question that constitutionally- and theologically-guaranteed freedoms raised: what does governance look like in a society of equals?

Therefore, using the issues of unity and just war criteria raised at the beginning of this paper in Madison's war-time speech as a jumping-off point, this analysis will explore how American Baptists dealt with these themes at such a critical moment in American history. The purpose of this exploration, conducted through the lens of a collection of churches loosely fitted under the rubric of denomination, is to set forth a theological explanation for the consequences that the second battle with England had for the burgeoning nation. For the Baptists during that time, a war with British North America was about more than maritime rights, economic concerns, or even nationalism; it was about an understanding of how God planned to use America to manifest his divine plan. Therefore, concepts like denominational unity, religious freedom, personal morality, national sin, and even fund-raising for missions took on eternal significance and, through them, the Baptists constructed a theology for war,

---

4. Madison, not coincidentally, was one of the definitive translators and implementers of Jefferson's Third Amendment guaranteeing Freedom of Religion.

governance, sanctification, and eschatology that was uniquely their own and uniquely American.

JUST WAR

THE ENGLISH AS EVIL

The first section of the paper will explore how many Baptists, acknowledging that only God could deliver them from something as deadly as the war, examined the morality both of the war and of the nation in order to insure divine favor. While both England and America claimed God defined their national mandate and had blessed them in times past, the two had very differing opinions about what constituted the character of a Christian nation. For Spencer Houghton Cone, the oppression of Ireland highlighted Britain's lack of integrity and Christian character. For Anglophiles like Rev. John Strachan of York, Upper Canada, it was the American treatment of Natives and their invasion of Canada that illustrated the avarice and violence of the newly-formed Republic.[5] Thus, Upper Canadian clergy of the Anglican and Presbyterian persuasion frequently labeled America the "satelite [sic] of Napoleon,"[6] desirous of a similarly secular and ungodly revolution.[7] Despite America's almost identical dislike of French policies at that time, the American attempt to seize British territory while the Crown

---

5. For a fuller treatment of this see Robertson, "Children of Nature."

6. "[O]ur neighbours blinded with ambition; and arrogant, from the great wealth and extensive trade which they had acquired by the miseries of Europe; and tempted by views of immediate aggrandizement, became traitors to the peace and happiness of mankind; and anticipating the downfall of the last citadel of liberty, hastened to seize upon a part of her territories. They have been sadly disappointed, and are about to meet with the punishment which their baseness deserves. The same victories which have prostrated the Tyrant of Europe [Napoleon], will prostrate *his Satelites*[sic] *in America*" (Strachan, *Sermon Preached at York*, 33; italics added).

7. The following are just a couple of quotes from Samuel Stillman. They show how the war of empires was viewed by him as leading to a new land much like America: "It ought not to be said, That the friends of the French revolution approve of all the circumstances attending it. They love the cause of liberty, and with its *universal triumph*, but lament every event that checks its progress and injures its reputation" (Stillman, *Thoughts*, 26). "May Almighty God make them [the French people] glad according to the days wherein he hath afflicted them, and the years wherein they have seen evil; and cause these great events among the nations, to terminate in the universal establishment of the rights of man, and the peaceful kingdom of Jesus Christ" (Stillman, *Thoughts*, 27).

was in a life and death struggle against France seemed too coincidental and too morally repugnant to be ignored.[8]

Therefore, the propaganda war that transpired in the papers[9] also took place in the pulpits of America as some Baptist Associations sought to show the obviously anti-Christian nature of their enemies. Returning briefly to Cone, one can see the moral indignation he felt against the British in the early days of the conflict. In the following letter he wrote of a recent experience:

> I have been listening . . . to a farewell address delivered by the Rev. Jn Hargrove to the Balt Volunteers who have rec orders to march tomorrow morning. The address was a very animated one, and produced many a burst of indignation and revenge coming from the lips of an old Revolutionary character, whose only son was press'd on board an English frigate, and in an attempt to escape found refuge in a watery grave. When I beheld the tears of bitter anguish rolling down the venerable cheeks of a disconsolable grey headed old man . . . I must confess my feelings were too agonizing for feeble words to describe.[10]

Not only was such a story inflammatory and one that created "many a burst of indignation and revenge" but it also allowed room for the servants of Christ to cry "foul!" against another nation and initiate combat without stain to the soul of the country.[11]

    8. Strachan is, once again, a useful source for an Anglican perspective in Upper Canada as to the calamitous nature of the American invasion. He preached: "[America has] threatened with unblushing arrogance to subdue this fine colony; to separate us from that heroic nation which enjoys the gratitude of the world. They mocked our attachment to the best of kings; and tho' born to the most exalted freedom and independence, they reproached us with being slaves" (Strachan, *Sermon Preached at York*, 37).

    9. Alan Taylor has done an excellent job in his book *Civil War*, showing how the political struggles within America led to a vast amount of both pro- and anti-war propaganda in various politically biased newspapers. After each battle, in many cases irrespective of the actual outcome of the battle, the Republican Party would "spin" the battle to win popular opinion in order to keep the often floundering war effort afloat. The same could be said of the decidedly antiwar Federalist party in their own newspapers.

    10. Cone, "Letters to Sally," 27 Sept 1812.

    11. However, it should be noted that there were those who did not believe such a thing was possible, as William Gribbin records the words of Ariel Kendrick (pastor in Cornish New Hampshire) who lamented following the war, "[I] drank into the war spirit, and delivered addresses and harrangues upon the conflict which swallowed up morals, men, and money, and fixed an indelible stain upon the Christian character of both nations" (Gribbin, *Churches Militant*, 85).

Even though the war was officially begun by America, some Baptists were able to see that while "War in any shape is a curse," the history of British atrocities and tyranny coupled with the continued threat to American sailors, commerce, frontiersmen, and citizens left the nation with no choice. America had "to resist the lawless aggressions of our vindictive enemy . . . We are contending for rights ever dear to freemen; and let this motto be engraved upon our hearts, 'United we stand, Divided we fall.'"[12] For the *Massachusetts Missionary Baptist Magazine* the issues that needed to be faced in 1812 were none other than the ones that had defined America's earlier and celebrated contest for independence. The laudable goals accomplished in that conflict were not simply the right to vote, taxation with representation, or even the overthrow of political tyranny but "We were then oppressed; we have now full liberty to worship God according to the dictates of our own consciences."[13] The glory found in the character of a nation defined by freedom of religion was a concept worth celebrating and, if necessary, worth killing and dying to defend.[14]

Once again, it cannot be stressed enough that within the writings of the Baptist associations such teachings were not simply about national pride in the political system or even the fact that an upstart people had won their independence from the acknowledged super-power of the day. For these Baptists, the only way the war could be fought with divine permission was in defense of what they held to be the core of the gospel message: freedom in Christ. The role of America in God's plan was truly global and the American Baptists seemed convinced that their message, supported by the successful experiment of their newly independent nation, had something God-honoring to offer to the world. Writing later in the war, Rev. Shackelford of the Georgia Association wrote out these ideals thus:

> Teach them to feel a general interest in the lawful prosperity of all men; and to commiserate the cases of the distressed. The laws of nature, and of God, announce that all men ought to be equally free both in civil and ecclesiastical governments. They know no

---

12. EKYA, "Circular Letter, Aug 1814," 5.

13. BMBA, "Address, Sept 1814," 14.

14. Therefore, Madison's conclusion to the declaration of war can rightly be called a political justification for Just War Theology: "The decision before Congress was whether the country would 'continue passive under these progressive usurpations,' or would respond with force and 'commit a just cause into the hands of the Almighty Disposer of events'" (Borneman, *1812*, 49), quoting from Hunt, *Writings of James Madison*, 191–201.

difference between the rich and the poor, the wise and the simple. Therefore, suffer not those committed to your care, to tyrannise over and reflect on those, who, in other respects, may be their inferiors, because they are such; but teach them the equal rights of man, and the love of liberty, according to the golden rule, '*do unto all men as ye would that they should do unto you*.'[15]

Within this is an understanding that the freedom of the individual is at the heart of Jesus' so-called "Golden Rule" and that America, more than England, had enacted that principle in their national governance.

America as the New Zion

Elkanah Holmes, who had been charged with treason for his support of the war from his Upper Canadian pulpit before escaping to the States, is an important Baptist to view, specifically because of his experiences in Upper Canada.[16] He had deliberately, and at great risk to his own safety, chosen to side with the land of his birth over the land of his residence when the war began. In his rationale, he cited America as God's "favoured Zion" in respect to its place in the plans of the Almighty. With such an understanding, the calamity of war, the wrath of England, natives, or even the staunchly anti-war Federalist Party of his own country whom, he believed, were undermining the hope of their nation in the name of peace, could not sour his mood because "God helping of me, I will not trouble myself about what 'the British, Indians & Devils,' of those that falsely stile themselves the Peace party can do: for with an unshaken faith I believe with you, that 'the Lord will arise & plead his own cause in the appointed time to favour Zion.'"[17] Holmes's belief that America occupied a special or favored place in God's purposes was perfectly in keeping with other Baptist writings from the time of the American Revolutionary War, up to and including the sometimes-called second Revolutionary War of 1812.[18] The strength behind such teachings was in the view that the

---

15. GBA, Shackleford, "Georgia Circular Letter, 1814," 3. Italics part of the original.

16. For more information on the role Baptists in Upper Canada played during the War of 1812, see Heath, "Ontario Baptists."

17. Holmes, "Letters, 1814."

18. John Taylor was known to refer to the War of 1812 as the second revolutionary war. See Taylor, *Baptists on the American Frontier*.

tyrannical government of England had been replaced by the Republican American Zion.[19]

The internal struggles to redefine America as an independent Christian nation had arguably created for the first time in Western civilization, "citizens [that] could claim as their fundamental right their religious beliefs to be nobody's business but their very own."[20] However, for the Baptist writers who reflected on this, the case was not simply one of national pride but one of divine destiny.[21] Spencer Houghton Cone's son once stated that his father believed the United States was "the grand theatre of [God's] mercy to His people, the peculiar place in which His truth expanded under the benign influence of civil and religious freedom."[22] England embodied Christian principles through established churches helping to dole out proper respect and a spiritual mandate to follow their constitution that, they argued, was as close to a gospel-centered political mandate as could be found in the world. For the States, the same was to be found in the more Republican ideas of freedom of religion and personal, non-coerced conversion as well as the rejection of any tyrannical overlords in favor of individual rights and freedoms.

The Elkhorn Kentucky Association would not even permit the appearance of both war and famine—two events frequently attributed in the Bible as punishments brought by God on unfaithful nations—to override their belief in God's pleasure with America. Acknowledging the calamities of 1814, they remained adamant in their claims that their land remained blessed in the sight of God and that "we are yet, a people highly favored by the Lord" before summarizing: "we possess a still greater blessing—Religious freedom constitutionally secured."[23] It was within their

---

19. As Hudson puts it: "This faith of the new republic was neither sectarian nor parochial. Its roots were Hebraic" (Hudson, *Religion in America*, 112).

20. Gaustad and Schmidt, *Religious History*, 125.

21. "The war, with all its vicissitudes, is illustrating the capacity and the *destiny* of the United States to be a great, a flourishing, and a powerful nation" (James Madison to Congress, 7 December 1813; italics added). "Manifest Destiny as an American idea is probably as old as the 'sea to sea' charters of the earliest colonies. The Puritan's sense of divine mission soon added a spiritual dimension to these grandiose ideas—a dimension that grew in importance after 1776, when nationalistic ambitions superseded the apocalyptic visions of an earlier day. In the antebellum decades evangelical dreams of a vast Christian republic brought prophetic certainty to the idea. Manifest Destiny became the catchword of an epoch" (Ahlstrom, *Religious History*, 878).

22. Gribbin, *Churches Militant*, 84.

23. EKYA, "Circular Letter, Aug 1814," 4.

constitutional guarantee of freedom of religion that the Elkhorn Baptists found their cause to celebrate regardless of their present circumstances. The Madison New York Association argued that the constitution created a nation "uncontaminated with a religion" and that it was such an uncontaminated land that would dispense with duty and provide the proper atmosphere for Christian love to flourish because "Our religion, like its Divine Author, speaks to the language of mercy & humanity—It teaches us charity to our brother, love to our enemies, hospitality to strangers, liberality to the distressed, and awful reverence to the God of Israel."[24] The religious freedom of Zion produced an environment better suited than its English predecessors to not only create, but foster, a land devoted to that which was greater than Christian duty: Christian love.

UNITED WE STAND

The Struggle to Create a Denomination

For the burgeoning denomination, "unity" was the watchword of the hour. Supporting such notions was the republican ideal that individual rights bestowed not just freedom but responsibility upon each citizen. Thus could the Elkhorn Association remind its member churches in the circular letter of 1813 that the Christian's duty in times of national crisis was to, "promptly render to Cesar the things that are Cesars [sic]." The meaning behind this was not simply an allusion to a teaching of Christ, but a demand that deference to the elected assembly was essential because, "The strengths of the nation cannot be wielded to advantage without confidence in the administration. Nor is it possible to excite distrust, or diminish confidence in the Executive, without essentially serving the purposes of the enemy."[25] Though couched in gospel language, the message was one of political significance as the associations recognized that internal squabbling during wartime threatened the very existence of the country.[26]

With the newly-found freedom came questions pertaining to what the individual's responsibility and relationship was to the nation. As Walter Borneman correctly declares, "In this early period of American history, the idea of states seceding from the Union was not nearly as cataclysmic

24. MBA, Peck, "Circular Letter, Sept 1813," 9–10.
25. EKYA, "Circular Letter, Aug 1814," 5–6.
26. "Thus, for Cone, participation in the war was 'as much the duty of the Christian as the honor of the soldier'" (Gribbin, *Churches Militant*, 84).

as it would be deemed two generations later."[27] During a tense period of the conflict, the Cumberland Maine Association challenged its members: "never . . . consider political sentiment as a criterion by which to try the sincerity of the profession of others; for while we conscientiously differ from them in political sentiments, we trust we are interested in the Saviour's merits, and have received pledges of his love"[28] In the early days of the war, the association from Massachusetts saw this potential for politics to undermine their efforts at denominational unity and commented, "We are in danger of losing that *harmony among ourselves*, on which the comfort and prosperity of our churches so much depend." As the association went on to remind its readership: "We do not all subscribe to the same political creed. We differ in common with our fellow-citizens at large, in the opinions we entertain of state affairs." Without offering a theological plea for unity, the circular letter admitted that "we have felt the pernicious tendency of this political licentiousness." And after appealing to the more pragmatic side of its readers, the association reminded them that should this situation "be suffered to proceed without control, it must eventually destroy the peace, if not the visibility of many churches."[29]

Such arguments illustrate what Rufus Weaver argues in his book on the Baptist Missionary Luther Rice that "while holding to common principles and doctrines, there was no visible union, no co-operative action and in reality no Baptist denomination; only a congeries of scattered churches loosely connected through membership in some local Baptist Association."[30] For the Union, New York Association, the divisions provided an excellent teaching opportunity for its members and one year into the war they recorded:

---

27. Borneman, *1812*, 11. The idea that the states, and not the federal government, were responsible for any success in the conflict is seen in the following statement by Daniel Webster in his speech before the House of Representatives in what would prove to be the weeks before the official end of the war: "That every town on the coast is not now in possession of the enemy, or in ashes, is owing to the vigilance and exertions of the States themselves, and to no protection granted to them by those on whom the whole duty of their protection rested" (Daniel Webster, "Speech before the House of Representatives, 9 December 1814," as found in Polner and Woods, *We Who Dared*, 4). The Republican Party had won their election based on the promise of lower taxes and the refusal to form a national military in order to keep those taxes low. However, that meant that the bulk of the military responsibility fell to the state militias.

28. MCA, Boardman, "Corresponding Letter, Oct 1814," 8.

29. BMBA, "Circular Letter, Sept 1812," 11. Italics part of the original quote.

30. Weaver, *Luther Rice*, 9.

we shall now address you on the topic of Brotherly Love. We think it of the first importance, at this critical and awful period, to impress your minds with this heavenly subject. God seems to be pouring out the vials of wrath, the world is agitated with the deepest commotions; nation is rising against nation, which shocks the harmony of creation and the happiness of mankind. The confused noise of war is heard in our land; garments are rolled in blood, "Iniquity abounds, the love of many is waxing cold"; Satan is raising up bulwarks in the Churches of Christ, and political discord prevails in our great national family.[31]

Their Boston counterpart, likewise, saw the pervasive power of political issues but reminded its readers, "In all free governments the people are bound to watch over their liberties with a jealous eye . . . [but] we will venture to say, you cannot feel the ardour of a political partizan [sic], and that of a humble, spiritual christian at the same time."[32] The role of the associations was, by their very nature, to promote unity between churches that had chosen to define themselves as autonomous entities. In that, the tension between individual rights and collective responsibility that was defining America could be seen. The American Baptists functioned as a microcosm of their nation as they struggled to unite without the "hierarchical structure [they considered] a mark of ecclesiastical corruption."[33]

Rev. Shackelford issued his own commentary on the political situation but reminded his Georgian readers that theirs was a solvable problem if only the base unit of any civilization—the family—would share the responsibility. Seeing the lack of attendance in churches as indicative of larger societal problems he chastised: "Were parents more particular in the education of their children, we should have less disorder in our families, neighborhoods, and religious assemblies." He then concluded the argument by stating that such attention would yield, "fewer political divisions and altercations in our government."[34] Minor Thomas of Cayuga agreed with Shackleford's assessment that the true evils of society lay in the hearts of its citizens and not in the incompetence of the governing bodies. He instructed his constituents to change their hearts

---

31. UBA, "Circular Letter, Sept 1813," 5–6.

32. BMBA, "Circular Letter, Sept 1812," 10.

33. Gribbin, *Churches Militant*, 110. "This belief [in the dangers of established churches] was as much a fact in the worldview of American Baptists as the horrors of impressment and the savagery of Indian raids" (ibid. 88).

34. GBA, Shackleford, "Circular Letter, 1814," 3.

to become more in line with that of Christ so that, "Instead of the rage of sin, holiness will prevail and reign in the minds of men, and God will dwell with them on earth." For it was the corrupted heart of humanity that created destruction, but a heart renewed by the grace of Jesus had the power to usher in a new world order where, "instead of wars, ill will, and revenge, all will be possessed of love, and kindness: for the great ones of the earth will bow, and the kings cast down their crowns in submission to the sceptre of Lord Jesus, and songs of Zion will be heard in every corner of the world."[35] In such calls to personal, familial and national holiness, the Baptist belief that the grace of Christ was both the key to the betterment of society and the glue that could hold their collection of like-minded churches together was shown.[36]

Indicative of such sentiments, the Boston Baptist Association printed the following to show that although the war effort was proving taxing and unsuccessful in 1813, grace was evident in the unity that existed among the churches of the region. To that end, Rev. Baldwin wrote:

> [A] good degree of harmony prevails among us; and considering the circumstances of the times, the changes which are taking place in the world, and the civil and political concussions which shake the earth, we have reason to bless God, for the unanimity and stability which characterize our Churches at this portentous and eventful crisis in the history of human and ecclesiastical affairs.[37]

As Baldwin, Thomas, and Shackleford reflected on the "Brotherly love" needed to create a denomination, the question still remained whether fiercely independent Baptists would desire such unity if it meant sacrificing church autonomy. Would this denomination experience the same ruptures as their nation or would the lordship of Christ form a union strong enough to withstand such challenges to their much-lauded independent and frontier-style governance?

THE MISSIONS CONTROVERSY

Ironically, the way in which such tensions manifested themselves had little to do with association membership and more to do with the growing

---

35. CBA, Thomas, "Cayuga Circular, 1812," 11.

36. Therefore, almost every Association Circular Letter began with thanksgiving to God for his providence that allowed another annual meeting.

37. BMBA, Baldwin, "Corresponding Letter, Sept 1813," 11–12.

desire for missions in some sections of the nation. In 1812, Luther Rice was championed by some as the founder of the Baptist Mission to other nations, but demonized by others because his Presbyterian origins threatened to undermine the traditional independent governance that many saw as a cherished and historical pillar that upheld Baptist beliefs.[38] So great was the Baptist concern in some corners that, after 1818, the so-called "Anti-mission" movement referred to support for missionaries in the west as, "taxation, presaging a state church" in an effort to rally condemnation against those Baptists who desired money for missions.[39] Although the following was written after the war, this excerpt from the 1819 pamphlet *Thoughts on Missions*, by Kentucky wilderness preacher John Taylor, exemplifies the concerns that many Baptists had regarding placing too much authority in a central system of government and how "un-Baptist" such a concept was. He wrote:

> the Pope of Rome and the Mother of Harlots were at their zenith . . . Money and power are the two principal members of the old beast. That both of these limbs are found in this young beast is obvious and exemplified in the great solicitude of correspondence with all Baptist associations . . . I consider these great men as verging close on an aristocracy, with an object to sap the foundation of Baptist republican government.[40]

---

38. "About China, Hindostan & 'other nations': We are further told that they lie, cheat, steal, and use all the little mean arts of fraud: and, when detected, only say, 'It is the custom of the country.' Now compare the state of society in Europe, at the present day, with its state previous to the diffusion of the Gospel among them . . . It is impossible for them to say in justification of their conduct, as is said in some of the heathen nations of the present time, *It is the custom of the country*" ("The Importance and Advantages of Itinerant and Missionary Efforts." *MBMM* 4, no. 1, March 1814, 41).

39. Along with missions there were various other voluntary societies such as Sunday Schools, tract societies and Bible printers that also required funding. Because the Baptists, like most other Protestants in America, lacked government support, they depended on a spirit of voluntarism. Therefore, societies sprang up to do the work of the church that had to operate without tapping into any structural coffers. This would give birth, out of necessity, to many ecumenical endeavors because few denominations had the financial support to run a mission, temperance, or Bible and tract society out of its own pockets. The energy and enthusiasm from the revivalistic meetings was channeled into such societies, as Protestants, though divided in many aspects, worked towards a Protestant nation. For more on the necessity of ecumenical endeavors based on economic realities in nineteenth-century America, see Bulthuis, "Preacher Politics"; also, William Westfall's *Two Worlds*, in which he famously quips: "Who will underwrite the kingdom of God?" (Westfall, *Two Worlds*, 91).

40. Taylor (ca. 1819) as found in Clark, *Small Sects*, 200.

Such adamant rhetoric opposed the seemingly benign (and actually beneficial) missionary society based on, among other things, the idea of individual money finding its way into a communal pot. This was no small matter as it threatened the very heart of the Baptist ideology of independence from what Taylor labeled "an aristocracy," and smelled a little too much like centralized—and non-republican—governance.

It was a question of organization—not validity—that provoked opponents of the missionary venture. The outspoken Taylor condemned such a mission as antithetical to Baptist convictions and contrary to the Scriptures themselves when he posited the question "whether the gospel was sent to the heathen land of America by a Missionary Society, or the providence of God?" For him, the actual means by which the Holy Spirit had spread the gospel since the days of the early church was "persecution in some shape for sending the gospel from one country to another."[41] What kind of persecution he is referring to is not known but what is clear from his writings, as well as those of his supporters, is that the idea of communal coffers and centralized control over the missions movement was seen as a threat that far outweighed any benefit.

However, other Baptists offered up arguments in support of a church-sponsored centralized and concerted missionary effort. At the close of the war, the Franklin New York Association wrote that "[When we observe] the missionary spirit that prevails in Europe and America, we conclude that it is a hopeful symptom of better times."[42] Their rationale was that peace brought increased opportunity for spreading the gospel in lands ignorant of Christ's salvific message. The Sturbridge Association echoed such sentiments when they wrote:

> Let us offer unto God thanksgiving; and pay our vows unto the most high. For he has caused the day of trouble to pass from us: he has delivered us from the destruction of the sword, that wasteth

---

41. Circular Letter to Primitive Baptist churches, Mississippi (ca. 1810), as found in Clark, *Small Sects*, 202.

42. FBA, Bostwick, "Corresponding Letter, June 1815," 11. The following quote shows an American Baptist response to a British Baptist desire that the two groups with strained relations would be united in mutual affection again. It is an important quote because it was printed in the *Massachusetts Baptist Missionary Magazine* during the war. The quote, originating in England but reprinted in America, states: "I long to hear from you and other American brethren! Yes, brethren we are in Christ, which neither seas, nor governments, nor politics can divide" (William Johns, "Excerpt from a Letter to Mr. Bolles of Salem, dated Birmingham, [Eng.] March 7, 1814." *MBMM* 4, no. 3, Sept 1814, 85).

> at noon and once more, the silver trump of peace is heard in our land . . . Do we feel [peace's] happy effects? Then from this may we learn to appreciate the invaluable worth of that gospel, which proclaims "peace on earth and good will to men." Permit us from this to call your attention to those heathen climes, which, as yet, have never been blessed with the gospel of peace.[43]

Therefore, the missions controversy brought to the forefront a uniquely American theological conundrum: how could Baptists faithfully discharge Jesus' command to "make disciples of all nations" without betraying the independence and freedom that, they asserted, defined them as God's light to the nations?

The answer to this question begins with an important recognition that there were many frontier Baptists of the southwest who shared their northern co-religionists' feelings on the subject. In Taylor's state of Kentucky, the Elkhorn Association referred to the missions movements as a "laudable Institution" and lamented the loss of printing presses at Serampore, India, to fire, where William Carey was ministering, before encouraging their people to donate to a rebuilding campaign and explaining that "any money received [for the purpose of rebuilding will be sent on] to the general agent in Philadelphia."[44] The Salem Kentucky Association likewise voted favorably "that all monies which may be intended for the use of Foreign Missions if forwarded to Brother Lewis our Secretary, shall be forwarded by him to the Corresponding Secretary of the Baptist Board of Foreign Missions."[45] Such official writings may not seem like much but must be read in the light of a changing denomination concerned to maintain their unique place within Zion while also exploring ways in which their version of the faith could be spread abroad. For American Baptists, centralizing something as vital as missions during that critical national and denominational time is worth noting because, as Warren Mild comments in his book *American Baptists*: "Missions made American Baptists into a denomination."[46]

While perhaps a touch overstated, Mild's words are not wrong. Vocal agitators called into question the wisdom and character of those who asked Baptists to pool their money and defer leadership to a centralized body. The problem was germane to the topic at hand because America

43. SBA, "Circular Letter, Sept 1815," 7.
44. EKYA, "Minutes, August 1813," 3.
45. SKBA, "Decision 25-Minutes, October 1815," 3.
46. Mild, *American Baptists*, 32.

was at war against an empire that embodied such principles. The political reality of the American nation granted the anti-mission movement the potential to divide the uniting denomination. Northern and southern churches were able to find common ground on this matter and the *Massachusetts Missionary Magazine* was "happy to learn" in December of 1813 "that missionary societies are forming in our Southern States . . . Let us, brethren, not cease to offer up Zion, that the knowledge of the Lord may cover the whole earth, and the church appear in her millennial glory."[47] The Elkhorn Association adopted an "ask for forgiveness rather than permission" mentality with regards to the spreading of missions pamphlets "[that] were afterwards distributed to each Church through their Messengers and paid for, which the Association hope will be satisfactory to the Churches, as they contain much useful information on the state of the Society."[48] However, it was the Miami/Ohio Association that offered the most impassioned plea for the endeavor when they composed, at length, the following apology for the necessity of missions:

> When we take into consideration, the state and situation of Mankind, in general, throughout the world, it furnishes an extensive field for the christian's contemplation. Has not every Christian in this Gospel Land, the greatest reason to bless and adore Zion's King, for having favoured us above any nation on the earth, that he has not left us to roam in the fields of nature, without the advantages of Civilization and Education; but that we are highly favoured of the Lord, in that we have the Gospel preached, in its purity and have free access to the written revealed will of God, and every mean[s] necessary (agreeably to God's appointment) for the furtherance and advancement of the Gospel. Notwithstanding we are blessed in so peculiar a manner, there are thousands of the human race, that are left in the wilds of nature on our frontiers, with no other guide or direction, than that of instinct, while many more who have the advantages of science among them, are deprived of the blessings we enjoy, by their lots being cast in remote regions, where the blissful sound of salvation has but seldom, if ever been proclaimed; in addition to these, there are almost innumerable multitudes, who are led astray by the cunning artifices of fanatic teachers who go about to establish their own righteousness, which is calculated to allure the world in general, and if it were possible, to deceive the

---

47. "Missionary Societies." *MBMM* 3, no. 12, Dec 1813, 379.
48. EKYA, "Minutes, Aug 1815," 2.

very elect. Ought not we, Brethren, who are so distinguishable favoured, to try to unite our energies and use every mean[s] within the compass of our power for the advancement of the Redeemer's Kingdom, by establishing institutions, and casting in our mites for the support of Missionaries, who are willing to go forth and proclaim the joyful sound of Salvation to the Heathens, or to any of the human family, who shall be destitute of a preached Gospel, whether saint or sinner.[49]

Although wars raged in Europe and at home, many Baptists saw not cataclysm but the hope of a new and deeper Christian world being birthed—a world that required missionaries at such a critical juncture.

For these men and women, the missionary movement was the remedy for the social ills that so obviously plagued the world, and the gospel was the only tool that could change the heart of humanity and bring hope. Such a thing, it was argued by the *Massachusetts Missionary Magazine*, superseded denominational governance because, in direct opposition to Taylor and his ilk, the benefits far outweighed the potential threat or loss of Baptist identity. To that end it was argued, "Review these advantages, brethren, that are the results of generous efforts for the propagation of the Gospel among the destitute and unenlightened, and we trust they will approve themselves with force to your minds. A reformation of morals among the degenerate descendants of a degenerate progenitor."[50] The degenerate and war-like race of Adam needed the peace-loving message of the second Adam that could only come from the work of missionaries.

The Democratic Bible

However, the content of the message to be delivered to the descendants of the degenerate progenitor is yet another example of the unique character of American Baptist theology. In the words of Mark Noll, "Warfare—and the more cataclysmic the better—has sometimes been the mother of theological profundity."[51] Therefore, what Baptists viewed as essential theology at such an early period in the republican experiment bears close examination. In March of 1814, the *Massachusetts Missionary Magazine* published an article titled "The Light of Divine Revelation Spreading"

49. MOBA, "Circular Letter 1816," 3.

50. "The Importance and Advantages of Itinerant and Missionary Efforts," *MBMM* 4, no. 1, March 1814, 41.

51. Noll, *Civil War*, 14.

in which it was argued: "As the sacred Scriptures are the foundation on which all our religious hopes are built, they must necessarily contain whatever is to be believed and practiced towards God and our fellow-men ... the HOLY BIBLE should be circulated among all nations, and in all languages."[52] While that statement seems simple enough, the act of interpreting the Scriptures for the "nations" could prove very complex.

William Miller, after the almost inexplicable British loss at Plattsburgh on Lake Champlain, "could only attribute his country's amazing salvation to divine intervention. This evidence of providence in history persuaded the young officer to turn his back on fashionable deism and join a Baptist church."[53] Miller became prominent in Baptist circles later on in the nineteenth century as the namesake of the apocalyptic Millerite movement. Regardless of the group's controversial eschatology, he serves as an excellent example of the American ability to step beyond the traditions that dogged biblical interpretations of Christian Europe when he wrote the nuanced statement: "I believe the Bible is the revealed word of God to man ... [However] what may be understood today might not have been necessary to have been understood 1,000 years ago."[54] Written closer to the time of the war, Lucius Bolles's reflections on the importance of Scripture frame a decidedly democratic understanding of the Bible. Acknowledging the critiques of the more hierarchical churches that tradition prevents heresy, Bolles argued that individual interpretation actually increased the prestige of the Bible. He believed that appeals to the Bible (as opposed to tradition) were a more effective means to bring the wayward back into orthodoxy. In 1822 he wrote:

> We consider it an acknowledged principle, that we have no right, by coercion, to restrain the liberties of men, on the subject of religion, and yet the effects of their differences are such, both on believers and unbelievers, as we may justly lament. On some unbelievers, at least, if we credit their declarations, it produces neutrality of feeling and conduct. They know not what to believe, or whom to follow, and therefore determine to believe nothing. And among the avowed disciples of Christ it produces bitterness and strife, evil speaking and evil work ... Under such

---

52. "The Light of Divine Revelation Spreading," *MBMM* 4, no. 1, March 1814, 18.

53. Howe, *What Hath God Wrought*, 289. The church he joined was the Low Hampton Baptist Church in New York.

54. William Miller's synopsis of his beliefs, c. 1840s, as found in Handy, *Religion*, 166.

circumstances the utility of the Bible becomes apparent to all . . . it is of no sect or party, is biased by no prejudice or self interest, changes with no change of time, or men, or measures; and what it speaks once, it speaks forever. To this standard the erring christian may be brought by his fellow christian . . . But what is more to us personally, to this standard we may bring our own scruples of conscience.[55]

Later on in his *Discourse*, he would locate such beliefs squarely within the nation he called home: "The fathers of our churches in this country have told us, what God did by them: How he wrought with them, and made the administration of his word and ordinances his wisdom and power to the salvation of many souls, and greatly enlarged their borders, so that from a little one they became a thousand, and from a small one, a strong nation."[56] The reason behind the success of Bolles's "strong nation" was the early republican Baptist idea of liberty being the seedbed from which the most authentic Christianity could grow.

David Jones, a Baptist American military chaplain, in writing his autobiography about coming to America, "of which I had often heard a good account," laid claim to American freedom as his incentive for the journey because "it was a land of freedom. I had, at that early age, adopted the maxim, 'Where Liberty dwells, there is my country.'"[57] Such freedom gave a mandate for the Baptist cause to become involved in the war, because, as the Cumberland Association put it, "A person once put in possession of liberty, has no authority to surrender that right—hence in the injunction, 'let no man take thy crown.'"[58] However, fighting for the above-mentioned freedom was not a *carte blanche* excuse to engage in the carnality of battle. The women of the Boston Female Society for Missionary Purposes were reminded that "We are not, dear sisters, called to go into the field of battle and expose our lives to the devouring sword." These women were warriors of a different sort, pleading with God so that "divine displeasure may be averted."[59] Such a calling was not reserved for women, who could not serve as soldiers anyway, but, according to the Franklin Association, was the calling of all believers in a time when

55. Bolles, *Importance of the Scriptures*, 10–11; italics original.
56. Ibid., 21.
57. Jones, *Biographical Sketch*, 4.
58. MCA, "Circular Letter, Oct 1814," 6.
59. Mary Webb, "An Address from the Boston Female Society for Missionary Purposes to Females Profesing [sic] Godliness," *MBMM* 3, no. 8, Dec 1812, 283.

the madness of war threatened to overwhelm their spiritual duties. The Circular Letter of June 1813 reminded its readers that "while the nations of the world are contending with carnal weapons for their civil rights and privileges . . . let us, who have professedly turned our backs upon the world, and enlisted under the banner of King Jesus, put on the whole armour of God and fight manfully under him who is the great head and captain of our salvation."[60]

Over a year later, as America was falling to the steady march of British regulars, the Madison Association reminded its adherents that "While our land, (at a time when the nations of Europe, so lately, and so largely agitated, generally enjoy tranquility) is involved in the most complicated troubles," theirs was a calling to speak into the world of violence because "though sheltered under the wings of the ALMIGHTY, [we] must necessarily participate in the common calamity." The association then reminded its fearful readers that the faithful churches possess "an inheritance beyond the reach of cannon, or the power of any hostile invasion; an inheritance reserved in heaven for believers, who are kept by the power of God, through faith unto salvation; ready to be revealed in the last time."[61] Therefore, according to the Elkhorn Association, attention to passages like 2 Timothy 3:16, which states that Scripture is excellent for reproof and biblical teaching, was of the utmost importance to steer the nation into godly paths, for "inasmuch as our journey through life, is a state of tribulation and warfare, and we have enemies both powerful and subtle to encounter, it may not, perhaps, be unprofitable, at this time, to summon your attention . . . to this important and interesting subject."[62] Thus, the arguments for denominational unity, missions, church governance, and religious liberty were each undergirded by the only instrument the Baptist churches saw fit to guide the churches—and the nation—through such turmoil: the Bible. American Baptist biblical interpretation of the war formed yet another unique aspect of their theology.

---

60. FBA, "Circular Letter, June 1813," 5.
61. MCA, Boardman, "Corresponding Letter, Oct 1814," 7.
62. EKYA, "Circular Letter, 1812," 3.

BIBLICAL INTERPRETATION OF THE WAR

War and Peace

In the early days of the war, the Madison Association cautioned its churches that "yea tho' wars and commotions, human carnage and blood-shed, fill the earth like a tempest; yet the ROCK of ages stands firm and immovable."[63] In the same month the Sturbridge Massachusetts Association echoed this sentiment: "And while we hear of wars abroad and rumours of war at home, we are not troubled," because of the eternal plan of the God they served that, according to the Bible, would, "overrule all things for the display of perfections for the fullness of his purposes, in the accomplishment of his eternal plan."[64] A year later, Rev. Waters of Sturbridge reiterated such claims but expanded their meaning to show that as his readers were "formed by God in the truth," the biblical mandate for all Christians to love their enemies set them free to "give our fears to the wind, and be at peace with all men. Let us never render evil for evil, but contrawise blessing" in the hopes that such godly behavior might please God enough "that he shall make even our enemies to be at peace with us."[65] In such statements, and the themes we are about to explore, the Bible acted as the interpretive agent of the national conflict. In the absence of creeds or hierarchical governance, the Bible functioned as a "flag" around which those desirous to be called Baptists could gather. This is not to say that there existed any kind of interpretive uniformity—far from it—but it was acknowledging the ultimate supremacy of the Bible and the use of biblical allusions and motifs that united many Baptists even if their words and interpretations differed.

An example of this existed in certain Baptist attitudes towards war and peace. While the official letters appeared more conciliatory, personal correspondence from several presiding leaders communicated a more war-like attitude; equally couched in biblical language. William Gribbin notes that Baptist William Parkinson provided a month after the declaration of war a "thorough defense of both Madison and the war."[66] He also cites Elisha Cushman's Just War ideology as being found in Jesus' refusal to condemn the soldier. Therefore, "[While some] Christians might op-

---

63. MBA, "Circular Letter, Sept 1812," 10.
64. SBA, Waters, "Corresponding Letter, Sept 1812," 7–8.
65. SBA, Waters, "To Corresponding Associations, Sept 1813," 8.
66. Gribbin, *Churches Militant*, 81.

pose the present war [they] should not denigrate those who took up arms in it."[67] Spencer Houghton Cone provided one of the more impassioned letters giving support for the war when he wrote:

> Success to our cause! And may all who have enlisted units support, "Remember the Heroes our Fathers . . . In the day of distress side by side—when the grass of the vallies [sic] grew red with their blood they stirr'd not, but conquer'd! or died!" My heart pants with anxious solicitude for the fate of our gallant little navy. Rodgers and Decatur will certainly cover themselves with glory! They will fight like heroes of the past, and die as brave men ought. I tremble for their immediate safety—opposed as they are by overwhelming numbers—But let us confide in the God of Battles, who will ultimately crown the cause of virtue with success![68]

It was for freedom they fought, first in the eighteenth century, and then, as Cone argued, again in 1812. Throughout both contests, the Bible tied the faithful into the deeper meanings of what the war was about, what they as Americans were defending, and how the average Baptist could utilize Scripture to make sense of the violence and confusion brought on by such conflict. Because of that, there is some support for William Gribbin's controversial assertion that "Baptists knew the war was more than justified; it was holy."[69] However, while the Baptists saw their nation as blessed with civil and ecclesiastical freedom, how did they react to a government desirous of mandating spiritual activities in the name of the country?

HOLY WAR

In July of 1812, President James Madison and his congress declared a national day of prayer and fasting to plead for divine assistance in the war effort. As the war proved largely unsuccessful and the morale of the nation plummeted, the celebrated separation of church and state diminished and that had the potential to invite criticism from ecclesiastical circles. However, the churches responded to the presidential plea and "recommend[ed] to the Churches that they observe the 2d Wednesday of December next, as a day of Humiliation, Fasting, and Prayer, on the

---

67. Ibid., 83.
68. Cone, "Letters to Sally," Letter 27, July 1812.
69. Gribbin, *Churches Militant*, 89.

account of our National Calamities."⁷⁰ Randolph Hall of the Southern District Association honored the presidential request to his readers stating: "And whereas the President of the United States, at the request of Congress, has recommended a day to be observed with religious solemnity, as a day of public humiliation and prayer; and has by his proclamation set a apart [sic] the 2d Thursday in September: we do earnestly advise and recommend to you to observe this as a day of prayer and fasting."⁷¹ All associations eagerly participated in the request⁷² but it was the Massachusetts Association that most ardently expressed their belief that it was prayer that would save the nation:

> We cannot close our letter without referring to the state of our nation. The present is a momentous period. The safety of our towns and cities is endangered by a powerful foe; and the lives of our citizens are in jeopardy every hour. These considerations solemnize our minds. We feel the importance and necessity of prayer . . . May we not hope then, that, in our united prayers, the Lord will bless our land? And, are we not sure, that He will

---

70. MCBA, "16th Resolution—Minutes, 1814," 6.

71. SDAB, Hall, "Circular Letter August 1813," 4.

72. The following series of quotations provides an overview of some of the other Associations writing about this topic in order to illustrate the congruity between them: "15th. From Nolin—would it not be advisable for this association to encourage and appoint days of *'Humiliation and Prayer'* under the distressing circumstances that we as a nation are under—Answer, Yes—and appoint the 25th day of December next, as a day of *Humiliation, Fasting and Prayer*" (SKBA, "Minutes, October 1814," 2; italics original). It is interesting to note that the day of prayer was actually on Christmas Day. "8. Voted, that we recommend to the Churches of this Association, to observe Thursday, the 29th day of the present month, as a day of fasting, humiliation and prayer, on account of the present afflicted state of our country, and the low state of Zion" (BMBA, "Minutes, September 1814," 5). "13. At the request of several Churches for a day of fasting and prayer—It is recommended to observe the 3d Thursday in this instant in that way: being the day set apart by the Executive of the United States—and also the 1st Friday in October, as recommended by the North District Association" (EKYA, "Minutes, August 1812," 2). "13. Resolved in consideration of the awful and distressing calamities of war in which we, as a nation are involved, that it be recommended to the churches we represent, to set apart the second Wednesday in December next, as a day of humiliation, fasting and prayer to Almighty God" (MBA, "Minutes, Sept 1814," 9). "Conformable to the request of several churches and of the President of the United States, we recommend that the second Thursday in September next be observed throughout the churches as a day of fasting and prayer" (EKYA, "Minutes, August 1813," 3).

unquestionably bless all those who engage in service with sincerity, and humility of heart?[73]

Like the Zion of ancient times, the "land" in need of blessing needed to be understood as a physical and spiritual home where the faithful were creating a devout nation. Therefore, the war was also about more than just national or military goals; the sacredness of the American "Promised Land" made its defense a holy endeavor.

In 1813, the Kentucky Association—the same that refused to acknowledge war and pestilence as a sign of God's displeasure—challenged the citizens that in times of war, "It becomes our indispensible duty to examine ourselves as in the presence of the Lord, who is a heart-searching God." Once again, they needed to turn to the sacred texts of the Bible in order to learn "of those sins that have brought so many evils upon us as a nation, and let us repent, confess, and forsake them, and turn to the Lord, for he has graciously promised that if we draw near to him he will draw near to us."[74] In the identification of sin as a communal problem, the association did two things. First, it offered up a program of involvement based on personal reflection and repentance so that their members who were neither policy makers nor soldiers could, as repentant believers, impact the course of the war. Second, it found another unifying theme that stated that the individual was responsible not just to God, but to fellow believers and the nation as well. Brother Randolph of the Southern Baptists agreed and preached in August of 1813 "from Proverbs 14th chapter, and 34th verse—'Righteousness exalteth a nation, but sin is a reproach to any people.'"[75] The fate of the land was thematically paired with the biblical stories of Israel, so when scores of Redcoats landed it was easy to turn to the tales of apocalyptic judgment to find out what message the Baptists could deliver to embattled Zion.

The End of the World

The War of 1812 provided plenty of biblical allusions of judgment and doom that Baptists capitalized on to hammer home their message of national repentance and reliance on Jesus. The *Missionary Magazine* alluded to Christ's warnings regarding the end of the world when he told

73. BMBA, Baldwin, "Corresponding Letter, Sept 1814," 11.
74. EKYA, "Circular Letter, Aug 1813," 3–4.
75. SDAB, "Minutes, August 1813," 1.

his followers that they would "hear of wars and rumours of wars," but as dire as the situation appeared to be and the "great changes taking place in the civil and political affairs of mankind" they found purpose in their divine mandate to spread the gospel and that even "amidst all these scenes of apparent confusion and distress, such efforts should be so universally made to establish christianity and spread the gospel among all the nations of the earth!"[76] Juxtaposed to the Kentucky Association's belief that wars and famine were not signs of God's displeasure, the Cumberland Association offered up the war, and other struggles the nation was facing both agriculturally and politically, as a reproof against an American citizenry that appeared neglectful of God's law. Lamenting such trends within the self-professed godly nation of America they wrote:

> The general clash of nations abroad, the sound of war at home, the division and party spirit, now predominant amongst all the classes of our citizens, which have wrecked the happy union, once so prominent amongst the only free people on the earth: the unreasonable jealousy, acrimony, and illiberality manifested by partisans on both sides of the political contest . . . the rapid progress of falsehood, detraction, and almost every species of wickedness—The frowns of an incensed God, made manifest in the withholding . . . of the natural Sun . . . unintermitting rains . . . the slow progress of vegitation [sic], the unseasonable frosts . . . These considerations, with many others, which might be mentioned, combine to depress, the spirits and fill the mind with gloomy apprehensions.[77]

Although the times of war were terrifying and disheartening, the Cumberland article ended on a hopeful note as Rev. Boardman reminded the churches that "From the signs of the times we know that the day of Zion's redemption is approaching near."[78] Apocalyptic doom was not only matched but superseded by eschatological hope.

For the Franklin Association, the observable "tumults and commotions in our world," not to mention on their doorstep, were explained by the empirically unobservable, faith-based rationale that "because iniquity abounds and the love of many waxes cold, and clouds of darkness pervade our land, the judgments of God are abroad in the earth; he is correcting us for our sins, and we ought to be humbled under his

---

76. William Collier, "Report," *MBMM* 3, no. 7, Sept 1812, 221.
77. MCA, "Circular Letter, Sept 1812," 10.
78. MCA, Boardman, "Corresponding Letter, Sept 1812," 16.

chastisements."[79] Even though national sin as a concept appears negative upon first viewing, there existed deeper and more positive meanings. First, it reiterated the role of America as the new Israel; a nation chastised by God because it held a prominent place in the divine plan and needed to act accordingly. Second, if the people had wronged God as a community, it stood to reason that they could bring about his pleasure as a united collective as well. The Boston Association located their own land's struggle in the paradigm of other nations that had experienced the same:

> All the changes we are called to witness; the rise and fall of states and empires; commotions in the material and political world, however violent and extensive; all, all cannot essentially affect the happy state of the saints of the Most High . . . For in very deed, "nation is rising against nation, and kingdom against kingdom"; . . . And these things are the beginning of sorrows . . . But in view of the kingdom of Christ, may we not look for a second fulfillment of that prophecy; "I will shake all nations, and the desire of all nations shall come"?[80]

Therefore, like Cumberland's optimism, or Kentucky's refusal to relinquish America's status as "favoured," or the pro-missionary groups' understanding that missions were an integral part of the human assignment on earth, the Boston Association injected a message of hope that all political turmoil sped the temporarily terrifying, but ultimately desirous, arrival of the Kingdom of God.

As William Johnson and William Brantley noted in March of 1814, "Late events in Divine Providence prove, with convincing testimony, that this time fast approaches. Wars and rumours of wars, the overturning of the nations, the rapidly increasing destruction of the man of sin, and the spread of divine truth, events, predicted by the prophets, and represented by them as prelusive to the general diffusion of the Gospel, clearly shew that the universal triumph of Christ, the King in Zion, is not far distant."[81] Such quotes show the struggle to unify disparate churches for the communal good of Zion. Lake continued: "we earnestly desire to maintain and enlarge, not merely to become acquainted with each other as men, but as soldiers of the cross" for the deeper ecclesiastical reason "that we may understand each other in our views and belief of the doctrine of

79. FBA, "Circular Letter, Sept 1813," 4.
80. BMBA, Baldwin, "Corresponding Letter, Sept 1812," 14.
81. William Johnson and William Brantley, "Circular Address," *MBMM* 4, no. 1, March 1814, 7.

the gospel, the order of the churches, and discipline of the doctrine of the house of God." Thus, through Baptist theology the churches could be "united together" in order to experience the blessings of "Peace among ourselves."[82] Two years later the same song was being sung as Rev. Robinson echoed the words of his predecessor:

> while the nations of the world are dashing one against another and the inhabitants of the earth appear to be so deeply engaged in the concerns of this world. Dear Brethren—Let the cause of the Redeemer command our attention, and may we strive to maintain the unity of spirit, in the bond of peace—And amidst all the calamities that so convulse the world, may we learn to live near the Lord.[83]

Unity remained the key to Baptist survival. Thus, while numerous letters celebrated the fight for independence, both in the Revolution and during the campaigns of 1812–14, that independence was carefully and deliberately balanced with a humble submission to the interests of advancing the growth of Zion.

In such ways the Baptist associations used both the left hand of hope and the right hand of chastisement to gather together every disparate church that concurred with the published sentiments of the Association into a collective. Such shared understandings were capable of bridging the distances between individual churches to bind them together ideologically irrespective of physical distance. An anonymous pro-missionary writer explained: "The uncommon efforts which are now making to spread the *sacred word*, must be highly interesting to all lovers of pure religion. Presuming that most of our readers are of this description."[84] Although the quotation is a somewhat backhanded insult towards any who opposed the missionary movement, it also serves to illustrate an understanding that holding to a contrary viewpoint would sever such a person from the larger community that was in support of the ideal.[85] The

---

82. FBA, Lake, "Corresponding Letter, June 1812," 8.

83. FBA, Robinson, "Corresponding Letter, June 1814," 10.

84. "The Light of Divine Revelation Spreading," *MBMM* 4, no. 1, March 1814, 18.

85. Although discussing Puritans in Massachusetts, Janice Knight makes a similar comment that, for churches to function as teaching agents, a certain amount of assumed common knowledge was required. In her chapter "Charity and Its Fruits" (130–63) she writes: "Presuming a regenerate audience who needed only to be recalled to the moment of faith and united in works of fellowship, they developed a preaching style designed to provoke that memory and therein to re-member the congregation"

churches were to be united through specific theological constructs more than any other ideology and as the storm clouds of war darkened young America's skyline, ideas of collective sin, personal repentance, individual responsibility, and redemptive eschatology reminded the faithful that they were part of an eternal nation as well.

With such an understanding in place, the war lost some of its destructive finality and was changed by some of the associations into a powerful interpretive tool to increase readers' personal spiritual disciplines. Rev. Lake of the Franklin Association wrote to the churches in the same month that Madison issued his declaration of war that "when the signs of the times hold out a Luminous warning to the countless multitudes, bound to the Supreme tribunal; enforcing with resistless energy the Saviour's solemn admonition, Be ye also ready, for the hour of Judgment is coming" he encouraged the people to be "like the faithful soldier" in emulating the strict attentiveness to spiritual matters so as to remain, spiritually speaking, "at the post of duty, awake and active in the cause of righteousness."[86] With the hope that "we be stimulated to faithfulness and encouraged in the glorious warfare, let us put on the whole gospel armor, and exert our united efforts in support of the cause and interest of Zion's king."[87]

For the Georgians in 1814, the ultimate benefit of spiritual discipline was their ability to unite the faithful together under the Lordship of Christ. The Circular Letter stated:

> The second particular to which we invite your attention, is *a strict, practical use of Gospel discipline*. Where this is executed, in faithfulness and love, it never fails to effect its designs; which are to glorify the Great Head of the Church; reclaim from error; and strengthen the bands of mutual affection. Never let your pity, on the one hand, make you relaxed in this duty; nor pride, nor prejudice, prompt you to go beyond its limits, on the other; but let the cause of God lie uppermost in your hearts, and his glory be your polar star. Then you shall be as an army with banners, striking terror through your enemies, and proselyting many to the cross of your Saviour.[88]

Thus was militarism and the pressing calamity of war utilized to bring people together under God's banner to unite in the cause of proselytization

---

(Knight, *Orthodoxies*, 131).
   86. FBA, Lake, "Circular Letter, June 1812," 5.
   87. FBA, Lake, "Corresponding Letter, June 1812," 8.
   88. GBA, Shackleford, "Georgia Circular Letter, 1814," 3.

and the betterment of America's spiritual landscape. With that understanding the Boston Association could challenge its readers that their salvation could not be effected by "the wisdom of statesmen, or the valour and intrepidity of heroes" but that it was the attention of each believer to their spiritual disciplines and fidelity to the Almighty that alone could bring the required divine pleasure needed to achieve national and military success. Once again, calling on the nationally-sanctified memory of the Revolutionary War, the Boston Association argued that disunity was a threat to the land and that without God's aid "our country will continue sinking beneath the pressure of foreign aggression and civil discord, until it has reached the lowest stage of national degradation unless the Almighty arm, which wrought such wonders for our fathers, be now exerted in behalf of us their ungrateful and degenerate offspring."[89] The arm of the Almighty was shown to be the only instrument capable of stemming the tide of civil discord and the Independence captured by the preceding generation served as the best example of people uniting together for the common goal of achieving the God-given right of individual equality.

THE END OF THE WAR

Lament for War

However, it would be an overstatement to argue that the Baptists, as a group, united under a pro-war banner, because of the vast number of writings that lamented the war, not just for the damage it did to America, but because of the inherent evil present in such conflicts. Writing in 1814, when the nation was nearly bankrupt and had little to show for the war, the Boston Association pleaded: "Bear on your hearts in prayer to Almighty God, the state and situation of your beloved country, now experiencing the awful calamity of war, and its attendant horrors," not because the horrors of war scarred the nation physically but because war stunted the nation's mission spiritually. Thus they requested "that speedily we may have share in common with other nations, the blessings of a righteous, honourable and permanent peace, with its attendant smiles; that war may forever cease." For the Boston Baptists the motive for peace was so that "the precious gospel of the Son of God universally spread

---

89. BMBA, "Circular Letter, Sept 1812," 12.

and triumph."[90] Although it could be argued that such statements were most prevalent when the war was least popular, the Boston Female Society for Missionary Purposes made a very similar argument only a few months into the war. In the final address for the year 1812 the following was recorded:

> The present is a time, which calls loudly on the people of God, to exert themselves to their utmost, in every way which may be calculated to promote the cause of truth. In a day when iniquity abounds, and the love of many is waxing cold; when the most important and fundamental doctrines of the gospel are controverted and held in contempt by many who call themselves Christians; when our beloved country which has long been the seat of peace, and an asylum for the wretched of every description, involved in the horrors of war; when the ocean is discoloured, and the land crimsoned with the blood of fellow-men; it more than ever becomes the real disciple of Jesus to "pray without ceasing" that "the Spirit of the Lord may lift up a standard" against those floods of error and infidelity, and cause a reformation of heart and life, both in the church and in the world.[91]

Even earlier in the struggle, the Cumberland Association lamented war, arguing that it was abhorrent to even the spiritually ignorant, when they wrote: "The peculiarities, at home and abroad, both in Church and State, which mark the present era, seem calculated (religion aside) to produce dejection and despondency."[92]

However, 1814 was understandably a year when many official and personal letters mourned where the war had taken America as a nation. With the British army running roughshod over the eastern seaboard and the threat of re-colonization by Britain increasing every day,[93] Obed Warren wrote:

> The scene is now changed, as it respects our once highly favored country! While there is but little or no mitigation of the horrors which have attended the *European* nations, the cup of wrath has

90. BMBA, "Circular Letter, Sept 1814," 9.

91. Mary Webb, "An Address from the Boston Female Society for Missionary Purposes to Females Profesing Godliness," *MBMM* 3, no. 8, Dec 1812, 282–83.

92. MCA, "Circular Letter, Sept 1812," 9.

93. "Suddenly the young American nation was no longer fighting for free trade, sailors' rights, and as much of Canada as it could grab, but for its very existence as a nation . . . it looked as if the British Empire might regain its former colonies" (Borneman, *1812*, 2).

passed the Atlantic. War [the War of 1812] is waving her bloody banner over *our* land, while many of our brothers and sons are numbered to the sword; and the pestilence, which walketh in darkness, has, within the two last years made an extensive desolation among persons of both sexes and all ages; particularly ministers of our order. Elders Furman, Osburn, Whipple, A. Farmer, Brewster, Harris, Orcutt, King, Ledoit, W. Rathbone, Francis, Atwell, Winchell and Waterman, have within twenty months past, fallen asleep as we trust in Jesus. On the sixth of last March, our much esteemed brother, Elder Caleb Blood, who was many years (about 20) connected with this association, finished his course; and it may be truly said, *he kept the faith*; and although his loss is lamented by thousands, yet we have reason to believe he is gone to be with Christ, which is far better than to remain in this world of tribulation and adversity.

However, the Long Run Association, like many of their co-religionists, was able to both decry the war as well as find an opportunity for spiritual growth. Admitting "it appears to be a time of great darkness, and a time in which we ought to mourn; and although, the rumors and horrors of war, and national calamity hang over us" the tone then changed to offer them a chance to prove God faithful to America, if only America would prove itself faithful to him. Therefore, the circular letter of 1814 concluded with the challenge: "Oh! Brethren let us return to the Lord, with prayer and supplication of heart, for the vivifying influences of his holy spirit."[94] Far from being wholly supportive of the war effort, the American Baptists saw the struggle with Britain as lamentable because of the death, destruction, and chaos it created—which were things that ultimately hampered the spread of the gospel.

Divine Mission

The divine mandate given by Jesus to "go into all nations" was proving too difficult for the Baptists in a time when their nation was struggling to remain in existence. Without the money or stability to launch missionary endeavors into other lands, the American Baptists saw the conflict as draining resources that were to be used to further Zion and speed the return of Christ. Ironically, the war both strengthened the authenticity of Jesus' apocalyptic message while simultaneously threatening to thwart

---

94. LRKA, "Circular Letter, September 1814," 3.

the realization of that message because of its destabilizing impact on the nation. In few instances was the Baptist understanding of the importance of peace more clearly articulated than in the Madison Association Circular Letter. In the following excerpt, the reader glimpses that their understanding of the war was that it, quite literally, hindered the very return of Christ.

> The Lord has given us to understand that "this Gospel of the Kingdom must first be preached unto all nations for a witness unto them, and then the end shall come." And it appears that it is already gone into almost all the world; therefore this bespeaks "the end of all things at hand: wherefore be sober and watch unto prayer" . . . The Lord frequently in the new testament calls on his disciples to watch; and introduces the solemnity and certainty of his appearing, their not knowing the time of his coming, and the necessity of being prepared.[95]

The American Baptists of the early nineteenth century were uniting under a two-fold banner of theological orthodoxy and missionary activity. Theology taught its adherents that they could impact the divine plan and bring about the fulfillment of the biblical message because their personal relationship with God impacted the national character of America. National character was of supreme importance because only a Christian America could properly spread the message of individual freedom to other nations still struggling under oppressive political and religious tyranny. However, the practice of missions was also an act of worship because, it was argued, when every nation had a chance to hear the gospel Jesus would return in glory. Both the theological and missionary endeavors were threatened by the war, as the testing field of battle seemed to be undermining the teaching that America was favored by God to fulfill his divine plans. The eschatological hope that had given purpose to both the teachings and the actions of the denomination appeared on the verge of collapsing and being re-subsumed under the British system so antithetical to everything the Baptists, and to a lesser extent the nation, believed God had divinely designated them to be.

---

95. MBA, "Circular Letter, Sept 1812," 11.

Peace Restored

Thus was the return of peace in 1815 celebrated by the Union New York Association in theological terms as they jubilantly printed, "Let it be our united cry to the throne of Almighty Grace, that the glorious work may spread till every knee shall bow to the peaceful sceptre of Prince Immanuel, and his name become the praise of the whole earth."[96] Rev. Coley of Madison New York wrote that as "the horrors of war are withdrawn from our shores" America had survived the war and "the cheering blessings of peace are again enjoyed in our favored realm."[97] The Cumberland Association began its letter of 1815 with relief that the nation had been released "from the alarm and confusion of war . . . we have been mercifully delivered; and the Olive Branch of peace once more waves over our beloved country."[98] The letter then asserted that peace brought more than temporal blessings, for "amidst a profusion of other things of great importance, [it] tends happily to facilitate the spread of the Gospel among the destitute."[99] With the fickle, and often violent, nature of global politics that was coming to bear on the young nation, the Cayuga Association, in 1814, expanded the definition of peace as something "the world cannot give nor take away" and called its readers to remember that true peace was such a fleeting aspect of the world in which they lived because of the fallen nature of the human creature. However, hope was found, not in political or even national peace, but in the Christian understanding that while people were "enemies to the Crown and Prince of Heaven" they needed not be defined by such divine alienation because, "The sacred spirit of peace, reaches . . . with the peace-making blood of Jesus, saying . . . be still, at peace with God."[100] Therefore, the cessation of hostilities was a mere shadow of the deeper and more abiding peace that existed between God and humanity because of the sacrificial atonement of Christ.

As the Kentucky militia suffered more casualties and engaged in more battles than any other state militia in the war, the opinions and views of the peace of 1815 expressed by the state's Association carry special weight. In August of 1815 the Elkhorn Association referred to the "scourge of war" that had visited the land. However, the justification for

---

96. UBA, Bulkley, "Corresponding Letter, Sept 1815," 11.
97. MBA, Coley, "Circular Letter, Oct 1815," 11.
98. MCA, "Circular Letter, Oct 1815," 6.
99. Ibid.
100. CBA, "Minutes, Oct 1815," 8–9.

the battle was found, not surprisingly, in the values for which the men fought, "that it was to vindicate rights ever dear to freemen; rights for which our forefathers fought and bled, and which was obtained by the helping hand of a kind Creator."[101] Once again, God and the Revolution were paired together to show that divine favor fell to America specifically because of the constitutionally guaranteed rights born in the wake of Independence. In his sermon on the French Revolution over twenty years earlier, Samuel Stillman arrived at the similar conclusion that the American system of government was something to be celebrated, especially in contrast to that of Britain. In November of 1794 Stillman preached:

> Let us unite in giving glory to God for our Federal Government, which hath already raised the United States to wealth and eminence. The experiment hath realized the expectations of its warmest friends . . . Our prosperity as a people cannot be denied, notwithstanding the depredations that have been committed on our commerce by the powers at war, especially by the rapacity of Great Britain.[102]

He would go on to preach that "The present war in Europe is a war of kings against the people, of *power* against *opinion*" before defending the superiority of the democratic system because "Power must be supported by fleets and armies; these cost immense sums of money . . . But opinion is easily propagated, and can never be conquered by power." Thus were the ideals of the Revolution an American export that had "already passed . . . to France, and pervaded the millions of its inhabitants; who have risen in a mass to oppose those powers, that are at war against their opinion of the rights of men." The beliefs of Stillman's eighteenth-century sermon were echoed throughout the Baptist Associations a generation later. For Stillman, the financial wisdom and ideologically unstoppable mass movement that had set America free from tyranny and appeared to be doing the same for the French people found the zenith of its value in the foundational belief "that every man is at liberty to worship God according to his conscience" because such an environment of personal choice would help create "a spirit of inquiry, and at least a readiness to encourage [religion] as good for the state."[103] For the Baptists, so accustomed to persecution at the hands of government-sponsored churches,

---

101. EKYA, "Circular Letter, Aug 1815," 3.

102. Stillman, *Thoughts*, 25.

103. Stillman, *Thoughts*, 22–23; italics original.

religious freedom was for them what the conversion of Constantine was to the earliest Christians in the Roman Empire.[104]

The War of 1812, much like the Revolution of the preceding generation, furnished proof in the testing ground of war for the theological theories espoused by the American churches; namely that the republican experiment appeared to be overthrowing the British constitution as the most godly government in the world. On the popular and official level, Baptists wrote of the superiority of religious freedom over a religious oligarchy as is evidenced by Daniel Merrill's statement that "[When Madison] declared war [he] vindicated the inestimable rights of our own nation against the tyranny and cruelty of that government which may, for the present, be styled the bulwark of national religion; that bane of Christianity, and principle support of Babylon the great, the mother of harlots, and abominations of the earth."[105] Returning to the Elkhorn, Kentucky Association, while the violence of war was abhorred in the official organ of the Association, the reasons for the war were celebrated unapologetically: "We delight not in shedding the blood of man, it is only justifiable in extreme necessity. While we are prompt in declaring war as the only alternative to vindicate our rights, let us ever cherish the principles of peace with all nations."[106] Coupled with the Christian love of peace was a deeper and, arguably, more specifically American theology that peace found under the boot of an oppressor is no peace at all and can actually hinder the growth of true Christianity in favor of institutional religion. They celebrated freedom from British law and governance and argued that it was that very freedom that birthed the kind of environment where real faith could flourish. Such a message was worth dying to defend and, as peace returned to the war-torn land, was one that, according to the Baptists, needed to be spread to the farthest corners of the world.

CONCLUSION

This chapter has offered up four conclusions that can be reached from an examination of the source material related to the War of 1812 and

---

104. "For Baptists, the disestablishment movement had been one of their finest hours; and its veterans . . . became almost folk heroes for their contributions to it" (Gribbin, *Churches Militant*, 110).

105. Ibid., 88.

106. EKYA, "Circular Letter, Aug 1815," 3.

the growth of Baptist unity and American nationalism. The first was that, for Baptists, America could rightfully be considered a new "Zion," specifically because of the Freedom of Religion that was described in the Third Amendment to the constitution. Second, the sacred nature of the American nation meant that the defense of the land was lauded as a noble enterprise. While some nuances existed in the understanding of a Christian's role in the war, all of the writings agreed that America's identity needed to be defended against the aggressions of England. The strength of that argument was found in the realization that the American national "experiment" had valuable teachings to share with other nations that were living under oppressive government and religious regimes that limited true faith from being realized. If America fell, so too could the religious hopes of the entire world be hindered.

However, organizing the spread of that message threatened the very freedom the Baptists believed central to their message. That conundrum forms the third conclusion as it presents an idea that is not only uniquely Baptist but also uniquely American. The role of the American Zion was to spread the message of religious freedom around the world but those who stood opposed to the missionary movement did so because they saw the existence of communal missionary societies as antithetical to the message the churches were charged with delivering. A governing body with charge over the money and the missionary mandate echoed too closely the structures the Baptist Churches argued they abhorred, and this caused true friction that threatened to undermine the movement and further divide the autonomous churches. Added to that was the simple fact that while these debates were transpiring, their nation was at war against an empire that maintained that such top-down governance was the way God wanted a nation to be ruled. The missions controversy struck at the heart of the issue: how could a group celebrate religious freedom as a definitive characteristic and then legislate their adherents to give money to a cause they might not agree with? Therefore, with coercion removed as an option, the fourth conclusion that can be offered is that voluntary missions and the Bible became the "flags" around which the Baptist "states" could unite. In order to accomplish that, the Baptists, like the nation, used common ideology to unite disparate groups and showed the individuals how they too could benefit from such mutual interdependence. In so doing, they were developing a unique American-Baptist identity/culture that was bound inseparably with their nation and the war.

Therefore, as the title of this chapter states, the American Baptist church was not a house divided, as the nation was, by pervasive ideological strife that threatened its security and unity. Nor was it a house united, because the physical distance between the churches alongside the lack of identifiable creeds or an overarching governing structure prevented such obvious and definable unity. The American Baptists of early nineteenth-century America were a house uniting through ideologies that made them, like the nation in which they resided, an unproven experiment in what religious freedom looked like at an institutional level. Through the war and beyond, these churches and associations struggled to define themselves and find a voice that was flexible enough to honor the American celebration of voluntarism but strong enough to bind churches from New York, Kentucky, Ohio, Massachusetts, and beyond under a common theological banner of brotherly and sisterly affection that could rightly be called Baptist. In a way, the term "American Baptist" was actually less a title and more a combination of two names, as both Americans and Baptists in America had yet to prove whether or not they could survive and thrive in the world they had fought so hard to create.

Bibliography

Primary Sources

Documents and Manuscripts

Bolles, Lucius. *The Importance of the Scriptures to a Teacher of Religion: A Discourse Delivered in the Meeting House of the Second Baptist Church in Boston, Sept. 18, 1822, Before the Boston Baptist Association.* Boston: Lincoln & Edmans, 1822.

Cone, Spencer Houghton. "Letters to Sally: 1812–1814." Located in the American Baptist Historical Society Archives, Atlanta, GA. Call no. RG-1243.

Holmes, Elkanah. "Letters, 1814." Located in the American Baptist Historical Society Archives, Atlanta, GA, 2011. Call no. RG-1109.

Hunt, Gaillard, ed. *The Writings of James Madison.* Vol. 8, *1808–1819.* New York: G. P. Putnam's, 1908.

Jones, David. *Biographical Sketch of David Jones, Written by Himself: With a Continuation and Additional Remarks by Two of His Friends.* Philadelphia: American Baptist Publication Society, n.d.

Polner, Murray, and Thomas E. Woods, eds. *We Who Dared to Say No to War: American Antiwar Writing from 1812 to Now.* New York: Perseus, 2008.

Stillman, Samuel. *Thoughts on the French Revolution. A Sermon Delivered November 20, 1794: Being the Day of Thanksgiving.* Boston: Manning & Loring, 1795.

Strachan, John. *A Sermon Preached at York, Upper Canada, on the Third of June, Being the Day Appointed for a General Thanksgiving.* Montreal: William Gray, 1814.

Taylor, John. *Baptists on the American Frontier: A History of Ten Baptist Churches of Which the Author Has Been Alternately a Member: Annotated Third Edition*, edited and introduced by Chester Raymond Young. Macon, GA: Mercer University Press, 1995.

Association Minutes and Magazine

BMBA – *Minutes of the Boston, Massachusetts Baptist Association, 1812–1848.* Located at the American Baptist Historical Society Archives: Atlanta, GA.

CBA – *Minutes of the Cayuga Baptist Association, 1812–1815.* Located at the American Baptist Historical Society Archives, Atlanta, GA. 286.1747 C31V.

EKYA – *Minutes of the Elkhorn, Kentucky Association of Baptist Churches, 1809–1819.* Located at the American Baptist Historical Society Archives: Atlanta, GA.

FBA – *Minutes of the Franklin, New York Baptist Association, 1811–42.* Located at the American Baptist Historical Society Archives: Atlanta, GA.

GBA - *Minutes of the Georgia Baptist Association, 1814-1815*. Located at the Southern Baptist Historical Library & Archives: Nashville, TN.

LRKA - *Minutes of the Long Run, Kentucky Baptist Association, 1803-1916*. Located at the Southern Baptists Historical Library & Archives, Nashville, TN. Pub. No. 884.

MBA - *Minutes of the Madison, New York Baptist Association, 1808-1855*. Located at the American Baptist Historical Society Archives: Atlanta, GA.

MBMM - *Massachusetts Baptist Missionary Magazine*, 1812-1815.

MCA - *Minutes of the Cumberland, Maine Association, 1811-1865*. Located at the American Baptist Historical Society Archives: Atlanta, GA.

MOBA - *Minutes of the Miami-Ohio Baptist Association, 1816*. Located at the Southern Baptists Historical Library & Archives, Nashville, TN. Pub. No. 884.

SBA - *Minutes of the Sturbridge, Massachusetts Baptist Association, 1802-1848*. Located at the American Baptist Historical Society Archives: Atlanta, GA.

SDAB - *Minutes of the South District Association of Baptists, 1813*. Located at the Southern Baptists Historical Library & Archives, Nashville, TN. Pub. No. 884.

SKBA - *Minutes of the Salem, Kentucky Baptist Association, 1802, 1804, 1808, 1810-1880*. Located at the Southern Baptists Historical Library & Archives, Nashville, TN. Pub. No. 884.

UBA - *Minutes of the Union, New York Baptist Association, 1813-1859*. Located at the American Baptist Historical Society Archives: Atlanta, GA.

Secondary Sources

Ahlstrom, Sydney E. *A Religious History of the American People*. New Haven: Yale University Press, 1972.

Borneman, Walter R. *1812: The War That Forged a Nation*. New York: Harper-Collins, 2004.

Bulthuis, Kyle T. "Preacher Politics and People Power: Congregational Conflicts in New York City, 1810-1830." *Church History* 78, no. 2 (June 2009) 261-82.

Clark, Elmer T. *The Small Sects in America: An Authentic Study of Almost 300 Little-Known Religious Groups*. New York: Abingdon, 1949.

Gaustad, Edwin, and Leigh Schmidt. *The Religious History of America: The Heart of the American Story from Colonial Times to Today*. San Francisco: Harper, 2002.

Gribbin, William J. *The Churches Militant: The War of 1812 and American Religion*. New Haven: Yale University Press, 1973.

Handy, Robert T., ed. *Religion in the American Experience: The Pluralistic Style*. New York: Harper & Row, 1972.

Heath, Gordon L. "Ontario Baptists and the War of 1812." *Ontario History* 103, no. 2 (Autumn 2011) 169-91.

Hickey, Donald R. "The War of 1812: Still a Forgotten Conflict?" *The Journal of Military History* 65 (2001) 741-69.

Howe, Daniel Walker. *What Hath God Wrought: The Transformation of America, 1815-1848*. Oxford: Oxford University Press, 2007.

Hudson, Winthrop S. *Religion in America: An Historical Account of the Development of American Religious Life*. 2nd ed. New York: Charles Scribner's, 1973.

Knight, Janice. *Orthodoxies in Massachusetts: Rereading American Puritanism*. Cambridge, MA: Harvard University Press, 1994.

Mild, Warren. *The Story of the American Baptists: The Role of a Remnant*. Valley Forge: Judson, 1976.

Noll, Mark A. *The Civil War as a Theological Crisis*. Chapel Hill: University of North Carolina Press, 2006.

Robertson, James Tyler. "The 'Children of Nature' and 'Our Province': The Rev. John Strachan's Views on the Indigenous People and the Motives behind the American Invasion of Upper Canada, 1812–1814." *Ontario History* 104, no. 1 (Spring 2012) 53–70.

Taylor, Alan. *The Civil War of 1812: American Citizens, British Subjects, Irish Rebels, and Indian Allies*. New York: Alfred A. Knopf, 2010.

Weaver, Rufus W. *The Place of Luther Rice in American Baptist Life*. Washington, DC: Luther Rice Centennial Commission, 1936.

Westfall, William. *Two Worlds: The Protestant Culture of Nineteenth-Century Ontario*. Montreal: McGill-Queen's University Press, 1989.

4

The Nile Expedition, New Imperialism, and Canadian Baptists, 1884–1885[1]

Gordon L. Heath

THE 19 MARCH 1885 edition of the *Canadian Baptist* included a map of the Egyptian Sudan and Abyssinia for readers who wanted to be able to picture the recent events surrounding the British advance on Khartoum.[2] Just a few weeks before, a Baptist pastor at First Baptist Church, Montreal, preached a sermon on General Gordon, the British leader and hero who recently had been killed in Khartoum. A summary of the sermon was also printed in the *Canadian Baptist*.[3] While Britain had been involved in a number of imperial conflicts in the preceding years, this particular imperial engagement deep in Africa along the Nile was of special interest to Canadians. There were almost 400 Canadians involved in the Nile Expedition, and their participation in a far-flung imperial conflict, as well as reactions on the home front to their exploits, indicate a significant degree of imperial fervor. As for Baptists, the map and the sermon were just two examples from many that indicate support for the "new imperialism."

---

1. I am grateful to *The Baptist Quarterly* for permission to reprint this article. See "The Nile Expedition, New Imperialism and Canadian Baptists, 1884–1885," *The Baptist Quarterly* 44, no. 3 (2011) 171–86.

2. "Map of the Egyptian Soodan [sic] and Abyssinia," *Canadian Baptist*, 19 March 1885, 8. The *Canadian Baptist* was a weekly paper published by Ontario and Quebec Baptists.

3. "General Gordon," *Canadian Baptist*, 26 February 1885, 1.

CANADA AND THE NEW IMPERIALISM

The Canadian Protestant churches were ardent supporters of Canada's involvement in the South African War (1899–1902).[4] During that imperial conflict they revealed their passionate support for the empire, and indicated that their concept of Canadian nationalism was inseparably intertwined with imperialism. In fact, their activities and attitudes during the South African War were precursors to the ways in which the Protestant churches supported the war effort during the First World War. But what about the Nile Expedition that occurred fifteen years before the South African War? What did the churches think of empire then?

Both Robert Page and C. P. Stacey assert that in the years immediately following Confederation (1867) English Canadians were loyal to Britain, but not all that excited about specific imperial ventures, and imperialism in general.[5] What the following research indicates is that imperialism in the churches—in this case among Baptists—was already fairly well developed by 1884–85. The South African War may have led to the most ardent expressions of imperial zeal in Canadian history up that point in time, but, if the coverage and commentary in the Baptist press is any indication, new imperialism was an ideology that had begun to capture the imagination of a number of Canadians more than a decade before Canadian troops embarked for their baptism of blood in South Africa. Perhaps not surprisingly, the Canadian response mirrored the Australian colonial response, although one important difference was that the Australians actually sent troops to the Nile.[6]

What little has been written about Canada and the Nile Expedition has dealt with either its political or military features.[7] Furthermore, no one has explored the churches and the birth of new imperialism. "New imperialism" was marked by a dramatic intensification of imperial expansion and conflict between the end of the Franco-Prussian War (1870) and the start of the First World War (1914). When did the churches begin to support this more aggressive, expansive, and competitive form of

---

4. Heath, *Silver Lining*.

5. See Page, *Boer War*, 3; Stacey, *Conflict*, 40–44. For French-Canadian views of imperialism, see Silver, "Quebec Attitudes."

6. See Inglis, *Rehearsal*; Saunders, "Inaccuracy." The men sent by Canada were not troops (see below).

7. Stacey, "Nile Expedition"; Stacey, "Macdonald"; Stacey, *Records*; Bumsted, "From the Red to the Nile"; Boileau, "Voyageurs"; Michel, "Represent the Country"; Pigott, *Canada in the Soudan*; McLaren, *Canadians on the Nile*.

imperialism that was so prominent during the South African War? This research into post-Confederation imperialism demonstrates that it was in place—at least among Baptists—by at least 1884–85.[8]

A brief comment on sources is in order. This research is based primarily on Canadian Baptist newspapers.[9] As noted elsewhere, the late-Victorian Canadian Protestant press acted in a nation-building role.[10] And while the press in 1885 did not expend the same amount of space on political concerns as it did in 1899, the press was on a trajectory towards developing into a nation-building press. For instance, the Baptist press in the 1870s was devoted primarily to church-related matters, but increasingly throughout the 1880s its pages included political commentary. By the time of the Nile Expedition, every week had cable news that outlined international events in great detail, and increasingly the editors included commentary or articles on political matters. The impact of the undersea cables on newspapers should not be underestimated, for not only did the cables bring immediate news to readers (and subsequently make the papers a valuable source of imperial propaganda),[11] but they also helped to bind together the widely scattered regions of the empire into a global community, or nascent imperial federation.[12]

---

8. Among the four largest Protestant denominations in Canada (Methodist, Presbyterian, Anglican, and Baptist), Baptists were the smallest, comprising approximately 6.5 percent of the population (although in the Maritimes they comprised 20–25 percent of the population). Consequently, there is a need for some comparative work to be done on the much larger Anglican, Methodist, and Presbyterian communities, not to mention some of the even smaller denominations. For a study of Canadian Baptist history, see Renfree, *Heritage*.

9. This research makes use of the following Baptist periodical publications: *Canadian Baptist* (Toronto, Ontario), *Religious Intelligencer* (Saint John, New Brunswick), the *North West Baptist* (Winnipeg, Manitoba), and the *Christian Messenger* (Saint John, New Brunswick). In January 1885 the *Messenger* merged with a Maritime Baptist paper called the *Visitor* to create the *Messenger and Visitor*.

10. For a discussion of the nation-building role of the press, see Heath, "Forming Sound Public Opinion."

11. John MacKenzie has noted how in Britain there was no pressing need for government agencies to be involved in imperial propaganda, for a number of non-governmental agencies were enthusiastically doing it for them. See MacKenzie, *Propaganda*, 2–3.

12. For developments in cable and communication, see Potter, "Communication." The London origins of most news reports also no doubt played a part in the English-Canadian papers being decidedly pro-British, whereas reports in French-Canadian papers were primarily from Paris-based wire services. For instance, little more than a decade later, these different sources contributed to different views of Canada's

COMMENTARY ON KHARTOUM AND THE SUDAN

When General Garnet Wolseley was faced with the daunting task of relieving Gordon in Khartoum, he thought that the best way to get there was to advance up the Nile. Remembering the help he had received from Canadian voyageurs during the Red River Rebellion (1867–70), he sent a letter to Canadian Governor General Lansdowne on 20 August 1884 requesting the assistance of voyageurs. The request was for boatmen, not soldiers, and the men were to take a strictly non-combatant role. The recruitment and organizing was efficient, for shortly thereafter, on 15 September 1884, 386 men departed Quebec City for Egypt. On 7 October 1884 the Canadians arrived in Alexandria. They soon joined Wolseley and his 5400 troops, and once united they headed south up the Nile.[13]

For a number of years the press had been printing cable reports on international events. The reports were often quite extensive, and contained disparate information on numerous imperial conflicts and political situations around the globe. This coverage of imperial events continued during the Nile Expedition, usually with weekly coverage. Initial events surrounding the call for the expedition,[14] the advance and conditions of the relief force,[15] various battles,[16] and Gordon's condition and fate[17] were the main types of printed reports.

---

involvement in another imperial conflict. See Page, *Boer War*, 17.

13. For a discussion of the larger strategic position, especially in regards to India, see Preston, "Wolseley."

14. For instance, see "English and Foreign," *Religious Intelligencer*, 11 July 1884, 3; "English and Foreign," *Religious Intelligencer*, 8 August 1884, 3; "English and Foreign," *Religious Intelligencer*, 15 August 1884, 3.

15. For instance, see "English and Foreign," *Religious Intelligencer*, 21 November 1884, 3; "English and Foreign," *Religious Intelligencer*, 28 November 1884, 3; "English and Foreign," *Religious Intelligencer*, 5 December 1884, 3; "English and Foreign," *Religious Intelligencer*, 12 December 1884, 3.

16. For instance, see "English and Foreign," *Religious Intelligencer*, 7 November 1884, 3; "English and Foreign," *Religious Intelligencer*, 23 January 1885, 3; *Religious Intelligencer*, 6 February 1885, 2; "English and Foreign," *Religious Intelligencer*, 27 February 1885, 3; *Messenger and Visitor*, 28 January 1885, 1; *Messenger and Visitor*, 4 February 1885, 1; "British and Foreign," *Messenger and Visitor*, 4 February 1885, 8; "News Summary," *Messenger and Visitor*, 11 March 1885, 8; "News Notes," *Canadian Baptist*, 26 March 1885, 8.

17. For instance, see *Canadian Baptist*, 12 February 1885, 1; "Death of General Gordon," *Canadian Baptist*, 12 September 1884, 5; *Canadian Baptist*, 19 February 1885, 1.

While information on the performance of the boatmen was limited, the Baptist press tried to follow their progress. Their departure from Canada, arrival in Egypt, and return from Egypt were all noted.[18] A few reports on their performance were printed,[19] as was personal correspondence.[20] A report on deaths made it into press,[21] as did a brief comment on the Queen's "hearty thanks" to the contingent.[22]

Despite the best efforts of the relief expedition, and the fact that they were just a few days away, they could not get to Gordon in time. On 26 January 1885, the defenses of Khartoum were breached and Gordon was killed. His death was a shock to people used to hearing about imperial victories and believing in the superiority of Anglo-Saxons over against "natives." The news of his death in Britain led to passionate denunciations of the Gladstone government for its lackadaisical support for Gordon, and eventually led to its downfall. His death also fueled war fever in Britain and parts of the empire. In Canada, there was a minor epidemic of volunteering for overseas service to recapture the Sudan and punish the Mahdi, but this abated relatively quickly when Britain decided to abandon the Sudan.[23] The Baptist press briefly mentioned this surge in volunteering, but did not actively recruit for the war effort.[24]

Although coverage of the Nile Expedition continued into mid-1885, the events with Riel in the Canadian West, as well as a looming British-Russian war, began to eclipse the events in the Sudan.[25] The British

18. "English and Foreign," *Religious Intelligencer*, 1 May 1885, 3; "News Summary," *Messenger and Visitor*, 11 March 1885, 8; *Christian Messenger*, 15 October 1884, 5; *Christian Messenger*, 29 October 1884, 5; *Christian Messenger*, 12 November 1884, 4.

19. "The Canadian boatmen have done grand work, —fully justifying their selection." See *Christian Messenger*, 12 November 1884, 4. "Reports from up the Nile show that the Canadian boatmen are experiencing more difficulty in getting their boats up the cataracts than they had anticipated." See "News of the World," *Christian Messenger*, 19 November 1884, 5.

20. "Dominion of Canada," *Christian Messenger*, 26 November 1884, 5.

21. *Canadian Baptist*, 4 June 1885, 4; "Dominion of Canada," *Christian Messenger*, 24 December 1884, 5.

22. *Religious Intelligencer*, 27 February 1885, 2.

23. MacLaren, *Canadians on the Nile*, 129; Morton, *Military History*, 109; Stacey, "Nile Expedition," 325–26.

24. *Religious Intelligencer*, 27 February 1885, 2; "News Summary," *Messenger and Visitor*, 11 March 1885, 8.

25. For instance, see "Russia and England," *Canadian Baptist*, 26 March 1885, 4; *Canadian Baptist*, 30 April 1885, 4; "What Shall the End Be?" *Canadian Baptist*, 16 April 1885, 4; "Wars and Rumours," *Religious Intelligencer*, 17 April 1885, 2.

evacuation of the Sudan after Gordon's death was also a factor in the Nile Expedition eventually disappearing from the pages of the press.

IMPERIAL ASSUMPTIONS

The response to the conflict exposed a number of assumptions held by Baptists. The war commentary revealed an ardent, expansionist, and militant imperialism, significantly similar to that displayed a decade and a half later during the South African War.

Much has been written about Canada's relationship to the empire in the late-Victorian period, and by the end of the nineteenth century the churches' nationalism was inseparable from imperialism.[26] Baptists cherished their connections to Britain, praised their "motherland," followed British politics as though they were their own, and looked forward to imperial victories. Hope was expressed regarding the formation of a grand alliance of Anglo-Saxon peoples that would bring peace to the world, and positive commentary on some type of imperial federation was presented to readers.[27] Based on the commentary in their papers, it is difficult to see Baptists imagining themselves as anything but both Canadian and British, whose national identity was fused to their imperial destiny. The degree of war commentary during the South African War allows for a clear picture of Canadian nationalism in 1899–1902. Nevertheless, the glimpses of nationalism during 1884–85 are certainly on the trajectory towards what would be seen in the South African War.

It was clear in the press that the conflict in the Sudan was just one conflict in the much larger imperial competition in Africa and around the globe. European nations were in a race for empire, and, for Baptists, the best thing for the "natives" in Africa was that the British Empire would win the race. The reason given, of course, was that the British Empire was a blessing to all it ruled.

Commentary on the Berlin Conference, where Europeans parceled out much of Africa, reveals the connection between the spread of empires and the advancement of civilization. The superiority of European culture,

---

26. See Berger, *Sense of Power*; Penlington, *Canada*; Page, "Canada and the Imperial Idea"; Page, *Boer War*; Page, "Berger"; Cole, "Imperialists"; Cook, "Parkin"; Buckner, "Whatever Happened?"; Buckner, "Canada"; Heath, *Silver Lining*, ch. 4.

27. "The British Empire," *Religious Intelligencer*, 24 July 1885, 2; "England and Her Colonies," *Religious Intelligencer*, 22 August 1884, 2.

with its manifold blessings, was now to be extended even more, but this time with a coordinated effort devoid of past conflicts.

> The blessing of civilization long bestowed in rich abundance in Europe and North America, and in measure in Asia and South America, seem now destined to overflow, flood with a new life and light the long oppressed, dark continent, with its swarthy races so long victimized by every nation possessed of ships and colonies. Never before in the annals of history of our race, has such a hopeful prospect exalted for the inhabitants of an uncivilized region brought for the first time into contact with strong and civilized peoples.[28]

Injustices were to end, slavery was to be abolished, and "black men and whites" were to be "equal before the law." Of course, much of the power of this sentiment came from the belief that "a higher will than that of man" was behind the rise of European empires, and that ultimately the advance of empire would lead to the spread of Christianity. The optimism in the motives and mandate of nations involved in the Berlin Conference can been seen in a brief article extolling Belgium's King Leopold II's missionary passion for the Congo.[29]

While European culture in general was considered to be more advanced than non-European cultures, the British were deemed to be superior to all. British rule, with the help of other English-speaking nations, would eventually be able to bring peace to the world.[30] The Anglo-Saxon people had a unique mission as a Christian people, one considered to be superior to that of other imperial competitors:

> The historic relation of the Anglo-Saxon to Christianity, and thence to civilization alike, is pronounced . . . The French, the Germans, the Spanish and the Portuguese, pale before the Anglo-Saxon race as qualified by nature, by education, and by all the forces of a long formative discipline, for the planting of new colonies, promising development into communities, and thence into States, into commonwealths, and like our own, into independent nationalities . . . But preeminently the Anglo-Saxon is

---

28. "The Results of the Berlin Conference," *Canadian Baptist*, 23 July 1885, 1.

29. "King Leopold and Africa," *Messenger and Visitor*, 28 January 1885, 2. While Baptists could not have known it at the time, Leopold's rule in the Belgian Congo became atrocious and one of the worst examples of exploitation and abuse in Africa. See Hochschild, *King Leopold's Ghost*.

30. "The British Empire," *Religious Intelligencer*, 24 July 1885, 2.

practical; and being practical, he naturally is more devoted to the arts of peace than to those of war ... It is this characterizing and this distinguishing feature which has made, and which will continue to make the Anglo-Saxon such a marked force and factor in that migratory and extending civilization which constitute the crowning glory of the nineteenth century.[31]

Rev. Dr. Wheaton Smith's message on 15 February 1885 at First Baptist Church, St. Catherine Street, Montreal, provides a vivid example of this belief in the blessing of British rule. The event was the commemoration of Gordon, the text was John 12:24: "Verily, verily, I say unto you, except a corn of wheat fall into the ground and die it abideth alone; but if it die it bringeth forth much fruit." A great deal of the message was about the life and successes of Gordon in China and Egypt. Tragic as Gordon's death was, Smith concluded, it would lead to the betterment of Africa.

> And now for the fruit which the dead seed would bring forth. God meant that the slave trade in Egypt should be abolished ... The death of Gordon and the fall of Khartoum would not soon be forgotten. They would live in the memory of the civilized world. Thousands of human beings each year would no longer march in misery the arid sands of the Behuda desert. England had drawn the sword, and justice should be done to humanity. The talismanic name of Gordon would electrify the forces of mankind. Regiments without number, he believed, could be enlisted to march to the Soudan and suppress the inhuman Madhi [sic].[32]

After promoting Gordon to relative sainthood (at least as much as Baptists were able to), and pointing out the immense good that would come from the inevitable British victory, the message ended with a prayer for the safety and success of the troops in the Sudan.

Not only would the expansion of British rule lead to the spread of civilization and justice, it was also argued that the expansion of empire would eventuate in the spread of Christianity. European empires in general, and the British Empire in particular, had contributed to the global spread of Christianity. Two overt examples of the connection between imperial conflict and the advancement of the gospel reveal remarkable precursors to the response to the South African War. First, while war was deemed tragic, it was still considered to be one way in which God

---

31. "The Anglo-Saxon Mission," *Messenger and Visitor*, 8 July 1885, 1.
32. "General Gordon," *Canadian Baptist*, 26 February 1885, 1.

advanced the cause of Christianity.[33] This connection between the progress of Christianity and imperial military success was more fully realized and developed among Baptists during the South African War. Second, the annexation of Burma in 1885 by the British was supported because it was considered a boon for mission work.[34] Brian Stanley proposes that British missionaries in the later nineteenth century entered the political arena to protect their interests.[35] It was assumed, Stanley argues, that British imperial control could best bring about the much-needed stability and rule of law (not to mention commerce and technology) that would aid the work of the missionaries. Like many British missionaries,[36] Canadian Baptists defended imperial expansion when deemed necessary for the expansion of the gospel: in the case of Burma it was. It would also be a significant reason for supporting the future war in South African.[37]

Stanley also argues: "If you wish to mobilize Baptists (and evangelicals as a whole) on an issue that divides the nation down the middle politically, the way to do it is to persuade them that liberty to preach the gospel is at stake."[38] The examples noted above affirm his claim. Baptists had a vigorous commitment to personal conversion and evangelical missions, and the events of the late nineteenth century fuelled that passion. Carl Berger has identified how Canadian English Protestant imperialism was "infused" with religious emotion.[39] It seemed as if God had providentially established an empire that aided in the growth of the church, and Baptists were not ones to argue with God. The empire was good for missions, so how could its expansion be bad?

This support for the expansion of the empire was directly related to Canada's growing national identity and concomitant providential calling. Berger notes that Canadian imperialists "made the realization of

---

33. Rev. Elbert S. Todd, "War and the Progress of Christianity," *Religious Intelligencer*, 8 August 1884, 2.

34. "But however mixed may be the motives that lead to the invasion, and however doubtful its justification, there can scarcely be a doubt that, like many other extensions of civilized government, will redound to the highest good of the benighted natives. A new door will be opened for missionary enterprise." See "The Annexation of Burmah," *Canadian Baptist*, 5 November 1885, 4.

35. Stanley, *Flag*, ch. 5.

36. Greenlee and Johnston, *Good Citizens*, 108–10.

37. See Heath, *Silver Lining*, ch. 5.

38. Stanley, "Baptists, Antislavery," 289.

39. Berger, *Sense of Power*, 217.

Canadian nationhood contingent upon the acceptance of racial responsibility and fulfillment of the mission." For imperialists, and a number of them were Baptists, mission was central to Canada's purpose. Canada, they said, "could only be a nation if she acted and functioned like one, and, to them, this meant that she must assume her share of the civilizing work within the Empire and be ready to defend that agency of progress."[40]

The fusion of the advance of Western civilization with the spread of Christianity can be seen above. The inverse of that equation was that Christianity brought civilization. This sentiment can be seen in an article on the effect Christianity had on civilizing peoples. The article that portrayed the gospel as the "true civilizer" dealt with imperial advances in the Pacific, Australia, and Tasmania, and how commercial and government methods were not always the best suited to deal with "barbarous peoples." Commercial interests were selfish, and government was often paternalistic; the most effective way to bring civilization to indigenous peoples was to bring the gospel first. In fact, if the gospel arrived first, the civilizing task would be made easier and safer.[41] It was noted that in New South Wales, the government had expended enormous amounts of money to relieve the suffering of the "natives," but had failed. In Tasmania, it went on, despite the best intentions of British authorities for the past sixty years, the entire indigenous population had been exterminated. The best way to protect people and introduce civilization was to bring the gospel first.

> The Gospel will not always save aboriginal peoples from decay, but it does delay the process, preserve the language, redeem a goodly number of the people, and prepare these lands for a better stock, under better auspices. The Sandwich Islanders may become extinct—but if so, it may be said, without wavering, that the Gospel puts brakes upon this process if it did not quite reverse the wheels, and saved scores of thousands unto God and transferred them from the realm of darkness into the Kingdom of God. If we would civilize the nations, give them the Gospel of Christ.[42]

---

40. Ibid., 231.

41. "Hence it has come to be said that the missionary is the best possible police force in the islands of the Pacific; and even in Ebon, no long time since a cannibal island, human life is safer than in San Francisco." See "The Gospel the True Civilizer," *Canadian Baptist*, 6 August 1885, 1. For a discussion of the variety of views among evangelicals regarding the need for civilization before Christianity, or vice versa, see Stanley, "Christianity and Civilization."

42. "The Gospel the True Civilizer, *Canadian Baptist*, 6 August 1885, 1.

Missionaries, in this type of discourse, were imperial agents, preparing the way for a benevolent and civilizing imperial rule.[43]

Associated with the benevolent role of empire was the idea of national righteousness. The idea was rooted in the Old Testament concept of God's covenantal expectations for the nation of Israel. If the nation followed God's commands, God would bless the nation. If the nation sinned, then God would foil the plans of rulers and generals. In other words, the temporal success of the nation depended on its spiritual condition. The same idea was applied to Britain, Canada, and the entire imperial enterprise.

As a new nation with vast resources and a sound government, Canada had great potential, but that potential could only be reached if Christians did all that they could do to make the nation truly righteous. As one article concluded: "The duty the Christian owes to his country is amongst his most solemn obligations. Righteousness, alone, can truly exalt a nation, and every Canadian Christian must desire to see Canada exalted by righteousness."[44] Because Canada was such a new nation, and because the "Canadian national character" was just being formed, it was imperative that Christians exert themselves to shape the nation's character in order to shape the nation's destiny.[45] If Christians were to make Canada truly a Christian nation, then the nation would be successful, prosper, and live up to its divine calling. On the other hand, if Canada failed to act justly, unrest and even war would be wrought upon the nation.[46]

It was this sense of righteousness that justified the spread of empire and could make for such a potent degree of confidence going into battle. The "God of battles" could be called upon for victory in the Sudan because God would ultimately come to the aid of the side of "right."[47] When it looked in early 1885 as if Britain and Russia were going to go to war the same principle applied:

---

43. For a broader treatment of missionaries in advance of empire, see Barker, "Missionary Frontier." Interestingly, it has been recently noted that Christian missions have contributed to the preservation of indigenous languages and culture. See Sanneh, "Christian Missions," 331–34.

44. "National Exaltation," *Canadian Baptist*, 3 April 1884, 4.

45. Ibid. See also "Christian Statesmanship," *Canadian Baptist*, 14 May 1885, 4.

46. For instance, the events with Riel in 1885 were seen to be due to the unchristian actions of the Canadian government towards the indigenous peoples of the West. See ibid. For a poignant Canadian example of this attitude during the South African War, see Heath, "Sin in the Camp."

47. *Messenger and Visitor*, 11 February 1885, 1.

> To those who view the matter from the loftiest standpoint, a question of still greater moment than that of victory or defeat is that of right and wrong. Will the war, if waged, be on the side of either a righteousness war? Can the British forces, for instance, go forth to the conflict feeling that they are clad in the triple steel of the just cause, and that the Lord of Hosts is with them?[48]

If right was on their side, those within the empire could have the unshakable faith in ultimate victory, for God, they believed, would ultimately aid the imperial cause.

For those uncomfortable with this language of righteousness bolstering the imperial cause, it needs to be remembered that it was that very same demand for righteousness that led to denunciations of jingoism and abuses of empire.[49] Over the past number of decades there has been a considerable amount of energy expended exploring the relationship between missions and imperialism, a relationship most often explained in terms of power. While power certainly is an important part of the analysis of missionary attitudes and actions, Jane Samson argues convincingly for a more nuanced approach to power and motives.[50] Andrew Porter's recent book on the history of British Protestant missionaries is an example of such an approach.[51] Porter's work shows that the relationship between British missionaries and empire was more complex and ambiguous than previously thought. Baptist commentary during the Nile Expedition reveals that while Baptists were supportive of empire, their support was not unqualified.[52]

Harsh words were printed for the waves of jingoism in Britain, and it was hoped that the "leaven of Christian purity will be found sufficient to purge the land speedily of so gross abomination."[53] The spread of military parades in Canada on Sunday was troubling for churches so committed

---

48. "What Shall the End Be?" *Canadian Baptist*, 16 April 1885, 4.

49. In this regards, Baptists were not alone among evangelical Protestants. For a discussion of the connection between righteousness, sin, and the support for (and criticism of) empire in Britain, see Bebbington, "Atonement."

50. Samson, "Problem of Colonialism."

51. Porter, *Religion versus Empire*. Porter's introductory essay on missions and empire also provides a sense of this complexity. See Porter, "Overview."

52. For examples of Baptist criticism at the end of the nineteenth century, see Heath, "When Missionaries Were Hated."

53. "The Mother Land," *Canadian Baptist*, 23 July 1885, 4.

to maintaining the Sabbath, and the practice was discouraged.[54] "Land grabbing" by France and Germany was criticized.[55] One article even had kind words for the Mahdi.[56] The Mahdi's rebellion against the British in the Sudan was described as a legitimate reaction to the corrupt rule of the Egyptians, and he was described as a freedom fighter in the likes of Cromwell, MacKenzie, or Papineau. If Britain was going to smash the Mahdi, it had better be for righteous reasons.

> If England is not in the Soudan to terminate the slave trade, nor to establish a government and civilization; if she stays there now with no other object than the popular brutal one of revenge— that of killing the prophet and making Arab blood flow—if the England of the nineteenth century goes back to that old law of "eye for eye," she will be guilty of a crime before heaven and the law of love. Why cannot she, in the moral strength that refused to revenge the death of Colley and the Majuba death, on the Boers, leave those Soudanese to themselves, so long as she feels she has no mission nor evangel to proclaim.

In other words, Britain could not just be in the Sudan for conquest and revenge; there needed to be a higher and nobler moral purpose.

The concern for righteousness cut both ways: if the cause was righteous, then they could confidently wage war and expect to win with God's help, but if the cause was unrighteous, then the cause could be criticized and would most likely fail. Of course, Canadian Baptists, in an imperial twist to nation-building, were to do all that they could to encourage the nation and empire to pursue righteousness.[57]

CONCLUSION

Almost a decade and a half later, Gordon's death was avenged on 2 September 1898 when the British under the leadership of Major-General Kitchener captured Khartoum. This battlefield success that made

---

54. *Canadian Baptist*, 23 April 1885, 4.

55. *Messenger and Visitor*, 11 February 1885, 1. This criticism seems somewhat disingenuous (or at least very inconsistent), for if Britain could grab territory why not France and Germany?

56. "The Mahdi," *Canadian Baptist*, 5 March 1885, 1.

57. The nation-building theme so prominent in Canadian religious historiography has neglected the imperial element of national identity. For instance, see Airhart, "Ordering a New Nation."

Kitchener famous allowed for the expansion of British imperial rule in the Sudan. As the following announcement of the victory in the *Canadian Baptist* indicates, it was believed that British control would better the lot of the Sudanese:

> Following the advance up the Nile and the capture of Khartoum and Omdurman, comes a proposition from the victorious General that a college and medical school be established at Khartoum in memory of General Gordon. The whole to cost about $300,000, which General Kitchener thinks the British public would gladly provide. Such a memorial would avenge the murder of Chinese Gordon in a spirit akin to his own, and would show the barbaric tribes of the Nile tributaries the great difference between the religion of Christ and the cruel fetishism of the Mahdi.[58]

By 1898 the new imperialism had captured the imagination of many Canadian English Protestants, and the acquiring of Khartoum fit quite nicely into the paradigm of British advances and blessings. The following year would see Canadians embark for South Africa to wage an imperial war against the Boers, and at that time imperialism among English Protestants reached a feverish pitch. However, the beginnings of such imperial zeal can be traced back to the Nile Expedition of 1884–85.

Of course, the events of 1884–85 need to be appreciated in their own right, not just seen as precursors to something greater down the road. Nevertheless, the Baptist press's response to the Nile Expedition does provide glimpses of an ardent passion for empire that indicates support for the convictions of the new imperialism. It appears that what kept Baptist commitment to imperialism from reaching a feverish pitch at that time was more the circumstances of the conflict than a lack of imperial passion. If Canadian soldiers had been sent (many volunteered to do so after Gordon's death, but were not needed), if the British had not abandoned the Sudan, and if the domestic dealings with Riel had not drawn attention away from foreign events, the imperial zeal of the South African War may very well have been seen during the Nile Expedition.

---

58. "Editorial Note," *Canadian Baptist*, 22 September 1898, 1.

Bibliography

Secondary Sources

Airhart, Phyllis D. "Ordering a New Nation and Reordering Protestantism, 1867–1914." In *The Canadian Protestant Experience, 1760–1990*, edited by George A. Rawlyk, 98–138. Burlington: Welch, 1990.

Barker, John. "Where the Missionary Frontier Ran ahead of Empire." In *Missions and Empire*, edited by Norman Etherington, 86–106. Oxford: Oxford University Press, 2005.

Bebbington, David. "Atonement, Sin, and Empire, 1880–1914." In *The Imperial Horizons of British Protestant Missions, 1880–1914*, edited by Andrew Porter, 14–31. Grand Rapids: Eerdmans, 2003.

Berger, Carl. *The Sense of Power: Studies in the Ideas of Canadian Imperialism, 1867–1914*. Toronto: University of Toronto Press, 1970.

Boileau, John. "Voyageurs on the Nile." *Legion Magazine*, January/February, 2004. Online: http://legionmagazine.com/en/2004/01/voyageurs-on-the-nile/ (Accessed: July 2010).

Buckner, Phillip. "Canada." In *The Impact of the South African War*, edited by David Omissi and Andrew S. Thompson, 233–50. Houndmills, UK: Palgrave: 2002.

———. "Whatever Happened to the British Empire?" *Journal of the Canadian Historical Association* 4 (1993) 3–32.

Bumsted, Michael. "From the Red to the Nile: William Nassau Kennedy and the Manitoba Contingent of Voyageurs in the Gordon Relief Expedition, 1884–1885." *Manitoba History* 42 (Autumn/Winter 2001–2002) 19–26.

Cole, Douglas. "Canada's 'Nationalistic' Imperialists." *Journal of Canadian Studies* 5 (1970) 44–45.

Cook, Terry. "George R. Parkin and the Concept of Britannic Idealism." *Journal of Canadian Studies* 10 (1975) 15–31.

Greenlee, James G., and Charles M. Johnston. *Good Citizens: British Missionaries and Imperial States, 1870–1918*. Montreal and Kingston: McGill-Queen's University Press, 1999.

Heath, Gordon L. "'Forming Sound Public Opinion': The Late Victorian Canadian Protestant Press and Nation-Building." *Journal of the Canadian Church Historical Society* 48 (2006) 109–59.

———. "Sin in the Camp: The Day of Humble Supplication in the Anglican Church in Canada in the Early Months of the South African War." *Journal of the Canadian Church Historical Society* 44 (2002) 207–26.

———. *A War with a Silver Lining: Canadian Protestant Churches and the South African War, 1899–1902*. Montreal and Kingston: McGill-Queen's University Press, 2009.

———. "When Missionaries Were Hated: An Examination of the Canadian Baptist Defense of Imperialism and Missions during the Boxer Rebellion, 1900." In *Baptists and Mission*, edited by Ian M. Randall and Anthony R. Cross, 261–76. Milton Keynes, UK: Paternoster, 2007.

Hochschild, Adam. *King Leopold's Ghost: A Story of Greed, Terror, and Heroism in Colonial Africa*. Boston: Houghton Mifflin, 1998.

Inglis, K. S. *The Rehearsal: Australians at War in the Sudan, 1885*. Sydney: Rigby, 1985.

MacKenzie, John M. *Propaganda and Empire: The Manipulation of British Public Opinion, 1880–1960*. Manchester: Manchester University Press, 1984.

McLaren, Roy. *Canadians on the Nile, 1882–1898: Being the Adventures of the Voyageurs on the Khartoum Relief Expedition and Other Exploits*. Vancouver: University of British Columbia Press, 1978.

Michel, Anthony P. "To Represent the Country in Egypt: Aboriginality, Britishness, Anglophone Canadian Identities, and the Nile Expedition, 1884–1885." *Social History* 39 (2006) 45–77.

Morton, Desmond. *A Military History of Canada*. Edmonton: Hurtig, 1990.

Page, Robert. *The Boer War and Canadian Imperialism*. Ottawa: The Canadian Historical Association, 1987.

———. "Canada and the Imperial Idea in the Boer War Years." *Journal of Canadian Studies* 5 (1970) 33–49.

———. "Carl Berger and the Intellectual Origins of Canadian Imperialist Thought, 1867–1914." *Journal of Canadian Studies* 5 (August 1970) 39–43.

Penlington, Norman. *Canada and Imperialism, 1896*. Toronto: University of Toronto Press, 1965.

Pigott, Peter. *Canada in the Soudan: War without Borders*. Toronto: Dundurn, 2009.

Porter, Andrew. "An Overview, 1700–1914." In *Missions and Empire*, edited by Norman Etherington, 40–63. Oxford: Oxford University Press, 2005.

———. *Religion versus Empire? British Protestant Missionaries and Overseas Expansion, 1700–1914*. Manchester: Manchester University Press, 2004.

Potter, Simon J. "Communication and Integration: The British and Dominions Press and the British World, c.1876–1914." *Journal of Imperial and Commonwealth History* 31 (2003) 190–206.

Preston, Adrian. "Wolseley, the Khartoum Relief Expedition and the Defence of India, 1885–1900." *The Journal of Imperial and Commonwealth History* 6 (1978) 254–80.

Renfree, Harry A. *Heritage and Horizon: The Baptist Story in Canada*. Mississauga: Canadian Baptist Federation, 1988.

Samson, Jane. "The Problem of Colonialism in the Western Historiography of Christian Missions." *Religious Studies and Theology* 23 (2004) 2–26.

Sanneh, Lamin. "Christian Missions and the Western Guilt Complex." *Christian Century*, 8 April 1987, 331–34.

Saunders, Malcolm. "A Case Study of Historical Inaccuracy: New South Wales and the Sudan Campaign of 1885." *Journal of Australian Studies* 8 (1984) 29–38.

Silver, A. I. "Some Quebec Attitudes in an Age of Imperialism and Ideological Conflict." *Canadian Historical Review* 57 (1976) 440–60.

Stacey, C. P. *Canada and the Age of Conflict*. Vol. 1, *1867–1921*. Toronto: University of Toronto Press, 1992.

———. "Canada and the Nile Expedition of 1884–85." *Canadian Historical Review* 33 (1952) 319–40.

———. "John A. Macdonald on Raising Troops in Canada for Imperial Service, 1885." *Canadian Historical Review* 38 (1957) 37–40.

———. *Records of the Nile Voyageurs, 1884–1885*. Toronto: Champlain Society, 1959.

Stanley, Brian. "Baptists, Antislavery and the Legacy of Imperialism." *Baptist Quarterly* 42 (2007) 289.

———. *The Bible and the Flag: Protestant Missions and British Imperialism in the Nineteenth and Twentieth Centuries*. Leicester, UK: Apollos, 1990.

———. "Christianity and Civilization in English Evangelical Mission Thought, 1792–1857." In *Christian Missions and the Enlightenment*, edited by Brian Stanley, 169–97. Grand Rapids: Eerdmans, 2001.

5

The Call to Arms: The Reverend Thomas Todhunter Shields, World War One, and the Shaping of a Militant Fundamentalist

DOUG ADAMS

> Thou, therefore, endure hardness, as a good soldier of Jesus Christ.
>
> 2 TIMOTHY 2:3

THE DECADE SPANNING THE years 1910 to 1920 were the first ten years of a remarkable thirty-five year pastorate for Reverend Thomas Todhunter Shields. T. T. Shields was the renowned pastor of Jarvis Street Baptist Church, one of the premier churches in the Baptist Convention of Ontario and Quebec until its departure in 1927. Shields remained pastor at Jarvis Street until his death in 1955. This opening decade of ministry also delineated the pivotal period of Shields's life and career. Undoubtedly there was some continuity with his previous pastorates in the manner of his pastoral oversight and governance of Jarvis Street Baptist Church. However, radical changes were in the offing, both in the character of Shields's ministry and in his own personal attitudes and deportment. Furthermore, it could be argued that by the midpoint of his first decade of ministry in Jarvis Street Baptist Church all was not well for Shields. His prestige in church and denomination was rapidly rising but the fundamentals of his earlier pastoral vision were severely compromised. Most significantly, his evangelistic zeal had been almost entirely curtailed and his administrative control over the affairs of the church was seriously limited. This paper seeks to identify and evaluate the changes that occurred in the ministry of Shields during this period with special attention being given to the impact of the First World War. A guest of Britain's Ministry of Information during the final stages of the war, Shields was confronted with images of violence and horror that forever reshaped his outlook on life and ministry. Walking among the dead on the French front in a terrain grotesquely desecrated by the horrific destruction of the world's first "modern" war, the excruciating shock impressed upon him the enormity of the struggle with "modernism" in which he was engaged. Shields's internalization of these experiences was a traumatic call to war in the context of war. The militancy of Shields's Fundamentalist construct was born as he recoiled from the dark revelation of modernity's deadly fruit.[1]

HISTORICAL CONTEXT

The events of this decade provided a startling contrast with much that had gone before. Prior to 1910, Shields was above all else an evangelist. Historically, every new pastorate had begun with an ambitious and dynamic evangelistic campaign. Successive campaigns blitzed the immediate and extended locale of his pastoral oversight until, metaphorically, he had pumped the well dry. Then the geographic sphere of his ministry would shift and the process would begin anew. He had little interest and no time for anything but the proclamation of the gospel. Even his holidays were devoted to evangelistic ministry in some other locale. Later in life he would boast of how he regularly worked through the night in study and preparation, beginning the next day refreshed as though having slept the whole night through. At 77 years of age he was chagrinned that he could no longer maintain such a pace.[2] However, in his early ministry, evangelistic outreach consumed him, and by 1903 he actually left the pastorate for a time to pursue evangelistic endeavors. The following ten months were a virtual whirlwind of activity for Shields. He conducted in

---

1. For more on Canadian Baptist reactions to the First World War, see Haykin and Clary, "Battles."

2. Shields, Letter to Miss Ethel Shields, 1 March 1951, in "Shields Correspondence," JSBCA.

that time fourteen evangelistic campaigns, going from one church to the next in immediate succession. His practice was to preach three times on the Sunday and then every week night except Saturday. Seven of the campaigns ran for two weeks while the rest were carried on for three weeks or more. Throughout this period he preached every Sunday, including once at home in Hamilton on the Sunday of his Christmas break. The period of his full-time evangelistic endeavors spanned 329 days, during which he preached 309 times. Over the course of the forty-four weeks, thirty-six were spent actively campaigning. On a few occasions he enjoyed a week's break between the last Sunday of one campaign and the first Sunday of the next. In those thirty-six weeks of active campaigning, then, he preached an average of 8.5 times a week. Nor was he idle during the weekdays before his evening sessions. During the day it would seem that he led an aggressive visitation blitz of the area. Speaking years later of his experience in one of the towns he visited, he shared how he was able to educate the pastor there as to how to run an evangelistic campaign:

> I immediately proposed to him that we should visit together from house to house throughout the entire town, not omitting a single place of human residence. We printed some invitation cards, with an announcement on one side; and, on the other side, a simple setting forth of the way of salvation, with the names of the Pastor and his helper subscribed. We then began each morning about nine o'clock, and went from door to door. Where it was possible, we entered the house, engaged the people in religious conversation, and, where they were willing, we read the Scripture and prayed. Where that was not possible, we bore our testimony at the door, gave the people a warm invitation to attend the services, and left a card as a reminder. We continued this until every house in the entire neighbourhood had been visited, and not an individual in the town had been left without an invitation.[3]

This Pastor said to me, "I have been a minister in this town for ten years: you have been here but a few days. But you have introduced me to the town. I have met hundreds of people I did not know. I have entered many homes I had not even seen. You have shown me possibilities of work of which I had never even dreamed; and I am most grateful."[4]

For Shields, the evangelistic campaign was the answer to everything. His growing renown as a conciliator demonstrated another function of

3. Shields, *Plot*, 297.
4. Ibid.

active evangelism. Employed for a time by the denomination as a mediator in church disputes, Shields turned again to the evangelistic campaign, which figured prominently in his efforts to restore harmony to the congregation.[5] Harmony and growth, then, were the distinguishing marks of his early pastorates.

A statistical analysis of his early ministry demonstrates the significant growth that accompanied his evangelistic efforts. In his first church at Florence he was able to post a 40 percent net increase in membership in a single year of ministry. In Dutton he baptized sixteen people in a year and saw a net increase of 36.5 percent. In Delhi, he posted an increase of 46 percent in the first year. In subsequent years the growth fell off and Shields was soon to leave for greener pastures. Perhaps his most successful ministry, from a church growth perspective, was in Wentworth Street Baptist Church in Hamilton. Using the congregation's size at the time of his coming as a benchmark, Shields posted gains after a year of 83 percent, after two years of 125 percent and after three years of 168 percent.[6] He was able to boast of having baptized ninety-four people in the course of this pastorate.[7] Furthermore, he led the congregation in expanding its current buildings and to becoming self sufficient, free from home missions support. In London, his successes were equally astonishing. Over the course of his ministry there, the membership grew by 71 percent. That number did not reflect the significant number of people sent out from the church to establish Egerton Street Baptist Church. Church growth was so rapid that the church had to be expanded three times to provide sufficient capacity and on at least one occasion they had outgrown their expanded facilities before they even moved back in.

In light of this, the record of the next ten years is astonishing. Not only were the earliest years of the Toronto pastorate devoid of evangelistic campaigns, but it was over eleven years before a single campaign of such character was conducted within the walls of Jarvis Street Baptist Church. In fact, over the next eleven years, only three such campaigns can be identified from Shields's records. The first was nearly two years after the outset of his Toronto ministry and was conducted on the other side of the American border in Jackson, Michigan. Another two years passed before Shields

5. Ibid., 298–99.

6. All the statistics discussed in this paragraph were taken from those recorded in the *Baptist Year Book*.

7. Shields, "Sermons Preached" (this was the title Shields gave to his sermon diary), JSBCA.

undertook evangelistic work. However, once again his work was done a long way from home, this time in Kingston, Ontario. After Kingston it was not until 1920 that Shields was once again engaged actively as an evangelist, this time even further from home, in New York City. To be sure, Shields spent a good deal of time in 1919 going about the Convention in behalf of the Forward Movement to make an appeal for evangelistic outreach, but the evangelistic campaign itself was curiously absent.

The results in church growth were predictable. Though Leslie Tarr boasts of an average growth of 114 people a year or 10 percent, this figure is misleading.[8] Tarr reports only additions to the church and ignores losses. Over the course of ten years the church posted net losses in four of those years. Also Tarr's numbers do not accurately reflect evangelistic success in Shields's ministry. They do not take into account the 273 received by letter in 1913 when the church amalgamated with Parliament Street Baptist Church. Nor do these numbers reflect the fact that of the nearly 1200 people who did join the church over the ten year period, 64 percent were received by transfer from other churches and only 36 percent through conversion and baptism. *The Baptist Year Book* in the year that Shields became pastor recorded the congregation's size as 1069. Unlike in every previous pastorate, Shields posted a net loss in membership for his first year of ministry. At the end of ten years, the figures provided to the *Year Book* recorded a congregational size of 1144, a net gain of seventy-five or only 7 percent after ten years of ministry.[9] By previous standards, Shields's record for the first ten years of ministry was dismal indeed.

The first key to understanding the shift in Shields's ministerial record has to do with the congregation he now faced. At Jarvis Street, those beliefs and practices that he took for granted in his previous ministries were now under attack. The otherworldly focus of kingdom ministry was challenged on every front by the insidious creep of secularization within a church governed by a culture of "respectability." This creeping liberalism from the pews of his own church coupled with the theological shifts so easily embraced by his liberalized parishioners were an assault on Shields's faith perspective that shook him to the core. Shields suddenly

---

8. Tarr, *Shields*, 62.

9. *The Baptist Year Book* published detailed membership records on an annual basis. Each year the numbers joining the church were identified as entering by baptism or by letter. Losses were represented as those transferring out by letter, those who died, and those who were excluded. It is very clear that after ten years of ministry, Jarvis Street had sustained very little real growth and had barely managed to hold its own.

found himself embroiled in a war not of his own making. Gradually, over the course of the decade, Shields was drawn into what he saw as the battle for "the faith which was once delivered unto the saints."[10] His evangelistic methodology was the first casualty of this struggle. Shields later complained: "I had to wait eleven years for my full liberty as a preacher of the gospel."[11]

His tenure at Jarvis Street convinced him that modernism was a "hydra-headed" monster that would invariably show itself in "its many-colored forms."[12] His first significant experiences with modernism came early in his Jarvis Street pastorate and were theological in nature. Controversy over the teachings of Dr. I. G. Matthews at McMaster had surfaced in the protest of Elmore Harris. Shields had played a minor role in that controversy by seconding a compromise solution in the 1910 convention.[13] By 1919 the seeds sown in that earlier period had come to fruition in open attacks on the inspiration and integrity of the Bible. In the Ottawa convention of that year, Shields successfully championed the cause of biblical orthodoxy.[14] He quickly discovered, however, that his attack on theological liberalism would have serious ramifications for his own church. He was gradually discovering that theological modernism had its counterpart in the cultural liberalism that characterized many of his own socially elite parishioners. When he began to confront and resist the culture of respectability that had been deeply ingrained into the very ethos of Jarvis Street identity, he discovered the beating heart of modernism. A nascent worldliness that revelled in the love of the ever-increasing amenities of modern urban society flourished under the vaults of the magnificent gothic cathedral that so effectively reflected their Baptist pride of place and accomplishment. "Modernism in vaudeville performances in Sunday School entertainments" and "Modernism in Church Choirs" were for Shields two of the most prominent symptoms of this

---

10. Jude 3.
11. Shields, *Plot*, 196.
12. Shields, "The Final Chapter," *Gospel Witness*, 10 June 1922, 3.
13. Shields, *Plot*, 44, 45. Cf. *Baptist Year Book 1910*, "Proceedings," 27–30.
14. Shields, *Plot*, "The Great Ottawa Convention," 139–48. For further reading on this controversy see "The Inspiration and Authority of Scripture," *Canadian Baptist*, 2 October 1919, 8; T. T. Shields, "Inspiration and Authority of Scripture," *Canadian Baptist*, 16 October 1919, 3; Charles J. Holman, "Those 'Settled Questions' in the Old Land," *Canadian Baptist*, 16 October 1919, 4; *Baptist Year Book 1919*, "Proceedings," 24–27.

culture within Jarvis Street. Outside its walls the participation of its congregants in the amusements craze of dancing, cards, and the theatre led Shields to his denunciation of "Modernism in the matter of amusements." Curiously absent in this liberalized crowd were the traditional marks of spirituality. Most significant was the total lack of interest in prayer and worship. While attendance upon the organs of culture and refinement came naturally, participation in prayer meeting and the celebration of the ordinances was neglected. This was but a first manifestation of what Shields would identify as a "Modernism in opposition to the Regular Baptist position in the matter of the ordinances." Shields's contest with the modernistic element within his own church climaxed in the conclusion of the annual meeting, 21 September 1922. With the exodus of 341 of his liberalized opponents, Shields was able to boast "Modernism was vanquished! Hallelujah." [15] Three weeks after this exodus, on the evening of 14 October 1921, Shields defiantly declared to a cheering congregation, "We will begin the fundamentalist movement now!"[16]

A second key factor in the reshaping of Shields's ministerial outlook, and the particular focus of this paper, related to the fact that at the same time he was beginning to come to an appreciation of the magnitude of the challenge facing him at Jarvis Street, he became an active observer of the events unfolding on the world stage. The shock of war's brutality and his own war experiences taught him further of the enormity of the struggle in which he was engaged. Shields's internalization of these experiences was a traumatic call to war in the context of war. The context of his own struggle was reshaped and the manner of his reactions was redefined. The militancy that so characterized Shields the Fundamentalist was born in him as he drove across the territories devastated by war on the French front.

OFF TO SEE THE WAR

When war broke out in August of 1914, Shields was away from the Jarvis Street pulpit for his summer holiday. His first opportunity to comment on unfolding world events was 6 September 1914, the first Sunday of his return. He preached a sermon "The LORD Is a Man of War" based on a

---

15. Shields, "The Final Chapter," *Gospel Witness*, 10 June 1922, 3.
16. Shields, *Inside of the Cup*, 17.

text from Exodus 15:3.[17] The text was something of a pretext that Shields used largely as an excuse to comment on the war. The sermon provided insights into Shields's perspectives at the outset of the war. Shields noted that it was his duty to show the religious significance of the war. He disputed with the man who insisted that the war had no religious significance and insisted: "Nothing is without religious significance if Christ is all in all."[18] However, Shields promised that hereafter his commentary on the war would be minimal:

> I have said this that you may know that this pulpit will not attempt to usurp the office of the military expert. From time to time it may be wise to try to read the events of the week in the light of the sanctuary; but in the main I hope we may find this place as a thick-walled, sound-proof castle, where at the King's table, we may gain wisdom and strength to worthily play our part in the battle which rages without.[19]

Such was Shields's intent at the outset of the war, but as his exposure to the events of the war increased so did his commentary upon it. Shields's promise, therefore, was short lived, and before long he was preaching regularly on the matter. By war's end he imagined himself something of an expert on the war and his commentary was increasingly posited as authoritative summations of the war's impact and significance.

Three times during the course of the First World War Shields undertook the hazardous voyage across the Atlantic Ocean to engage in ministry in London, England. His destination was Spurgeon's Metropolitan Tabernacle, where he spent his summer holidays ministering to this famous congregation as a pulpit exchange with his friend Dr. A. C. Dixon. Though the purpose of his trips was ostensibly ministerial, his fascination with Britain's war effort could not be contained. His correspondence to his family at home was filled with wartime observations and a barely concealed sense of excitement. Speaking for instance of the perils of traversing the Atlantic in this period he commented: "They were thrilling days, however, whether on land or at sea, and I have never enjoyed crossing the ocean more than during the war."[20]

---

17. Shields, "The LORD Is a Man of War."
18. A reference to Eph 1:23. Shields, "The LORD Is a Man of War."
19. Ibid.
20. Shields, *Plot*, 56.

The experiences of 1915 and 1918 particularly impacted Shields's outlook. In 1915, Shields's correspondence demonstrated a deep fascination with those who had been to the front. One young lieutenant told him of his experiences in the battle of the Marne. He had two horses shot out from under him, one of those having had its head blown off. He himself was wounded in the head.[21] Another told him of the German atrocities he had himself witnessed:

> He told me of the literal crucifixion of a friend of his and who was still alive. He was nailed by railway tie spikes to a door and a rope put around his ankles and the rope nailed down. He was found and taken down, but has lost the use of both hands. He says the Canadians now take no prisoners. The only thing to do with a German is to kill him where ever you find him.[22]

Shields's growing sense of horror at these ghastly fruits of war came to expression with his remarks after visiting the brother of one of his acquaintances in Edmonton Hospital. He had been wounded and "gassed" at Ypres. Shields noted that "a piece of shrapnel about 2 inches wide went into his right side and lodged in the left lung—it is there still. He is convalescent, but will never be strong. It will always be a menace to him and doctors say it can never be removed." Shields was deeply moved at seeing him and wrote: "When I looked at him I felt toward the Kaiser as I hope I always feel toward the devil."[23]

Not only was Shields's psyche being reshaped by the traumatic scenes he witnessed, but also, his self-image was being redefined by the reception he was given. The accolades he received in the environs of The Metropolitan Tabernacle were significant. However, the warmth of welcome that he experienced was not only ecclesiastical. Shields came to England armed with a letter of introduction from Sir George Foster to the Canadian High Commissioner, Sir George Perley.[24] Little is known now

---

21. Shields, "Circular, 6 July 1915."

22. Shields, "Circular, 6 August 1915." Note: The *London Times* printed a story May 10, 1915 about a crucified Canadian Soldier; "Torture of a Canadian Officer." The story became legendary and after the war the Nazis later used this as an example of British propaganda. The account related here by Shields differs in details, but quite likely reflects the growing legend. The significant point is that Shields believed it and used its propaganda value.

23. Shields, "Circular, 11 August 1915."

24. Sir George Foster had first served as Minister of Marine Fisheries in the government of Sir John A. MacDonald. From there he was promoted to Minister of

of the nature of the relationship between Shields and Foster, but clearly Foster's reputation carried great weight, and his recommendations were of such a character as to establish Shields before Perley as a Canadian of some distinction. Shields himself commented: "I don't know what Sir George Foster said about me in the letter which he gave me to Sir George Perley, but both Sir George Perley and Mr. Griffith are very good to me."[25] Perley's immediate response to the letter of introduction was a promise to process Shields's application for a passport which he hoped to use to go to Paris. Shields's fascination with the war was such that he wanted to travel as close to the front as possible. As matters worked out, in very short order Shields did receive his passport in good form but when he went to have it certified at the French Consulate he discovered "a mob" waiting to process their papers to go home for the "Bank Holiday."[26] Because of this and other opportunities that presented themselves before the end of his stay, Shields did not get to France on this trip.

Further gestures from Perley included a ticket to the House of Commons and a "ticket and a reserved seat . . . at the Guildhall where Sir Robert S. Borden was to be presented with the freedom of the City." Making use of both of these opportunities, Shields was able to report home in glowing terms of the speeches he had heard and the important men he had encountered. Some of these included "The right Honorable Herbert Asquith Prime Minister and first Lord of the treasury . . . Bonar Law, Austen Chamberlain, Bishop of London, Dean of Canterbury, and Earls and Lords galore."[27]

From his own perspective the greatest honor afforded Shields by the High Commissioner's office came in the form of an official invitation to the great ceremony "commemorating the commencement of the war" to be held at St. Paul's Cathedral on 4 August 1915. Shields had returned to the Commissioner's office hoping for a letter that might expedite his attempt to get into France. He was given the letter but in the course of conversation

---

Finance in 1888, a position he continued to hold through the governments of Abbott, Thompson, Bowell, and Tupper. In the Borden government he was given the portfolio of Trade and Commerce. In 1914 he was given a knighthood for his work on the Royal Commission on Imperial Trade. He was responsible for "the reorganization of Canadian industry on a war-time basis" and was appointed acting Prime Minister while Borden was in London. In 1919 he served as Canadian delegate to the Versailles Peace Conference. For more on Foster, see Wallace, *Foster*.

25. Shields, "Circular, 30 July 1915."
26. Shields, "Circular, 2 August 1915."
27. Shields, "Circular, 29 July 1915."

was apprised of the coming ceremony. The High Commissioner's agent noted that there were a number of tickets reserved for "distinguished Canadians" and that if Shields chose to stay in England one such ticket would be reserved for him. Shields decided to put off his trip to France and the ticket was delivered to his place of residence August 3rd.

Shields was almost mesmerized by the sequence of events that followed. Upon receipt of the ticket he immediately reported to his family "You will see by this that I am specially favored as a 'Distinguished Canadian.'"[28] The developments of the day were recorded in some detail as Shields tried to convey to his family at home something of the grandeur of the occasion. He rode in an open cab and was quite aware of the spectacle he must have presented: "Of course I was dressed in my best— my morning coat, and Top Hat and I felt quite important, able to wave aside all those officers of the law . . . by my Lord Chamberlain's warrant." Shields's reserved seat was among the best in the Cathedral. He prepared a detailed diagram of the seating arrangements, which he attached to his letter. He boasted of his proximity to the King and Queen. "If you examine the forgoing plan you will see that I had a better seat than Kitchener or Borden, for they were behind the King—whereas I was just to his right in front of him. And 'honest-injun,' he fixed his eyes on me and stared at me as though he wondered who I was. And so did Queen Mary too! That is really a fact. He did not offer to shake hands but he certainly ought to know me when we meet next time."[29]

Despite his excitement and sense of reverence concerning the significance of the proceedings, Shields was, however, less than impressed with the performance of the Archbishop. With comments suggestive not only of his inflated view of himself, but also of his growing tendency to elevate all war themes into the realm of the spiritual, Shields critiqued the Archbishop's performance. Having sent a bundle of newspaper reports of the event home to his family he left the reading of the sermon itself to them. His own conclusion was that "There is not so much in it, and as he delivered it, it seemed poorer still. Apart from his official position, and on his merits, if he always preaches in that strained and jerky style, he would not be invited to preach in some pulpits I know the second time."[30]

---

28. Shields, "Circular, 3 August 1915."
29. Shields, "Circular, 4 August 1915."
30. Ibid.

Shields was particularly critical of the Archbishop's failure to spiritualize the war or to see it in its religious aspect:

> he might at least have brought the matter into a strong religious light. Instead of that he talked a lot of thuddle about everybody having been made inheritors of the kingdom of heaven in holy baptism and urged upon them "To stand fast in the faith" to which they had been dedicated at a time when they "did not dream" what it meant. I looked across at the Giant Kitchener, then at Frey, then at Asquith, and considered what they thought of such piffle.[31]

By the end of 1917, Shields had travelled the hostile waters of the Atlantic four times. Adventures on the high sea had stirred his restless spirits. The very real dangers he encountered gave him a real sense of identification with the war effort. In retrospect, however, up to this point he had been merely a casual observer of the war. In 1918, all that changed with his introduction to the British Ministry of Information. By the end of 1918 Shields would lay claim to a measure of expertise on war matters that truly reshaped his own self-image and his ideals of ministry.

In August, 1918, Shields arrived safely in London to take up his summer ministry. Unfortunately, Shields's letter journal for this period is no longer extant. However, a number of letters do survive and his accounts of the events in his addresses on the war when he returned home summarized his experiences. Over the years, Shields often spoke of these experiences, either to validate his own prestige or to illustrate some spiritual principle that he was expounding. Shields again supplied the pulpit of London's Metropolitan Tabernacle, this time for the month of August. During his time in London, Shields was invited by the British Ministry of Information to "see Britain's war effort" and he became "a guest of the ministry . . . over a period of four months." Shields long viewed this privilege as recognition of his labors in behalf of Borden's Union Government and of his "unreserved support of the British cause."[32]

In September he awaited his pass to France but due to some unforeseen delays with the Ministry of Information he was unable to get to France until October 14. In the meantime, the church in London invited him to preach there while he waited his pass. In addition, since the

---

31. Ibid.

32. Shields, "The Censor and the Editor Exchange Letters," *Gospel Witness*, 2 January 1941, 11 (455).

Ministry of Information's transportation facilities in France were tied up for the "use of certain French journalists," the Ministry proposed a tour of Ireland. Shields readily accepted the invitation and in fact secured the inclusion of some ministerial friends, "Drs. Truett, Francis and Hoyt," and so went as a "party of four."[33] At the conclusion of his tour he could boast of an extended interview with Sir Edward Carson.[34] Through the years Shields bragged again and again of the insights that he had been able to share with Carson about the Irish problem.[35] Indeed, Shields came away from the experience believing that he was something of an expert on the Irish situation. He boasted that "in two weeks we met with the leaders of all shades of Irish opinion,"[36] and "saw more than perhaps one would ordinarily be able to see in ten years."[37] He added the observation that "the Ministry of Information tells us that to no others have so many Irish leaders spoken, and so freely as to us."[38] On the whole the trip left a lasting impression on Shields, and as time would show, contributed to a hardening of his attitudes toward the Roman Catholic Church.

Shortly thereafter Shields made two trips into France, ostensibly to find members of the Canadian troops "who were by this time on the march toward Germany as part of the army of occupation."[39] He explained that "The chaplaincy services were anxious I should see the Canadians in detail and carry back some news of their work." In his explanatory note to the deacons' board giving the reasons for his delayed return, he argued: "This seemed a very reasonable request, the more so, as I should expect to report my observations chiefly to Canadian audiences." These were of course the last days of the war and though Shields "motored fully 300 miles over the devastated part of France," he did not see much of the Canadian troops. What he did see however, left images seared upon his mind that even time could not entirely obliterate:

> I remember making a tour of the battle fields of France while the war was still on. Many returned soldiers are here this evening.

33. Shields, "To the Deacons."

34. Lord Carson was a leader of the Ulster unionist Party and held many positions in the Cabinet of the United Kingdom. The standard biography is Hyde, *Carson*. For more recent treatment see, Hostettler, *Sir Edward*.

35. For instance, Shields, "Hepburn's Alliance," *Gospel Witness*, 7 March 1935, 1.

36. Shields, "To the Deacons."

37. Shields, "A Lecture on Ireland," *Gospel Witness*, 7 March 1935.

38. Shields, "To the Deacons."

39. Shields, "The Fall of Lucifer," *Gospel Witness*, 7 March 1935.

You saw the horrors of it. When I saw hundreds of dead lying upon the ground; and miles, and miles, and miles of territory in the region of the Somme where not a living thing remained; where towns and villages had been blotted out of existence, and the whole face of the earth changed: and I said to some friends who were with me, "this looks as though something superhuman had been at work. It really looks as though hell had here been let loose.[40]

As Shields waited for his pass to enter France for a second trip, the First World War ended. Shields was on hand for the celebrations first in London and then Paris and later Brussels, where he was witness to the return of King Albert of Belgium to his capital. From Paris, Shields traveled to Boulogne from which point a car was standing by to drive him in pursuit of the Canadian troops. Though his time was limited, Shields was "most anxious to follow them . . . and get as far on the way toward Germany as possible." Though he did not expect actually to "set foot on German soil," he did hope to get as far as Brussels. This trip was among the most significant events in all of Shields's war experiences. With him on his drive was "an officer of 'the old contemptibles,'" Captain H. G. Gilliland.[41] Together they drove "thousands of miles" across French territory visiting one scene of devastation after another.[42] From first-hand observation Shields would relate: "Her [France's] losses have been colossal. I have seen tens of thousands of her graves. Her mining and industrial centres have been in the hand of the enemy. I have seen war's destruction. Cities reduced to ashes. Bethune, Bapaume, Peronne, Albert, many others. Villages obliterated. Land like the waves of the sea."[43] Perhaps even more significant than the scenes unfolding around him were the stories told to him by Gilliland. Gilliland, more than many, harbored a deep hostility toward the "Hun." The Captain had the great misfortune of being captured in the second or third month of the war. He was held as a prisoner of war in Germany for two and a half years, during which time he made three attempts at escape. He was successful on the third attempt.

40. Shields, "Great News," *Gospel Witness*, 13 November 1924, 4.

41. "The Old Contemptibles" was a name adopted by British troops of the regular army in 1914. It likely originated in a comment of the German Kaiser who in exasperation at the delay of German troops in France referred to "Sir John French's contemptible little army." Cf. "firstworldwar.com." Online: http://www.firstworldwar.com/atoz/oldcontemptibles.htm (accessed July 2, 2010).

42. Shields, "The Fall of Lucifer," *Gospel Witness*, 7 March 1935.

43. Shields, "Sword of Victory," 19.

When he returned to England, he wrote a book entitled: *My German Prisons: Being the Experiences of an Officer during Two and a Half Years as a Prisoner of War*. The book was published in 1918 and was a deliberate attempt to stir up animosity against the German State and to resist rising pacifistic sentiments among the British people:

> Further, there must be many who are already feeling war-weary and despondent, and who consequently may be ready to embrace any opportunity of making peace even on the basis of the *Status quo*. If the revelations disclosed herein bring home to these a knowledge of the infamous, relentless, and savage character of the Hun, deliberately dehumanised by the State for the purposes of the State, the writer will feel that his labour has not been in vain.[44]

Gilliland's stories filled Shields with a great animosity toward the Germans and were perhaps among the most significant instruments in producing within him the militancy that hereafter so profoundly characterized his ministry. Furthermore, Shields became more and more resolute in his own denunciations of pacifism, a resolve that hardened rapidly as he was confronted on all sides by these horrific evidences of human depravity. There can be little doubt that Gilliland's stories had a deep effect on Shields:

> He told me many things which the censor would not permit him to publish, and other things which are too horrible to print. But he saw the working of the German mind in the days when Germany thought she was winning. And from intimate association with him I learned that the fiendishly ingenious tortures of the dark ages, and the horrible mutilations of their captives by savage tribes, would rank as courtesies in comparison with the infernal inventions of the mind of a German prison commandant. They studied to inflict the most exquisite tortures upon the mind, to crucify the spirit, to drag the soul through all the filth of Prussian bestiality, to condense eternal torment into time, to throttle hope, and to drive their captives to the madness of despair.[45]

During the course of his four months as a guest of the Ministry of Information Shields was given a large number of opportunities to see and assess the strength of Britain's war effort. He visited a factory which "outside of Krupps," he was informed was "the largest munitions plant in the

---

44. Gilliland, *German Prisons*, preface.
45. Shields, "The Fall of Lucifer," *Gospel Witness*, 7 March 1935.

world."⁴⁶ Shields was also taken to one of the "principal aerodromes" and to England's first tankodrome. "I saw where the tanks were made, and where they were assembled and tested and by what means their secret was so cleverly kept." Later he was actually able to ride in one of the latest tanks through the Hindenburg trench. He told how it "rode over logs, and through shell-holes, and over all sorts of obstructions. It was not exactly like a Pullman car, but it was thrilling. It carried its bridge with it. Pushed it ahead and threw it across the canal, went over it, and picked it up, and carried it along for the next gap."⁴⁷

One of the most impressive sights that Shields experienced came with his visit to the Grand Fleet. "It was my privilege to visit the Grand Fleet, and to sail down between those miles of floating fortresses. I saw the Famous *Lion*, Admiral Beatty's flagship at the Battle of Jutland, a ship which the Germans officially sank four times!" He noted sarcastically, "That is the only way of sinking the British *Lion*—on paper!" He also saw the current flagship, "*The Queen Elizabeth*," and spoke personally over lunch with Sir Philip Watt, the ship's designer. He also spoke of the "many other famous ships" he passed as well as "the American battle-fleet." In these great ships Shields saw the last line of defense for the world's liberties:

> But what if I were to describe those long lines of gray hulls, their cleared decks, their heavy armour, their mighty guns, all ready to speak in righteousness and might to save the liberties of the world? . . . then these gray monsters are fused into an invincible whole; animated by one spirit, moved by one passion, directed toward one aim; a single weapon in the hand of a Free Democracy and mightily used for the weal of the whole world.⁴⁸

In December of 1918, Shields sailed from Liverpool aboard the Mauritania, the first ship to deliver American troops to the shores of the United States at war's end, and so he was once again on hand for the celebrations. He spoke of the trip in which he and his friend J. W. Hoyt were the only civilians aboard, and which was the roughest of all his crossings. Undaunted by the ferocious winds and towering waves, emotions stirred by scenes of war and celebration flowed unrestrained throughout his whole being:

46. Ibid.
47. Ibid.
48. Ibid.

The weather was terrific, high seas, and a seventy-mile gale, but as Neptune played his grand organ—the majestic open diapason, with all the magnificent orchestral harmonies of a storm at sea, to my ears the wind and the thunderous waves did but echo the acclamations of London, and Paris, and Brussels. And at New York, as ours was the first ship to bring American soldiers home, I heard it again, and louder than anywhere else. But it was the same exultant cry!

The scenes of victory that stirred his heart as he braved the storm fired his imagination with visions of the triumphs he hoped soon to see repeated in the spiritual and ecclesiastical realm. Coming home fully apprised of the immense cost by which "the Sword of Victory was forged and fashioned and how it was skilfully [sic] wielded until it was driven with fatal force to the heart of tyranny," Shields prepared himself to wield the sword to obliterate the last vestiges of Germanic influence from America's shores.[49]

HOME FROM WAR: EVALUATION OF A CHANGING PERSPECTIVE

The pivotal character of Shields's first decade at Jarvis Street resulted from a combination of two significant factors. The first factor was the restraint imposed upon Shields by the culture of respectability and his growing restlessness under its dictates. The second was the traumatic shock of a war in which he became deeply engaged. His observations of that war directly shaped the character of his response to the restraints facing him at home.

There can be little doubt that upon his return from England in 1918, things quickly changed in Shields's ministerial demeanor and outlook. Over the next few years, the man who had never suffered through a church split, and had been used by the denomination for his conciliatory skills, now witnessed a serious division within his own church and dragged his whole denomination into the bitterest rupture in its history. At home in Jarvis Street a faction was becoming increasingly restive under a ministry they found to be progressively more controversial. They complained: "Dr. Shields' ways do not appeal to a quiet peace-loving people, such as we are. He is a fighter all the time."[50] In the pivotal convention of 1926 in

---

49. Shields, "Sword of Victory," 1.
50. "Retired Deacons Tell of Jarvis Church Case," *Toronto Daily Star*, 12 October

First Avenue Baptist Church, one delegate was led to the observation: "Three years ago in the Emmanuel Baptist Church there was not a man who would not have voted for Dr. Shields and followed his leadership; today I challenge anybody to find a single man who has any confidence in any statement that Dr. Shields makes." Moments later the same delegate remarked: "These things are crippling the Lord's work. If slandering the brethren is Satan's work, if robbing men of God of their good name is dishonourable, if disrupting churches and sowing disunion is wicked, if undermining the health of noble and Christian men is cruel, then I beseech Dr. Shields to come to repentance, for he has committed every one of these offences."[51] It should be noted that both of these examples are expressions of those who were willingly blind to the issues Shields was trying to confront. However, both inside his church and outside, a new and more caustic Dr. Shields was emerging. Shields would have explained the changes in his demeanor as a necessary response to the enormity of the threat facing evangelical Christianity. Shields now viewed himself as a heroic warrior, set for the defense of the faith. While the import of the issues being fought over certainly contributed to the magnitude and speed of his metamorphosis, it is equally arguable that Shields's immersion in the affairs of war over the previous four years led to significant shifts in outlook and behavior.

War now increasingly became the defining metaphor in Shields's view of the Christian faith. Early in his career and before his involvement in the First World War, Shields had a much more "other-worldly" view of the warfare in which he was to be engaged. The connection between "great conflicts" of the physical and spiritual realms lay in the sphere of principles. In his early sermons Shields was quick to find illustrations in contemporary battles of spiritual realities. Nevertheless, the connection between the two realms was tenuous and served primarily to provide illustrative material. "In every great conflict," he argued, "the warring peoples are representative of warring principles, and from the issue of such battles useful lessons may always be learned."[52] For instance, at the

---

1921, sec. 1, 2.

51. Shields, "Ichabod, McMaster's New Name," *Gospel Witness*, 4 November 1926, 155–56. (This was an expanded issue of the *Gospel Witness*. In its earliest form the magazine commonly ran to eight pages. As controversy unfolded editions began to run over twenty pages. This particular edition was 176 pages in length and was printed as a separate booklet.)

52. Shields, "The End," Sermon # 659.

conclusion of the war between Russia and Japan, he impressed upon his congregation the importance of making peace with God. At that time, though, he was quick to note: "I am aware that the now historic conflict between Russia & Japan can only partially illustrate the battle between the soul and God."[53] However, with the advent of the Great War, the connections between physical and spiritual dimensions quickly deepened.

Arguably, one of the most dramatic consequences of this growing conflation of the spiritual and physical was the loss of the otherworldly aspect so characteristic of Shields's early ministry. While this element never entirely disappeared, it became less and less prominent in subsequent years. There was a subtle elevation in Shields's mind of the significance of contemporary events and a growing tendency to spiritualize such events. The war marked the genesis of this trend and set the trajectory towards his later absorption into political matters in the 1930s and thereafter. His fascination with the unfolding scenes of war increasingly diverted his attention from the eternal to the temporal. Shields's justification for his obsession with the temporal affairs of war was to find spiritual meanings in events, often so elevating the importance of temporal circumstances as to speak of them in a spiritual fashion.

Clearly, Shields spiritualized the war in almost every part. To his mind it brought into vital interconnection forces that were playing themselves out in the physical realm and in the spiritual realm. This was truly a war for righteousness, justice, and truth, and its battles were being waged simultaneously on both planes. On the practical level this allowed Shields to imagine himself a direct participant in conflict, offering leadership in the spiritual conflict that was unfolding and recruiting soldiers from his following for the physical conflict. From his pulpit, then, he thought to lead the spiritual charge against the enemies of righteousness. In a 1915 sermon entitled, "Germany and Future Punishment," Shields argued that Germany was the superlative embodiment of moral evil. He chose as his text Luke 11:50: "That the blood of all the prophets, which was shed from the foundation of the world, may be required of this generation." Citing the principle of accumulating guilt as taught here by Christ concerning his own death at the hands of the Jews, Shields drew a rather tenuous link to Germany's guilt:

> It would be easy to relate innumerable instances of German villainy, and thus to stir your emotions. But there is no time for

53. Ibid.

details, and I have no disposition to appeal to passion. Let me rather show you, in the light of this text, something of the heinousness of Germany's offence. What has she done? Ravaged Belgium and shed the blood of tens of thousands of others? That is the least of her offences. Her destruction of the University of Louvain was a symbolic act. With all her boasted culture, she has turned her back upon all the lessons of history, upon all human learning of morals; and, by her attempted conquest of Europe, she has taken upon herself the guilt of the blood of all who have died in the cause of freedom from the foundation of the world; she has entered into league with the spirit of every despot whose ambition ever cursed the earth.[54]

To Shields's way of thinking this amounted to nothing less than a second crucifixion of Christ. "The war involves, I say, the repudiation of Christianity, a second crucifixion of Christ, and an attempt to banish the principles of which He is the incarnation from the earth."[55]

Shields traced the genesis of the war to German rationalism which, in the physical realm, resulted in Germany's quest for world domination, and in the theological realm manifested itself as an all-out assault against the bastions of supernaturalism.[56] What would become the Fundamentalist contention with Modernism was merely the spiritual dimension of the First World War. Although the physical war in Europe ended in 1918, Shields believed that the struggle against "Germanism" in the spiritual sphere was only just heating up. When Shields gave the inauguration speech at the founding of the Baptist Bible Union in 1923, he identified the sole purpose for their union: "The Baptist Bible Union is designed to mobilize the Conservative Baptist forces of the continent, for the express purpose of declaring and waging relentless and uncompromising war on Modernism on all fronts. We are resolved that we will not surrender the faith once for all delivered to the saints."[57]

Another dimension of the eroded distinction between the carnal and spiritual spheres was Shields's growing identification of carnal opponents with spiritual enemies. With his justification of hatred in his 1915 sermon, "The Virtue of Hatred," Shields now began to focus his personal animosity

---

54. Shields, "Germany and Future Punishment," 57–58.

55. Ibid., 58.

56. This was a recurring theme in Shields's war addresses. For instance, see Shields, "The Fall of Lucifer," *Gospel Witness*, 7 March 1935.

57. Shields, "A Holy War," *Gospel Witness*, 21 June 1923, 5.

against personalities whom he saw as agents of the devil's work. While the sermon was a clear admonition to hate evil, at places it bordered on an appeal to hate the evildoer. He spoke approvingly of the late Dr. Parker's cursing of "the Sultan, Abdul Hammid." In light of subsequent events, Shields's advocated the same for the Kaiser.[58] While such sentiments were perhaps common in that era, it seems that this tendency to hate the personality behind the action became more and more pronounced in Shields's subsequent conflicts with Modernism and Catholicism.

The impact of the war on Shields's ministerial outlook can hardly be overstated. It provided a new defining metaphor for the Christian faith, it led to a deepening of the connection between spiritual and physical realms, it established a trajectory towards military and political involvement by elevating the significance of contemporary events, it illustrated a vital interconnection of forces operative in both physical and spiritual spheres, and it justified hatred as he equated spiritual and carnal enemies. It is not surprising then that, with his changing outlook, the war would evoke in Shields practical and significant changes in the manner of his ministry. These could be summarized as a new military leadership model, a new military service model, and a new military operational model.

MILITARY LEADERSHIP MODEL

The experiences of these years loomed large in his subsequent ministry. Having been honored in both secular and ecclesiastical realms and having been uniquely privileged in witnessing Britain's war effort, Shields was emboldened in his public demeanor. Hereafter he would always be quick to cite his credentials, believing his record endowed him with an authority that should not be challenged.

The development of Shields's military leadership model and concomitant superiority complex was linked to an accentuation of the prophetic aspect in his ministry. This provided the biblical justification for Shields's growing authoritarianism. To Shields's way of thinking, the Old Testament prophet was a warrior fighting against the inroads of apostasy among the people of God. He was God's mouthpiece to address the evils that threatened the Old Testament theocratic state. As Elijah was sent to rebuke wicked King Ahab, so the ministers of the New Testament era were to admonish transgressors within the church. As scenes of war stirred Shields to militant

---

58. Shields, "Virtue of Hatred," 2–3.

action, he solidified his authority by magnifying his prophetic office. As the battles erupted in church and denomination, Shields appealed more and more to the prophetic experience. Whenever he faced accusations of being a trouble-maker he remembered Ahab's retort to Elijah: "Art thou he that troubleth Israel?"[59] Responding on one occasion to accusations of obstructionism, he imagined himself an Elijah:

> They say they cannot move but Jarvis Street pulpit crosses their track. Well, sometime it has done. Someone said to Elijah . . . "Hast thou found me, O mine enemy?" and Jarvis Street pulpit has crossed the track of certain denominational tendencies; and tomorrow shall be as this day, and yet more abundant, in that respect.[60]

Shields's claim to prophetic standing was significant to his developing military leadership model at several levels. In the first place, as a prophet, his was an honored profession in direct succession from the Old Testament prophets, with autonomy "to prophesy as he believes the Lord requires."[61] By virtue of his prophetic office, Shields believed that the pastor's authority in the church was superior to that of the deacons. When Shields later wrote *The Plot That Failed* as a record of his struggles in Jarvis Street until the split of 1921, he made particular reference to this element:

> This story is written in an endeavour to show my brethren that there is no scriptural, or practical, warrant for regarding the deacons of the church as its superior officers. In the average church the deacons arrogate to themselves the function of directors and managers, to whom the pastor, forsooth, must be in subjection and subservience . . . The pastor is called an "overseer." Believers are exhorted to "obey them that have the rule over you"; and ministers were described to still other Christians as those who are "over you in the Lord."[62]

Second, Shields believed that the prophets of the Lord, by virtue of their calling, were gifted with special divine insight and even foresight. Shields was never one to shy away from such claims. He credited his victories in the Ottawa Convention of 1919 (Inspiration Controversy) and the showdown within his own church in 1921 as a fruit of this gifting.

---

59. Shields, *Inside of the Cup*, 3.
60. Ibid., 16.
61. Ibid., 21.
62. Shields, *Plot*, 308.

By the time of the Second World War Shields had placed his powers of discernment on a par with that of leading secular authorities: "It was difficult," noted Shields, "for Mr. Churchill and other prophets of discernment in Europe and elsewhere—among whom I would dare to include myself, as my printed utterances through the years would warrant—to convince Britain and the Empire and the United States of the malignant character of Europe's ailment, and of the menace it was to the rest of the world."[63] Even at that time his justification for such extravagant claims always came back to his understanding of his prophetic office. "The prophets were called 'seers' in ancient times. Noah saw something in his day that no one else saw . . . Abraham saw the destruction of Sodom before it came. Jonah . . . cried in the streets of Nineveh, 'Yet forty days, and Nineveh shall be overthrown.'"[64]

Third, there was also in Shields something of a martyr complex in his expectation of persecution in prophetic ministry. As he increasingly faced opposition in his struggle against the "evils of the day," he consoled himself with the thought that this was the plight of all the prophets up to and including Jesus Christ: "But always the prophets of truth are derided: they always have been."[65]

A fourth characteristic of Shields's prophetic outlook was the unimpeachable character of his office. Though the prophets were often martyred for their faithful testimony to God's truth, Shields believed that those who raised hands against the prophet would be held to account. Opposition to the prophetic utterance was resistance to Christ himself, for whom the prophet spoke. In his preface to *The Plot That Failed* Shields noted:

> This story is published in the hope that it will reach the eye of a Nicodemus or a Joseph; and that it will move them not to wait until after the crucifixion to act, not to be content merely with not consenting to the counsel and deed of those bent upon crucifixion; but that they will determine henceforth to obey the Scripture, "Touch not mine anointed, and do my prophets no harm."[66]

---

63. Shields, "Challenging Answer," 3.

64. Shields, "The Abiding Menace of the Frustrated Attempt to Sell Canada 'Down the River,'" *Gospel Witness*, 30 January 1941, 9.

65. Ibid.

66. Shields, *Plot*, viii. Joseph of Arimathea and Nicodemus were the biblical figures who prepared Jesus' body for burial.

The assumption that lay behind much of Shields's behavior, particularly his reaction to criticism from subordinates, was what he expressed in his observation about the authority he exercised within the church: "But neither pastor nor deacons exercise authority over each other, nor over the church, by virtue of their office; for if there be any precedence in rank in the Christian church, it must be attributable solely to a superiority in spiritual quality. *He who serves best will thus become chiefest of all.*"[67] As a prophet or as the general who had earned his stripes, Shields clearly had come to expect the unquestioning support of those under his charge. Criticism could be accepted from a superior but never from an inferior. Throughout the course of his ministry his response to any who dared criticize him was to remind them of their place. The more serious the criticism, the more virulent were his denunciations of their insolence. These denunciations, which in many cases amounted to out and out character assassination, often left the casual observer with lasting impressions of a hateful and vindictive character. To Shield's mind, however, this was the only possible response to insubordination. Whether from the point of view of an Old Testament prophet coupled with the Old Testament prohibition against touching the "Lord's anointed," or from the point of view of a military superior brooking no insubordination from those under his command, Shields would never lend legitimacy to criticism by answering the charges. His defense lay entirely in his imagined place—the office he had attained by his service record.

MILITARY SERVICE MODEL

By the end of Shields's first decade at Jarvis Street, his relationship with his congregation was becoming increasingly strained. Though the changing character of Shields's leadership style played a part in this tension, the heightened expectations that Shields was developing for those under his pastoral care certainly contributed to the friction. At least three significant factors played into these heightened expectations. In the first place was Shields's challenge of the social elite and their culture of respectability. The call to holiness in the matter of fiscal responsibility was his first battle. When, however, Shields began to attack the badges of social respectability that had for so long defined their "dear old Jarvis Street,"

---

67. Ibid., 168; emphasis mine.

such as the anthems performed by a professional choir, the war was on.[68] The second factor arose out of Shields's involvement with the Forward Movement. While visiting Convention churches to promote the Forward Movement, Shields quickly came to the conclusion that the biggest obstacle to revival was worldliness and the pursuit of amusements. In his public addresses Shields was soon issuing a call to "entire separation." Returning to his own church Shields preached a sermon on 13 February 1921 entitled "The Christian Attitude toward Amusements."[69] A storm of controversy quickly erupted as the social elite once again felt that Shields was targeting them. The third factor in Shields's inflated expectations was the contextualization of the whole struggle in terms of the world war that had just been concluded. Shields was determined to bring his new military perspective to bear on the question: "It were folly for anyone to join the army in wartime on condition that he be not required to leave his wife and family, business associates, and the country he loves! Hence our Lord insisted that no one could truly be His disciple who would not put allegiance to Him before all other considerations of life."[70] Having witnessed firsthand the depravations of war and the stupendous cost at which victory was achieved, he now firmly believed that the wars of the Spirit could be won with no lesser sacrifice:

> I have a vivid recollection of seeing the military trains leave Charing Cross and Waterloo stations in Old London during the War. I saw officers and men standing on the platform with their wives and children and other loved ones about them. And as the warning signal was given these splendid men each took his wife and his children into his arms, and often as tears streamed down their manly faces bade their loved ones good-bye. And after the doors of the carriages were closed, and the train began slowly to move out, I have seen them stretch out their arms that the wife and mother might once more put the baby into the father's arms for a parting kiss. In those great days, yes, GREAT, though terrible, no one was ashamed to shed tears. But why did these men go? Was it because they did not love their wives and children? Certainly not! It was because they loved duty more. *And for the sake of the world's freedom they separated themselves even from those they loved the best that, unhindered, they might,*

---

68. In the climactic battle to evict Shields from Jarvis Street, the rallying cry was "save dear old Jarvis Street." Cf. ibid., 240, 244.

69. Ibid., 216.

70. Ibid., 125.

> *amid scenes of blood, do their utmost to preserve the liberties of the world. And if we are to make progress in the work of the Lord the same principle must be applied, and the same spirit must be exemplified.*[71]

MILITARY OPERATIONAL MODEL

In vision and in practice the war significantly altered the way Shields approached day-to-day affairs of ministry. From this point forward in his ministry his outlook changed and hereafter he would be forever at war. The horrors of the First World War had imparted to Shields a new urgency in the way he envisioned the church and the work it did:

> And the war has done little for us as Christian men and women if it has not recalled us from some of the religious fallacies, the humanly complimentary and impossibly pretty religious dreams of our day, to the stern realities which now are so clearly shown to lie behind the martial figures and militant principles with which this Book abounds. Do we not know that the Christian church is at war? —not with flesh and blood but "against the principalities against us and powers, against the world rulers of this darkness against the spiritual hosts of wickedness in the heavenly places."[72]

Perhaps the most common New Testament image of the church is that of a body.[73] However, as Shields looked out upon his congregation, he envisaged an army: "But what a blessing it is in times of such stress to find saints who are steadfast and unmoveable! I discovered that God had given us a great army of people who had been attracted to Jarvis Street, not by its splendid choir, not by its reputation for wealth and social position, but only because of its biblical ministry."[74] It might be argued that Shields's choice of imagery was not of any great import, but it should be noted that this particular way of viewing the church directly impacted the way he thought the church should be governed. Using a military model for his ecclesiology had some serious ramifications. Hereafter, any hint of disagreement or discord within the church would be treated as treason and would be dealt with in severity.

71. Shields, "A Holy War," *Gospel Witness*, 21 June 1923, 3; emphasis added.
72. Shields, "Weapons of Our Warfare."
73. See, for instance, 1 Corinthians 10–12; Ephesians 4:12–16.
74. Shields, *Plot*, 311.

> We see no reason why one or two ill-natured people, born in the objective case, who absolutely refuse to co-operate with a ministry supported by the church generally, should be permitted to disturb its peace and hinder its progress. When the Empire was at war, no one who called himself a British citizen was permitted to lend aid or comfort to the enemy without. A New Testament Church is always at war—at war with the world, the flesh, and the devil; and it should ever insist upon unity within.[75]

In the decade that followed the war, many of the subsidiary ministries of the church took their final shape in accordance with Shields's new military model. As early as 1916, Shields began to portray different departments of the gospel ministry in these terms. For instance, in February of that year, Shields was the keynote speaker for the annual meeting of the British and Foreign Bible Society. The message he preached on that occasion was repeated two weeks later in the morning service at Jarvis Street. To Shields's way of thinking, there could be no more important agency than this. If the church and mission societies provided the army then the Bible society was the munitions supplier.[76] This also explained in part the tremendous hostility Shields demonstrated towards modernistic interpretations of the Bible that were prevalent during this period. If disunity was treason, so also was tampering with the weapons provided for the fight:

"The man who supplies defective munitions to the soldiers in the trenches is a traitor the heinousness of whose crime no language can exaggerate, and whose guilt no punishment can be severe enough to expiate."[77]

When, in the mid to late twenties, Shields reorganized the Sunday School of Jarvis Street Baptist Church, this too was given a military flavor. On the occasion that the editor of *The Sunday School Times* filled the pulpit for him, Shields could not resist the opportunity to brag about his own Sunday School in the hopes that Trumbull would showcase it in his publication. What was significant about his description of the Sunday School was the military element associated with bringing such a large number of children into the morning Service:

> Only last Sunday we inaugurated a new plan of having the [Sunday School] departments come into the service to the time and tune of a marching hymn. It worked admirably last Sunday,

75. Ibid., 334.
76. Shields, "Weapons of Our Warfare."
77. Ibid.

although we were without the mechanical aids which we have provided this week. Nearly a thousand marched into the church, the Pastor's class being there already. Since then we have had a temporary installation of amplifiers in all the Sunday School departmental buildings, so that when the organ plays it will be heard in all departments, and they will march to the same tune. This we had put in as an experiment on Monday, and tested it out Monday evening. It will remain over next Sunday, and then we shall have a permanent installation.[78]

The 1920s would see the establishment of two other significant tools for Shields in his assault upon the bastions of unrighteousness. The first was the *Gospel Witness*, a weekly magazine that Shields himself edited. This allowed him to make editorial comment upon nearly any matter that stirred his fighting spirit. When he later described the magazine he boasted: "The Gospel Witness has been a militant paper, and it is instructive to observe that the issues which have required the largest editions have been those which have come from the press with a great battle-cry."[79] The second institution was Toronto Baptist Seminary. Having lost McMaster to Modernism, Shields began his own training school. At its inception, Shields trained fighters to assault the strongholds of liberal theology. Over the years Toronto Baptist Seminary changed, but Shields always regarded it as an institution that would turn out militant ministers. By the forties, Catholicism was in his cross-hairs, and so Shields said of the school: "The Seminary is to be a religious commando training school. We shall aim to train our students in such a way that they will know what Roman Catholicism really is, and what the Roman Catholic Church is aiming to do, so that they will be qualified to deal with Romanism wherever they find it . . . In short, we shall aim so to instruct our students that they will not only be thoroughly evangelical, but that they will be informed and skilled militant Protestants."[80]

Shields's new operational model also came to expression in his inflated manner of proclamation. Not only was there a new fascination with military themes in the content of his preaching, but there was difference in style as well. His reflections on the war became increasingly jingoistic,

78. Shields, Letter to Dr. Charles G. Trumbull, 23 April 1929, in "Shields' Correspondence," JSBCA.

79. Shields, *Plot*, 350.

80. Shields, "Toronto Baptist Seminary Opens September 27: Canada's Only Distinctively Protestant Seminary," *Gospel Witness*, 16 September 1943, 1.

and his attitude of belligerent patriotism soon translated itself into a morally confrontational evangelicalism.[81] Richard Allen, in his discussion of the social passions stirred up in the post-war period, discovered "dubious elements" alongside the "high notes of social concern." These "dubious elements" included alarmist reactions concerning Bolshevism as well as a new jingoism: "Jingoistic Baptist publicity spoke alarmingly of 'enemies of righteousness' and the withering of 'fair flowers of virtue.'"[82] The *Canadian Baptist*, the official publication of the Baptist Convention of Ontario and Quebec, filled its pages in the first weeks of 1920 with reports of the Forward Movement. A central focus was the critical need for divine intervention because of the rapidly deteriorating social conditions. Several editorials were openly jingoistic in their militant denunciations of the evil rampant within society and the morally superior tone of advocates of the Inter-church Forward Movement who fought it: "The forces of evil are on the march. Can we not see them? They are destructive and profane. The Forward Movement is the marching out of the people of God to grapple with these terrible enemy forces . . . Our hope in is Christ. Without Him our souls, our country, and our civilization are lost."[83] What might better be defined as a Christian or Evangelical jingoism increasingly characterized the militant advocates of spiritual and moral reform.

Richard Price noticed a similar phenomenon among the members of the lower middle class in England at the end of the nineteenth century. As this class struggled with economic pressures and the erosion of Victorian morality, jingoistic protests erupted. These took the form of an appeal to "good old values" through a call to patriotic tradition as a sociological poultice against the breakdown of evangelical hegemony and the decay of "traditional respectability."[84] In Shields, we find a rather curious blend

---

81. "Jingoism" was also called "chauvinism." Both of these terms came into vogue in late nineteenth-century Britain. They were radical expressions of nationalism. To be chauvinistic or jingoistic meant that one saw one's own nation as superior to all others and one was ready to fight to prove it. A popular British music hall song of the period put it this way: "We don't want to fight, but by jingo if we do, we've got the ships, we've got the men, we've got the money too!" (Waites and Hunter, *Illustrated Victorian Songbook*, 180–84). For more on jingoism, see Price, "Society."

82. Allen, *Social Passion*, 139.

83. "The Forward Movement Is Not a Pretty Parlor Game," *Canadian Baptist*, 8 January 1920, 1; see also "The Years of the Greatest Battle," *Canadian Baptist*, 1 January 1920, 1; "Warning and Appeal by the Great Editor Richard H. Edmonds," *Canadian Baptist*, 10 January 1920, 2.

84. Price, "Society," 92–96.

of both elements; the Christian jingoism of the *Canadian Baptist* and the British jingoism of the late nineteenth century lower middle classes. In contradistinction to *Canadian Baptist* jingoism, Shields's jingoism contained an aggressively British and imperialistic note. For instance, while speaking of the metaphorical "Sword" with which Germany was defeated, Shields unabashedly spoke of British imperial superiority over her allies, a superiority that was the product of centuries of development:

> London, once a slave mart, is now a synonym for civil and religious liberty. Rightly to understand London at war you must remember that London is no stranger to war. You must reflect that many a battle has been fought on ground which now is trodden by the feet of London's millions. Briton and Roman, Saxon and Dane, and Norman, have all wrestled for the mastery here. And in the later centuries principles have found reincarnation in soldiers, and statesmen, in courtiers and kings, in lovers of freedom and lovers of power. London has not hesitated to buy its privileges with blood. True it is representative of the race and of other cities of Britain, but London has played its own part in the fortunes of the world. From the time of the Caesars she has refused to be ignored. As the highest expression of British thought and life she has touched the uttermost parts of the earth. Without deliberate design, her missionaries in search of spiritual wealth and conquest, her mariners and explorers in search of new adventures, her merchants, in quest of trade and gold, have put the whole world under tribute to her greatness.[85]

While Shields entirely supported the ideals expressed in the *Canadian Baptist's* jingoism, he believed that the righteous ideals the Forward Movement fought for were guaranteed by Britain which he saw as the "protector" of his religious liberties: "England," declared Shields, "at any time commands the attention of all who would trace the streams of civil and religious liberty to their source." It was at this point that his patriotic fervor burned brightest:

> But England in thoughtful and determined mood; Britain awake and girded for battle; John Bull with all the family resources mobilized, standing with sleeves rolled up, and fists clenched, and muscles taut, and eyes blazing, defying all the forces of tyranny and reaction—John Bull defending his own castle, and

---

85. Shields, "Imperial London," 21.

incidentally playing Big Brother to the whole civilized world, is incomparably magnificent.[86]

In Shields's mind Britain and empire then epitomized the civilization the Forward Movement sought to preserve and which he himself would spend the rest of his life defending.

British pride was always apparent in Shields, but there can be little doubt that under the influence of his war experiences, his pride morphed into open belligerence about British superiority. As his exposure to war increased, so did his belligerence until it became the stuff not only of content, but also of style. In the next decade, Shields's belligerent fundamentalism would not be far removed from the belligerent jingoism of the war years.

CONCLUSION

In his own pulpit at Jarvis Street Baptist Church, Shields's growing militancy came to expression in what many of his members identified as knocking, or "hitting."[87] The temptation towards a denunciatory ministry seems to have become a common one during this period. One correspondent to the *Canadian Baptist* noted: "During the war we developed a spirit of battle, and perhaps one of the results of that has been a tendency to fall into the way of opposing everyone with whom there may be any ground for a difference."[88] The "pew-sitters" in Jarvis Street were particularly sensitive to Shields's growing addiction to the trend. While there were very real issues at stake between Shields and his culturally liberal opponents, his personal conduct in these years left him open to their charges:

> The source of the trouble has at various times been attributed to various causes, all of which have been deliberate attempts to becloud the real issue and conceal the fact that the cause is Dr. Shields's own personal conduct which has alienated him from over half his church members. A small difference with him is never healed as he seems entirely devoid of any capacity for reconciliation. This, perhaps, is to a large measure accounted for by his inordinate egotism and vanity.[89]

86. Shields, "England in Wartime," 2.
87. Ryrie to T. T. Shields, 14 March 1918, in Shields, *The Inside of the Cup*, 49.
88. J. L. Gilmour, "Conference Impressions," *Canadian Baptist*, 13 March 1919, 8.
89. "Retired Deacons Tell of Jarvis Church Case," *Toronto Daily Star*, 12 October 1921, Section 1, 2.

Up to this point in Shields's ministry, the weapons of his warfare were primarily spiritual. He repeatedly preached on the text of Scripture "For the weapons of our warfare are not carnal, but mighty through God to the pulling down of strongholds."[90] In 1911, he had illustrated the absurdity of turning to "carnal" weapons by reference to the South African war:

> That is the meaning of this text: that the conflict is in another realm; that carnal weapons are no more effective against principalities and powers etc. than a British battleship against Pretoria. The armoured train was of value, but the battleship could not leave the sea—and would have been out of its element in such a war. And so carnal weapons are out of their element in Spiritual warfare.[91]

However, by 1919 Shields was adding new weapons to his arsenal that, arguably, were more carnal in nature, as he realized the power of proclamation both through the pulpit and the pen. Jingoistic demagoguery, hitting or knocking, graphic exposés and a general belligerence now became prominent features of his ministry.

Other aspects of Shields's new military operational model that could be identified would be the eventual politicization of Shields's ministry and the hardening of his Calvinistic presuppositions, especially the ideological tradition traceable to Calvin of "turning the world upside down." Those considerations must be reserved to another place.

In the early days after the conclusion of the First World War many attempts were made to reorganize the evangelical church on a war basis. What differed in Shields was the longevity of the military metaphor. Where others tired of war and its legacy, Shields fought on. In 1918, as he returned home from the traumatic scenes of war, he arrived with a grim determination to wage war on the rationalistic remnants of "Germanism" that continued to threaten both church and society. Stirred with patriotic pride and filled with a sense of British valor, he clearly viewed himself as representative of that British militancy discovered in John Bull "standing with sleeves rolled up, and fists clenched, and muscles taut, and eyes blazing, defying all the forces of tyranny and reaction."[92] The decade that witnessed the savagery of the First World War was about to pass, but for Shields a new decade of war was dawning. With the conflation of

---

90. 2 Cor 10:4.
91. Shields, "Weapons of Our Warfare."
92. Shields, "England in Wartime," 2.

the worlds spiritual and secular in Shields's thought and practice, latent tensions were brought to a head. In Ontario, and, indeed, across North America, Shields was about to fan the flames of fundamentalist fervor. He was quick to protest, "We don't want war," but his sentiments most clearly matched those of the popular British bar song by G. H. MacDermott "but by Jingo if we do, we've got the ships, we've got the men, we've got the money too."[93] In the history of T. T. Shields, the story of the 1920s chronicled the outbreak of the war of the worlds as he stepped up to lead the fight against "the world, the flesh and the devil."[94]

---

93. "Jingoism," *Encyclopædia Britannica*.

94. For instance, see Bruce West, "Shields vs Satan," *Globe and Mail*, 10 February 1975, sec. 3, 25.

Bibliography

Primary Sources

Newspapers and Yearbook

Baptist Yearbook, 1910–1920
Canadian Baptist, 1910, 1919, 1920
Gospel Witness, 1922, 1923, 1924, 1926, 1935, 1941
Toronto Star, 1921
Globe and Mail, 1975

T. T. Shields's Writings (not in the Gospel Witness)

JSBCA – Jarvis Street Baptist Church Archives, Toronto.
"A Challenging Answer to Premier King and Other Parliamentary Critics." In *Three Addresses*, 3–34. Toronto: Gospel Witness, 1943. (JSBCA).
"Circular Letters," July–August 1915. JSBCA.
"The End of the War, London 1905." Sermon # 659, in "Sermons and Lectures," Box #2, File #656-660, JSBCA.
"England in Wartime," 1917, in "Addresses," JSBCA.
"Germany and Future Punishment," In *Revelations of the War: Eight Sermons*, 51–59. Toronto: Standard Publishing, 1915.
"Imperial London at War," 1916, JSBCA.
The Inside of the Cup. Toronto: Jarvis Street Baptist Church, 1921. JSBCA.
"The LORD Is a Man of War: The LORD Is His Name." 6 September 1914, Sermon # 1098, in "Shields' Sermon Manuscripts," JSBCA.
The Plot That Failed. Toronto: Gospel Witness, 1937.
"Sermons Preached: The Sermon Diary." (Manuscript) JSBCA.
"The Sword of Victory." Early 1919. JSBCA.
"To the Deacons of Jarvis Street Baptist Church Toronto," 2 November 1918, in "Shields' Correspondence 1910-1928." JSBCA.
"The Virtue of Hatred." In *Revelations of the War: Eight Sermons*, 31–39. Toronto: Standard Publishing, 1915.
"Weapons of Our Warfare," 7 February 1916, Sermon # 1194, in "Shields' Sermon Manuscripts," JSBCA.

Secondary Sources

Allen, Richard. *The Social Passion: Religion and Social Reform in Canada 1914-28*. Toronto: University of Toronto Press, 1973.

Gilliland, H. G. *My German Prisons: Being the Experiences of an Officer during Two and a Half Years as a Prisoner of War*. Toronto: Hodder & Stoughton, 1918.

Haykin, Michael A. G. and Ian Hugh Clary. "'O God of Battles'": The Canadian Baptist Experience of the Great War." In *Canadian Churches and the First World War*, edited by Gord Heath, 170-96. Eugene, OR: Pickwick, 2014.

Hostettler, John. *Sir Edward Carson: A Dream Too Far*. Chichester: Barry Rose Law, 1997.

Hyde, H. Montgomery. *Carson: The Life of Sir Edward Carson, Lord Carson of Duncairn*. London: Heinemann, 1953.

"Jingoism." *Encyclopædia Britannica*. Encyclopædia Britannica Online Academic Edition. www.britannica.com/EBchecked/topic/303992/jingoism.

Price, Richard N. "Society, Status and Jingoism: The Social Roots of Lower Class Patriotism, 1870-1900." In *The Lower Middle Class in Britain, 1870-1914*, edited by Geoffrey Crossick, 89-112. London: Croom Helm, 1977.

Tarr, Leslie K. *Shields of Canada*. Grand Rapids: Baker, 1967.

Waites, Aline, and Robin Hunter. *The Illustrated Victorian Songbook*. London: Michael Joseph, 1984.

Wallace, W. Stewart. *The Memoirs of the Rt. Hon. Sir George Foster*. Toronto: Macmillan, 1933.

6

Reluctant Warriors: Australian Baptists in World War Two

Robert D. Linder

THE DAWN OF 1939 revealed that Australia was extremely ill-prepared to fight a major war. At that time the country had a permanent military force of only 3,000 troops, and munitions were mostly leftovers from the Great War. In addition, there were 80,000 reservists known as the Citizen Military Force or Militia. However, the experiences of the First World War had left many servicemen disenchanted with the British military machine, especially its officer class, because of its perceived arrogance and the class rigidities of English society reflected in their attitude toward the Australian Diggers.[1] Further, by the 1930s the vaunted war aims of 1914 now seemed as dross—a grand illusion that had brought Australia great personal costs but no permanent solutions to world problems. And the country had long forgotten that it had promised its heroes great "benefits" at their homecoming, such as full employment and free farmland under the soldier settlement scheme. Most of these so-called benefits never materialized or were inadequately planned and executed by the public service.[2]

Nevertheless, as in the First World War, so in 1939, the call went out for volunteers shortly after the war began when German forces invaded Poland in September of that year, and Prime Minister Robert Menzies announced that Australia was now at war. Approximately 100,000 young

1. Macintyre, "Succeeding Age."
2. Garton, *Cost*, 31–33.

Australians responded to this first call to arms. The reaction to this appeal was not as large or as enthusiastic as in 1914, but by the end of the war Australia mobilized nearly one million men and women out of a population of some 6.9 million people. Of that number, there were approximately 40,000 deaths in the war and more than 23,000 wounded in action. In addition, in the Second World War, Australia had nearly 29,000 men taken as prisoners of war (POWs), of whom 8,000 perished while in captivity. A comparison to the First World War is revealing. In that earlier conflict, Australia with a population of only four million mobilized 422,000, all volunteers, of whom approximately half were killed or wounded in action or taken prisoner.[3]

From a different perspective, population figures reveal that Australia was a far smaller country in terms of numbers of people on the ground in the Second World War era than today. There were about seven million people in the nation in 1939 as compared with twenty-two million in 2010.[4] This means that Australia was a far less-populated nation in the 1930s than it is now. Moreover, Australia's great cities, like Sydney and Melbourne, were far more cohesive, relaxed, and homogenous and far less impersonal in 1939 than they are today. However, in terms of religion, Australians do not seem to have changed much since the 1930s. As the Irish evangelist J. Edwin Orr observed after he traveled across the nation in 1936, "The average Australian is not religious: he is not antireligious either: he is just indifferent."[5]

However, according to my analysis of the available numbers, about half of the nearly seven million Australians on the eve of the war, at least nominally, identified with evangelical churches. Of that number, perhaps two million Australians had significant contact with such denominations through Sunday School or church services, while perhaps half of that number again, or about one million, would have been religiously active and possessed a genuine understanding of their faith. This figure of one million would mean that about 200,000 men and women out of the nearly one million mobilized during the course of the war were practicing,

---

3. http://www.awm.gov.au/atwar/statistics/world_wars.asp (accessed 9 August 2009); http://www.awm.gov.au/atwar/statistics/ww2.asp (accessed 9 August 2009); Grey, *Military History*, 152–53; and Radi, "1920–29," 358.

4. For the immediate background and the early years of the war, see Grey, *Military History*, 144–64. For general information on Australian involvement in the war, see Beaumont, *Australia's War*; Robertson, *Australia at War*; and McKernan, *Strength*.

5. Orr, *All Your Need*, 115.

knowledgeable evangelical Christians.[6] Interviews of Second World War Diggers indicated that "known believers" were always in a minority in any given military context during their time of service.[7] Practicing evangelicals appear to have been most frequently found in the medical corps, the intelligence services, or the Royal Australian Air Force (RAAF). Many of the interviewees also noted that there were a substantial number of "silent believers" among service personnel, as well as some who might be described as "fallen evangelicals."

In many ways, Australian Baptists, though not great in number, represented mainstream evangelical Christianity in Australia in the twentieth century. Their official church membership of 105,874 constituted only 1.6 percent of the general population in 1933, the last census year before the outbreak of the war.[8] Baptist figures, of course, are often deceptive because they do not count their infants or small children but only baptized believers who request local church membership. Australian Baptist congregations also contained relatively large numbers of non-members, that is, adherents who for various reasons had not requested baptism and/or membership. It is not known whether or not these "shadow Baptists" reported themselves as "Baptists" or not in the 1933 census. Therefore, the estimated number of Baptists in Australia on the eve of war was most certainly as high as 200,000, most of whom would have been active participants in a Baptist church, and perhaps even higher in terms of personal preference.[9]

Further, Australian Baptists and Roman Catholics in Australia have tended to be demographically younger than other denominations, especially in the twenty- to thirty-nine-year-old age group. Therefore, Baptists had more young men eligible for military service than most other

---

6. This analysis is based on statistics found in Vamplew, *Historical Statistics*, 37, 421–27. By 1939, theological liberalism had made serious inroads into the formerly evangelically-oriented Congregational churches and in some Presbyterian and Methodist circles. However, even in these churches the people in the pews were still basically theologically conservative and biblical in outlook and belief. Moreover, many Anglo-Catholics in the Australian Church of England held a basically conservative theology. Of course, at this time the large Sydney Diocese of the Church of England was overwhelmingly evangelical.

7. Barrett, "Questionnaire."

8. The next census occurred in 1947 when the official Baptist membership totaled 113,527, or about 1.5 percent of the population. All figures are taken from Hughes, *Baptists in Australia*, 38–39.

9. Ibid., 59.

denominations, with the possible exception of Anglicans and Catholics. In addition, whereas in the Great War, most Australian families had four to six children, many of them boys, in the Second World War, most Australian families thereafter produced only one son, or at the most two, who would have been eligible for service. Baptists, with their three or four children per household, proportionally contributed more men to the war effort than did other denominations.[10]

THE BAPTIST RESPONSE TO THE WAR

As in 1914, so in 1939, Baptist ministers and editors again offered spiritual advice to their younger members.[11] However, they had learned from their experience in the First World War and avoided the excesses of nationalism and did not actively recruit volunteers for the military. There had been no conscription in the First World War.[12] However, conscription was introduced in the Second World War because of the desperate situation in which Australia found itself in the wake of the Japanese advance toward the homeland beginning in 1941. But conscripts were distinct from the all-volunteer Second Australian Imperial Force, which could be deployed anywhere overseas. Those who were conscripted were not at first compelled to serve overseas. But this policy was later modified when the Japanese threat to Australian soil became increasingly apparent. Militia units were deployed and took part in some of the fiercest fighting in New Guinea, the government maintaining that the Australian colony was an appendage of the Australian mainland. Then, on 19 February 1943, legislation passed that extended the areas in which the militia units would be liable for service. These areas now included the whole of the southwest Pacific Theatre of Operations, excluding the Philippines, western Java, and northern Borneo.[13]

Many Baptist churches watched most of their best young men and women go off to war after 1939. Some churches were more patriotic than others, perhaps none so much as the Hobart Baptist Tabernacle in

10. Ibid., 50.

11. Dr. Ken Manley, the leading Baptist historian in Australia, is also the primary authority on Australian Baptists and their attitude toward war. See Manley, "Baptist Attitudes."

12. For an analysis of the fierce struggle over conscription in the First World War, see Linder, *Long Tragedy*, 83–97.

13. Grey, *Military History*, 183.

Tasmania. The Hobart Tabernacle was one of the denomination's largest and most prestigious congregations. It had as many as 300 active members. As in the First World War, so in 1939, the youth of the church flocked to the colors after the outbreak of war. Attendance at church services suffered severely because of the loss of so many of its young men and women to the armed forces. By the beginning of 1942, thirty members had already left for overseas duty and many others had been called up for Defence Corps work. At the peak, the church had over one hundred people involved directly in the war in one capacity or another. In order to keep its service personnel always in mind, a large board was erected in the church and on it were displayed the photographs of those on active service. Perhaps the church's most telling loss to the martial spirit was bomber pilot John Trevor (Jack) Soundy, son and grandson of longtime active church members and Hobart community leaders. Jack Soundy had enlisted in the RAAF in August 1940, and became a flyer shortly thereafter. He was killed in action, aged thirty, somewhere in the New Guinea area on 7 January 1943.[14]

Other key Baptist figures were lost in the war and not a few beloved sons of Baptist leaders perished while in uniform. For example, William Barnes, son of a Baptist minister and himself a Home Mission pastor, joined the RAAF early in the conflict and was killed in 1944 when his plane crashed in England.[15] Many other well-known Baptist names appeared on the casualty lists. Gunner Les Wilkin, grandson of dearly loved Baptist leader F. J. Wilkin and a member of Melbourne's Collins Street Baptist Church, died in combat in 1941.[16] Norman Gomm, cherished only son of leading Baptist minister Les Gomm, was killed in action in New Guinea in 1942, and Edward Hogg, a leader for many years among Perth Baptists, lost his only son Aubrey when his plane was shot down over Europe in 1944.[17]

Many Baptist ministers enlisted as chaplains, including twenty-three from New South Wales alone. Fifteen of these New South Welshmen served overseas, many of them in "the green hell" of New Guinea. Among the Baptist padres who served during the war were Robert Helmore, Norman Hansen, Allen Brooke, Robert S. Pickup, John Ridley,

---

14. Rowston, *One Hundred Years*, 46–47.
15. Newstead Baptist Church, *This Corner*, 16–17.
16. Collins Street Baptist Church, "Church Notes, September 1941," 3.
17. *West Australian Baptist News*, June, 1944, 5–6, 15.

Harry Orr, Alan Prior, John Drakeford, Les Gomm, Ern Milson, Malcolm McCullough, Neville Horn, Eric Marks, F. T. Smith, Keith Redman, Frank Starr, Norman Reeve, Arthur Wilkins, Reginald Kirby, Tom Keyte, Geoffrey Blackburn, Ernest Watson, J. C. Salter, Ted Roberts-Thompson, and Harold Law-Davis. All of these names would have been familiar to Australian Baptists, some before the conflict but most of them after the war when they became denominational leaders.[18] The Chaplains' Committee claimed that the proportion of Baptist pastors who served as padres during the war was "probably higher than that of any other church in the Commonwealth."[19]

Many other Baptist ministers served as welfare workers during the war, particularly in the Young Men's Christian Association (YMCA) and Everyman's Welfare Service (EWS). At that time, the YMCA in Australia was still basically "evangelical," rather than the secular institution that it is today. Among those who tried to do their part as welfare workers with the YMCA and EWS were many Baptist ministers and laymen who later became denominational leaders: Jack Manning, Tom Fleming, Les Taylor, S. T. Earl, Max Lord, John Hughes, Frank Peffer, Bill Clack, Val Bevis, Harry Black, Alan Dube and the brothers Andy, Sam and Jock Watson. After his discharge from the army, noted Australian Baptist evangelist John Ridley served along with Baptists Alex Gilchrist and Bruce Bryson in Everyman's huts in New South Wales and Queensland.[20]

A number of Baptist women also served in various branches of the armed forces during the war. Among the best known were Sergeant Margaret Patterson from Campsie in NSW who saw action in the Middle East where she served in the Army Medical Services and Flight Officer Ailsa Stewart from the Aberdeen Street Baptist Church in Geelong who became an RAAF pilot. Corporals Gwyneth Dedman and Edna Jacobs, high school friends and members of the Islington Baptist Church in Newcastle, joined the Army together and served together in Sydney during the war. Incredibly enough, the Dulwich Hill Baptist Church in Sydney contributed six women to the ranks of the military. Besides the forty-nine men from this church who experienced wartime service, five women enlisted in the RAAF while one volunteered for the Army. Two of the women, Sergeant Betty Shute and Sergeant Gladys Lockie, followed

---

18. Manley, *Woolloomooloo*, 504–5.
19. Brown, *Members*, 181.
20. Manley, *Woolloomooloo*, 504–6.

younger brothers into the armed forces. Three of the others, Sergeant Flora Hobbs, Corporal Elsie Wannan and Aircraftwoman Gwendolyn West, joined the RAAF, while Driver Gwendolyn Bagust enlisted in the Army and was assigned to a medical unit.[21]

Some ordained Baptist ministers found unusual ways to serve. Cyril Baldwin was such an individual. He was a missionary to India who had served in the Royal Australian Navy in the First World War. In 1942, he joined the Indian Navy and rose to the rank of Lieutenant Commander. While serving in the Second World War, he saw fierce fighting at sea, witnessing the destruction of the *Bismarck*, and its loss of more than 1,400 crew. After returning to Australia in 1952, he became the manager of the Sydney City Mission's Night Refuge.[22]

The following sections are a brief examination of two extremes of the Baptist response to the war: John Wyndham Quinn who served with courage and resolve as a sapper[23] in the Middle East early in the conflict, and Phil Hancox, who was Australia's best-known conscientious objector during the war.

JACK QUINN: A BAPTIST BOY WHO WENT RELUCTANTLY TO WAR

From 1982 to 1984, LaTrobe University historian John Barrett circulated an announcement as best he could across Australia, asking Second World War veterans if they were willing to fill out a questionnaire about their military experiences and return it to him. The original appeal simply asked them to respond affirmatively if they wanted to participate. If they did, the questionnaire was then posted to them, and they were asked to fill it out at their leisure and return it to Barrett in the envelope provided. The questionnaire covered their early lives before the war, and the experiences and ideas they had when they joined and when they served. It also gave them a chance to comment on their immediate postwar years and the lasting affects the war had on them. Among other matters, it included questions concerning religion and moral behavior. The announcement of

---

21. Ibid., 506; Nominal Roll, Australian War Memorial Museum; Interview with Gwyneth Dedman Allerton, 16 May 2001; Moore, *Dulwich Hill*, 149.

22. *Queensland Baptist*, September 2001, 7.

23. A sapper was an infantry rifleman with the rank of private who was assigned to an engineer unit.

the questionnaire was made in country and urban newspapers throughout Australia, and in the publications of churches, sporting bodies, automobile associations, trade unions, businesses, and ex-service and unit associations. According to Barrett, it was announced anywhere and everywhere that space was provided. Radio publicity worked badly and TV was never used. However, the print medium drew a heavy response. So did an invitation in the questionnaire to give the names of other returned men and women who might be approached. Several hundred additional individuals thus were nominated for attention by their mates. The exercise became known as "the army project." Behind it was the conviction that more should be recorded about ordinary people by ordinary people.[24]

The questionnaire was long and thorough. It posed some 180 questions and invited answers as extended as each person wanted to make them—an invitation that Barrett indicates many respondents took up with overwhelming enthusiasm. Some of them died before they could complete the questionnaire but often their spouses or children sent in what they had done. Some who received the questionnaire never returned their forms. Even so, more than half of the questionnaires sent to named individuals were returned completed, and a total of 3,700 individuals qualified as respondents. Barrett then produced a book titled *We Were There: Australian Soldiers of World War II Tell Their Stories,* published in 1987. The book was based on Barrett's selection of the most insightful and interesting replies, along with his connective narrative for the old Diggers' responses.[25] More important for my purposes, the original questionnaires with the returned men's responses have been deposited in the Australian War Memorial Archives where they are now available to historians like myself. They are the single richest collection of firsthand accounts of Australian soldiers in the Second World War of which I am aware. It was in these questionnaires in this archive that I first met John Wyndham Quinn.

Jack Quinn, like so many other Baptists during the war, was a young, idealistic and reluctant warrior. The twenty-year-old Quinn volunteered for the Second Australian Imperial Force (AIF)[26] in mid-1940 because, he said, he wanted to defend freedom and family. More than forty years later, as he answered a questionnaire sent out by Barrett and reflected

24. Of course, the Second World War generation in Australia was far from "ordinary." However, the questionnaire was aimed at men and women who had never had an opportunity to express themselves about their war experiences before.

25. All of the foregoing is explained in Barrett, *We Were There,* see esp. 16–20.

26. The First AIF had served in the First World War.

upon his enlistment, Quinn wrote in response to the historian's query "Did you have a personal desire to join?": "Not at all. I joined against my will." What Quinn meant was that he really disliked war but felt compelled to join in order to stop fascism and because he had been shocked by the German invasion of the Low Counties in Europe in 1940. At heart, he assured Barrett, he was a peaceful man. On the other hand, he confessed that: "I had little real knowledge, but thought in terms of 'I Love a Sunburnt Country' and 'The Waratah and the Wattle.' I had highly idealistic beliefs in the Empire standing for freedom and right."[27]

At the time of his enlistment in the AIF, Quinn was an active member of the North Sydney Baptist Church. He attended church regularly out of personal conviction, he said, and had little time for religious hypocrisy. Highly articulate and a bit brash, he was a unique yet quintessential young Baptist layman of the period. He thought for himself and spoke his mind. He had completed his Intermediate Certificate[28] and worked at several insignificant jobs, and considered himself to be a non-union member of the "working class" before his army service. Nevertheless, he was highly literate and later wrote eloquently of his army experiences.

His attitude and opinions on a myriad of issues were particularly interesting in light of his strong religious commitment. His analysis of conscientious objectors (COs), for example, reinforced his self-observation that he was a peace-loving Christian. When asked his view of COs, he replied that he "respected views of those who were 'Fair Dinkum,'[29] but found it hard to understand why they refused service, as my own views were sympathetic to their basic beliefs." Of army chaplains, he commented, "Well meaning but mostly useless and harmless. Some exceptionally helpful." When asked in what ways army life was a worthwhile experience to him personally, Quinn wrote, "I learned much about human nature, and developed a more realistic philosophy, became more self-reliant and had a better appreciation of my own worth."[30]

27. Barrett, "Questionnaire." For further background on how the average Digger saw the war, see Johnson, *At the Front*.

28. The Intermediate Certificate was awarded in Australia in this period for the successful completion of three years of high school, usually at around age fourteen. A student who wanted to be considered for a university needed a Leaving Certificate after the completion of another two years of high school. Both certificates were based on external examinations.

29. Australian adjective meaning true, genuine, or reliable.

30. Barrett, "Questionnaire." Also, see the index of Barrett, *We Were There* for references to Quinn in this study of World War II Diggers.

Quinn served with the 2/17th Battalion in Libya and later in Australia during his army career. He wrote with great feeling and insight concerning his experiences in India when he was on his way to the Middle East in 1940. His troopship paused briefly at Bombay[31] and the Diggers were allowed a day of shore leave before re-embarking for the trip to Egypt. Like most young men facing possible death and destruction in the near future, they wanted to see the exotic parts of the great Indian city. Years later Quinn remembered his impressions of the tour he and his mate took of the forbidden parts of Bombay. He wrote:

> Grant Road, Bombay, was strictly out of bounds. Therefore someone in our group on a day's leave suggested that we have a look at it. It was a brothel street where women were caged and I found myself looking into a pair of liquid brown eyes set in the face of an old-young woman. Once she had been beautiful. With desperation she held up three fingers on a delicate hand and called out, "Three annas." She would have given me her body for the price of a newspaper. Between us were bars like those on the cage of the chimpanzee at the zoo. I was young, full of hopes and ideals. What could I do to help her? Nothing I could think of, short of becoming a client—and at that thought my good lunch heaved in my stomach. She was one of the girls whose parents could not support her and who had sold her to those who put many like her into the cages of Grant Road. Hurt in my insides, I turned quickly away. We saw many things that day, and when the evening entertainment ended we rode back to the ship, paid off our guide and became soldiers again. Yet I was haunted by a pair of dark eyes, and a graceful hand holding up three fingers. Sometimes in the desert, breathing the clean night air, I would look up at the stars and think of brown eyes gazing through bars. After battle came, and they told us that we had "won a great victory," "set the pattern," "made military history," all six of us who teamed up that day in Bombay were dead or wounded. And the girl? What did the many words of politicians mean to her? She would not know. She would not remember us. Her slender hand would wave in no celebration of victory. I still wonder what became of her.[32]

---

31. Now called Mumbai.
32. Barrett, "Questionnaire."

Keep in mind that this deeply insightful and moving commentary came from a twenty-year-old Digger who was on his way to find out what his world was really like.

Jack Quinn eventually became one of the fabled "Rats of Tobruk," and was twice wounded in that battle, once only slightly but a second time severely. The second wound came in April 1941, during some of the fiercest fighting of the siege of Tobruk when his commanding officer surrendered his unit to the advancing Germans. Quinn did not agree with his lieutenant's decision and tried to flee. He was shot attempting to escape. As he described it, "The Germans finally withdrew, leaving me behind. I was in the outskirts of Tobruk, held for about 5 minutes before being shot, and then for another half hour afterwards." Quinn eventually made his way back to his own lines and survived, thanks to the newly developed sulfa drugs. However, he never recovered from his second wound and was repatriated to Australia where he spent two years in a hospital and endured eleven operations. The results of his second wound followed him to the end of his days and hindered his ability to stand for long periods of time. He was finally given a medical discharge on 21 December 1943.[33]

Among several "exit questions" on Barrett's questionnaire was one that asked what he thought of war after he was demobilized. Quinn replied that war was "evil, but sometimes the lesser evil." He also indicated that he found returning to civilian life "a bit hard." He explained, "There was a sense almost of bereavement and unreality." When asked to reflect on his experience as a demobilized soldier, Quinn "the reluctant warrior" clearly emerges. Writing in the context of the 1980s, he explained himself this way:

> The attitude of the community in general, and of my Baptist church in particular, has changed. These days the church sometimes makes me feel isolated because of my war service, and young people do not seem to understand that *we* were young in 1940 and that putting on a uniform was our way of *protesting*. Against what? For what? I believed I was fighting for freedom, and I believed I should do my *own* fighting. I believed that "truth," "right" and "freedom" were religious values. I believed that the empire was worth fighting for, and had been taught that at school. But I joined up against my will. When I decided to do so, I was so frightened I was gastric for a week, but I went on with it because I knew it had to be done. In the desert, after evening stand-down, we used to yarn and confide in each other, and many said that, basically, there were there because a job had

---

33. Ibid., and interview with Doreen Bovington Quinn, 13 November 2010.

to be done and "some bastard had to do it." Community rejection tends to push ex-servicemen back onto each other. Who else shows that they understand what we were about?[34]

However, the old Quinn sense of humor quickly emerged when he replied to the question about what his army experience had taught him about life. He responded: "It beats being dead."[35]

His local church and his wife Doreen Bovington Quinn, whom he married in 1948, aided him greatly in adjusting again to civilian life. However, before he finally found his niche in secular employment and in the life of his local Baptist congregation, there was a time of struggle and disappointment. He originally wanted to return to the Middle East as a missionary. Even though he attended a Bible college for two years and did well academically, he was rejected for the mission field because of his bad leg.[36]

Jack Quinn finally took up accountancy, and after four years of study was admitted to the Australian Associated Society of Accountants. He thereafter became one of Sydney's most reliable and productive members of that profession. His wife Doreen remarked that through it all, Jack never lost his great sense of humor nor resorted to self-pity. He, after all, had been a "good soldier."[37]

Both Quinn and his spouse eventually became thoughtful and loyal members of the Epping Baptist Church[38] in Sydney and great supporters of its Sunday morning Christian Education Fellowship, an adult education program at the church. On one occasion near the end of his life, Quinn was asked to teach one of the fellowship's lessons. It was based on 2 Timothy 2:1–7, 15, where Paul comments on being a "good soldier of Jesus Christ." Quinn usually wrote out his remarks in his own hand, and that day toward the end of the lesson, he observed:

> Some years ago, a brave soldier died and those who knew him had these words put on his gravestone:
> Here lies a soldier all may applaud
> Who fought many battles, at home and abroad,
> But the hottest engagement he ever was in,
> Was the conquest of self, in the battle with sin.

34. Barrett, "Questionnaire."
35. Ibid.
36. Ibid., and interview with Doreen Bovington Quinn, 13 November 2010.
37. Interview with Doreen Bovington Quinn, 13 November 2010.
38. One of Sydney's largest and most active Baptist churches.

Many believed that these were the words that Jack Quinn would have placed on his own tombstone.[39] Jack Quinn, the old Second World War Baptist Digger, died on 12 August 1986.

PHIL HANCOX: A BAPTIST BELIEVER WHO REFUSED TO SHED BLOOD

Phil Hancox was one of those "fair dinkum" Aussie conscientious objectors (COs) to whom Jack Quinn referred in his questionnaire. Hancox had accepted Christ as his Savior at an evangelistic meeting at the Brisbane Baptist City Tabernacle in September 1929 when a lad of fifteen years of age. He soon thereafter joined the Windsor Road Baptist Church, Red Hill, and developed a thirst for preaching. Soon he was a leading lay preacher and the local church's youth leader. As he notes in one of his books, that decision for Christ gave him a peace of mind and heart that lasted the remainder of his life.[40] It also launched him on an intensive study of the New Testament that eventually led him to take a dramatic stand for non-violent Christianity during the war.

In the decade before the Second World War, Australian Baptists had engaged in spirited debates concerning the issues surrounding peace and war. Baptist pastors W. H. Holloway in Melbourne, J. C. Chamberlain in Adelaide, and Gilbert Wright denounced war and argued that peace could be secured only through rendering justice to every nation. The Baptist World Alliance, meeting in Atlanta, Georgia, in July 1939, discussed what could be done to avert war and regretted that it appeared to be imminent and that they could do little about it. They seemed to know that they soon would be separated one from another by the protocols of war. The delegates claimed even if they became citizens of countries at war with one another, they still had an abiding fellowship of faith, hope, and love. On the other side, leading Baptist theologian Harold Dart argued that if war came with Nazi Germany, it would be a "just war." Others like young pastor J. B. Wilson explained the likelihood of a coming war by linking it to the biblical certainty that Armageddon was coming. Some of those who emphasized the Second Coming of Christ in their ministries rejoiced that the prospect of the Lord's return seemed to be near.

---

39. Quinn, "Path," 4.
40. Hancox, *Adventures*, 14–15.

When the war came in 1939, most of the peaceful evangelicals fell silent and the call for Christian non-violence melted in the harsh light of the threat to the Australian mainland. However, Phil Hancox and a handful of other evangelical believers kept their stand. There were very few COs in the entirety of Australia during the Second World War. In any case, as war clouds gathered over Europe in the late 1930s, talk of another world conflict complicated the lives of most young Australian men of the period, including Phil Hancox and the woman who was soon to be his bride, Helena Hull.[41] Hancox increasingly heard such comments as "anyone who plays tennis on Anzac Day should be taken out and shot" and "if a man won't fight for his country, he doesn't deserve to live in it."[42] These words fell heavily on the serious young Christian who in a typical Baptist manner had been studying his New Testament with great intensity since his conversion. The militaristic sentiments expressed in his hearing led him and his best friend, Henry Schuman, to discuss what they should do if they were conscripted for military service. After three years of study and thought, the outbreak of war in 1939 compelled Hancox to come to a conclusion concerning what war meant to a follower of Christ. He reported: "I did not consult any Bible commentaries nor read any books on the subject, apart from the Bible itself. Within a few weeks I became convinced that war had no place in the life of a professing Christian. This for me was now a strong conviction."[43]

This set the stage for Hancox's confrontation with the authorities over his determination not to participate in the war in any manner whatsoever.

As the father of two small daughters, Hancox did not receive his order to report for army service until 1942. He asked for and received CO status. However, this still left him liable for noncombatant duties, which he refused. Nor would he accept service in the Salvation Army's Red Shield or the Campaigner for Christ's Everyman's Huts. Therefore, he was hailed before a magistrate on 15 February 1942 to answer charges that he refused "to take the oath or make an affirmation for service in the defence forces." Moreover, he said that his religious beliefs would not permit him to undertake either combatant or noncombatant military duties. Whereupon the magistrate lectured the twenty-eight year old Baptist lay

41. Hancox married his high school sweetheart Helena Hull in March 1940 (Hancox, *Cavalry*, 29).
42. Ibid., 1, 14.
43. Ibid., 24.

preacher, and told him, "Mr. Hancox, you are a misguided young man," and sentenced him to six months at the Palen Creek Prison Farm about 110 kilometers from Brisbane.[44]

Hancox spent four months on the farm before he secured early release on grounds of good behavior. While there he discovered other evangelicals, but no other Baptists, among the thirty to forty members of the shifting prison population. The most outspoken of these other men, Harry Attwell, a Pentecostal preacher, became Hancox's closest friend while in confinement.[45] Other evangelicals included Methodist Les Hoey and an unnamed member of the Salvation Army. The other men in the prison at the time were various and assorted petty criminals serving sentences that varied from a few months to a few years.[46]

Only a few voices were heard in support of Hancox's decision to remain true to his conviction that all wars were wrong. The most prominent of those who expressed a similar concern was the Rev. Gilbert Wright, then pastor of the Epping Baptist Church in Sydney and later Principal of the Baptist Theological College of New South Wales (now Morling College).[47] Wright emphatically declared:

> There is little point in discussing the moral issues of the latest scientific discoveries as applied to war. "Thou shalt not kill" stands as eternal truth for all men for all time. One bomb is wrong, every bomb is wrong; war is the spawn of hell, and the sin of man while it abides in the heart will continue to create war and rumours of war, to man's misery and despair.[48]

In the years immediately following his release from prison, Hancox not only had difficulty finding a job but also endured much criticism and rejection by fellow Baptists. However, he maintained a kind and generous spirit and served his local church and the Baptists of Queensland well, finally winning back the esteem and affection of his fellow believers. Before his death in 2000, he had been a longtime Sunday School teacher,

---

44. Ibid., 45–54.

45. Apparently several Pentecostal Christians in Queensland rejected military service during the war. For example, Lloyd Averill, a newly converted Pentecostal believer, was a CO, as well as several of his friends. Averill was later a prominent figure in the Assemblies of God churches in Australasia. See Averill, *Go North*, 20–21.

46. Averill, *Go North*, 55–67; and interview with Phil Hancox, 16 June 1998.

47. Wright, as a minister of religion, was exempted from military service in the war. For Hancox, a layman, it was a different matter altogether.

48. Gow and Manley, *People*, 30.

choirmaster, deacon, and Baptist Men's Society president as well as twice president of the Baptist Union of Queensland, in 1964–1965 and 1972–1973. He spent his years following retirement in 1979 conducting evangelistic campaigns in Queensland, the United States, the Philippines, and Indonesia.[49] In 2007, Phil Hancox was one of sixty-nine representative individuals worldwide and the only Australian whose name was chiseled in the Conscientious Objection Commemorative Stone in Tavistock Square, Bloomsbury, London, England.[50]

CONCLUSIONS

First, it is clear that most Australian Baptists who participated in the Second World War did so reluctantly. Thus far, I have discovered no jingoistic war enthusiasm among Australian Baptists during the war. Many, like Jack Quinn, believed that it was their duty to defend freedom and family, and to do what they could, even though they would rather have stayed at home. They were at best "reluctant warriors." Second, Baptist experiences in the war provided an example of the negative consequences of war for the next generation to observe. That generation would be even less enthusiastic about supporting a war in Vietnam.[51] Third, according to Quinn, the main lesson that he learned was that war was "evil, but sometimes the lesser evil." Of course, if that view is correct, it means that there will always be wars because, until Christ intervenes with finality, there always will be evil in the world. Fourth, Australian Baptists were not vindictive after the war. There was a marvelous spirit of spiritual comradeship that made it possible for Phil Hancox to re-enter the Baptist mainstream and contribute substantially to his denomination's well-being in the years following the war. In fact, he became a revered leader among Queensland Baptists and served two terms as President of the Baptist Union of Queensland between 1945 and his death. In a like manner, Pastor Gilbert Wright, who fulminated against the war when most of his Baptist co-religionists supported it, emerged as a major leader among New South Wales Baptists after the war. He first became Vice-Principal in 1950 and then served as Principal of the important Baptist Theological College of New South Wales from 1964 to 1974. To their credit, there appeared to

---

49. He died in 2000.
50. Hancox, *Adventures*, 9–10; Hancox, "Conscientious Objectors."
51. See Linder, "Vietnam War."

be no lingering spirit of animosity or vindictiveness among Australian Baptists after 1945 because of serious disagreements over issues of war and peace.[52] Perhaps this was true because both those who fought in the war and those who opposed it knew at the end of the day how truly evil and destructive war can be. The experiences of the overwhelming majority of Australian Baptists who served in the war fell somewhere between those of Jack Quinn and Phil Hancox. Most were idealists and patriots but few were jingoists or excited nationalists. Most responded to the exigencies of the hour, and most were at best "reluctant warriors."

Finally, there is the lingering question of why Baptists in general, and Australian Baptists in particular, still in the main support war. Despite the clear commands of Christ to live non-violent lifestyles, most evangelical Christians persist in participating in what is almost universally acknowledged as one of the most "evil" enterprises in human history. This leads to the question of why politicians, hell-bent on war at any price, so easily seduce so many Baptists. Why is there so much enthusiasm for war among Baptists today when men like Jack Quinn and Phil Hancox have eloquently testified to its evils? In any case, it is best to discuss such issues before a war begins and not during its prosecution.

---

52. Hancox, *Cavalry*, 101–4; and Manley, *Woolloomooloo*, 751.

Bibliography

Averill, Lloyd. *Go North Young Man*. Springwood, QLD: Privately published, 1992.
Barrett, John. "Australian Army Questionnaire." In the Australian War Memorial Archives, PR89/135, Box 47.
———. *We Were There: Australian Soldiers of World War II Tell Their Stories*. rev. ed. St. Leonards, NSW: Allen & Unwin, 1995.
Beaumont, Joan, ed. *Australia's War, 1939-1945*. St. Leonards, NSW: Allen & Unwin, 1996.
Brown, Basil S. *Members One of Another: The Baptist Union of Victoria, 1862-1962*. Melbourne: Baptist Union of Victoria, 1962.
"Conscientious Objectors Celebrated on 15 May 2007." In *Conscientious Objection Commemorative Stone*, Tavistock Square, Bloomsbury, London, http://www.rrk.freeuk.com/COs.2007.htm (Accessed 4 July 2011).
Garton, Stephen. *The Cost of War: Australians Return*. Melbourne: Oxford University Press, 1996.
Gow, Harold, and Ken Manley. *People with a Purpose: Epping Baptist Church, 1933-1983*. Epping, NSW: Epping Baptist Church, 1983.
Grey, Jeffrey. *A Military History of Australia*. 3rd ed. Cambridge: Cambridge University Press, 2008.
Hancox, Phil. *Cavalry or Calvary? The Christian Dilemma*. West End, QLD: Christians For Peace, 1984.
———. *My Adventures in Evangelism*. Brisbane: Privately published, 1995.
Hughes, Philip J. *The Baptists in Australia*. Canberra: Australian Government Publishing Service, 1996.
Johnson, Mark. *At the Front: Experiences of Australian Soldiers in World War II*. Melbourne: Cambridge University Press, 1996.
Linder, Robert D. "Australian Evangelicals and the Vietnam War, 1965-1972," 2011. Unpublished essay.
———. *The Long Tragedy: Australian Evangelical Christians and the Great War, 1914-1918*. Adelaide: Openbook, 2000.
Macintyre, Stuart. "The Succeeding Age, 1901-1942." In *The Oxford History of Australia*. Vol. 4. Melbourne: Oxford University Press, 1986.
Manley, Ken R. "Baptist Attitudes to War and Peace." *The Baptist Recorder* 104 (November 2008) 1-8.
———. *From Woolloomooloo to "Eternity": A History of Australian Baptists*. Vol. 2, *A National Church in a Global Community*. Milton Keynes: Paternoster, 2006.
McKernan, Michael. *The Strength of a Nation*. Crows Nest, NSW: Allen & Unwin, 2006.
Moore, Beverly J. *Dulwich Hill Baptist Church: 100 Years in Witness & Ministry*. Sydney: Dulwich Hill Baptist Church, 2002.

Newstead Baptist Church History Group. *This Corner: Stories of Newstead Baptist Church, 1936–1996*. Launceston, TAS: Regal, 1996.

Orr, J. Edwin. *All Your Need: 10,000 Miles of Miracle through Australia and New Zealand*. London: Marshall, Morgan & Scott, 1937.

Quinn, John. "The Path of a Good Soldier." (Copy of the MS in possession of the author courtesy of Doreen Bovington Quinn).

Radi, Heather. "1920–29." In *A New History of Australia*, edited by Frank K. Crowley, 357–414. Melbourne: Heinemann, 1974.

Robertson, John. *Australia at War, 1939–1945*. Melbourne: Heinemann, 1981.

Rowston, Laurence F. *One Hundred Years of Witness: A History of the Hobart Baptist Church, 1884–1984*. Hobart: Hobart Baptist Church, 1984.

Vamplew, Wray, ed. *Australians: A Historical Library*. Vol. 10. *Australian Historical Statistics*. 12 vols. Broadway, NSW: Fairfax, Syme & Weldon, 1987–89.

7

Soviet Baptists and the Cold War[1]

Maurice Dowling

THERE IS SOMETHING ODD about including, in a book about "Baptists and war," a chapter that deals with what could be described as a non-war—albeit a conflict that was allegedly won by Ronald Reagan! The terms of reference for such a study are hard to define. The outlines of the Cold War itself may be described as follows. After the Second World War, the powers responsible for the defeat of Nazi Germany and of Japan—namely, the USSR and the Western allies—entered a period of heightened tension. Tension had not been absent in the pre-war period. In his masterly study of modern Europe, Tony Judt says that "in Europe the Cold War began not after the Second World War but following the end of the First."[2] He continues, "The years 1941–45 were just an interlude in an international struggle between Western democracies and Soviet totalitarianism."[3] However, Judt also comments, "In Europe before World War Two, the differences between North and South, rich and poor, urban and rural, counted for more than those between East and West."[4] The East-West ideological divide—which had a major impact on pre-war Soviet Baptist history—was undoubtedly exacerbated by the extending

---

1. Some of the material in this paper is taken from my chapter on "Baptists in the Twentieth-century Tsarist Empire and the Soviet Union," published in Bebbington, *Gospel*, chapter 9. The translations of extracts from Russian-language publications are my own.
2. Judt, *Postwar*, 103.
3. Ibid., 104.
4. Ibid., 195.

of a Communist empire and an "Iron Curtain" across much of central and eastern Europe, together with a new threat facing the world—the possibility of nuclear war. So 1945 ushered in a new era, one in which the United States of America would play a part in international (not least European) affairs significantly different from what had obtained before the war. The period saw many twists and turns, and the Cold War was in effect brought to an end by the reforming policies of the Soviet leader Mikhail Gorbachev in the mid-to-late 1980s.[5]

The topic that forms the title of this chapter entails consideration of, among other issues, the following: (1) relationships between the Soviet government and the Baptists during this period, and the extent to which these may have been influenced by the Cold War; (2) attitudes of Soviet Baptists towards the West during this period of tension; (3) relationships between Soviet Baptists and those in the rest of the world; and (4) perspectives today among Baptists who lived through the Cold War in the USSR on a difficult period in their denominational history.

EVANGELICAL CHRISTIANS AND BAPTISTS—THE 1944 MERGER

A key event in this survey is the birth in 1944 of the All-Union Council of Evangelical Christians-Baptists (AUCECB), a body with a rather complex gestation and, to the uninitiated, a mystifying title. Sergei Filatov has said that the AUCECB became in effect "the embodiment of Russian Protestantism."[6] Reasons for focusing on this body and its birth are expressed well by a modern Russian Baptist historian, Alexander Popov:

> It is difficult to overestimate the impact of this movement on virtually all Protestant churches within the territory of the former USSR. Even completely new congregations that have emerged since the fall of the Soviet Union are marked by the traditions, insights, and preferences that were formed within this stream of spirituality, which drew into itself the experiences of two Unions—the Evangelical Christians and the Baptists—within the Russian Empire and then later in the Soviet Union.[7]

---

5. As a reading of the contemporary Russian press indicates, a shadow of the Cold War clearly remains, but it has been largely upstaged by the "war on terror."

6. Filatov, "Protestantism," 94.

7. Popov, "Evangelical Christians-Baptists," 1.

Writing in 1945, and reflecting on the significance of the Baptist movement, Rushbrooke told the following story:

> I recall a word spoken to me by one of the most eminent of German Protestants as in the privacy of his own home he discussed the perils arising from the recent seizure of power by the Nazis: "Our trouble in Germany is that we have never had what you in England possess, a strong Nonconformity. If we had had that, our present situation would not have arisen."[8]

The point may be adapted to apply to the history of Russia and of the USSR. There was never "a strong Nonconformity" able to influence the nation's government and people in ways similar to those that unfolded in English and British history. However, a Nonconformity did exist, and one of the most interesting facts about it is that the Soviet government eventually felt that it had to take serious account of this movement that it had so savagely persecuted in the 1930s.

The story of the post-war relationships between the Soviet government and the Baptists begins shortly before the end of the Second World War. The 1930s were a period of savage persecution of religious believers. Official Soviet attitudes to religion changed during the "Great Patriotic War" (the standard Soviet name for World War Two).[9] One indication of this change in official policy was the restoration of the Moscow Patriarchate—by a decision taken in 1943. Another was the formation, in October 1944, of the All-Union Council of Evangelical Christians and Baptists. This measure brought together two distinct movements that nevertheless had a good deal in common and indeed overlapped to a certain extent: the Evangelical Christians and the Baptists. In 1946 the Council's name was changed to All-Union Council of Evangelical Christians-Baptists (AUCECB).[10] The term 'All-Union', which may sound rather clumsy and

---

8. Underwood, *History*, 8.

9. This point is discussed in a number of histories, for example: Chadwick, *Christian Church*, 93–95; Hosking, *History*, 236–37; Volkogonov, *Stalin*, 486–87; Bullock, *Hitler and Stalin*, 998–1001; Pospielovskii, *Russkaya*, chapter 7; Nikolskaya, *Russkii protestantizm*, 117–29.

10. An English translation of the original Statute of Unity can be found in Sawatsky, *Soviet Evangelicals*, 475–76. In English-language publications the name of the AUCECB sometimes appears as "Evangelical Christian Baptists". This form is misleading as it suggests that the words "Evangelical" and "Christian" are adjectives used to describe the Baptists. The Russian name makes it clear that what happened in 1944 was a merger of the Evangelical Christians and the Baptists. The AUCECB was formed without an explicit Confession of Faith. English translations of different versions of the

mystifying in English, was the standard Russian adjective (*vsyesoyuzny*) applied to any organization operating throughout the USSR, and indeed the use of the term "All-Union Council" for this new body does suggest a genesis in the minds of Soviet officialdom. Without the permission, and indeed the active encouragement, of the authorities, a religious body of this nature could not have come into being. As Owen Chadwick says of Stalinist regimes, "their only doctrine on government was force."[11] The Soviet news agency TASS and the newspaper *Izvestiya* (10 November 1944)[12] would hardly have reported the merger if there had been any doubt about such a body's right to exist. TASS and *Izvestiya* must have known that the merger had been initiated at the highest level.

As Walter Sawatsky has shown, the events surrounding the formation of the All-Union Council are hard to piece together.[13] However, it should be remembered that the uniting of the Evangelical Christians and the Baptists was not a new idea. In 1905, in Rostov-on-Don, there was a conference of the two groups, which formally adopted the label "Evangelical Christians-Baptists,"[14] and both began to participate in the world-wide Baptist movement. During the ensuing years the question of the uniting of Evangelical Christians and Baptists was constantly on the agenda; one serious step towards unity was taken in January 1920, with the formation of the Provisional All-Russian General Council of Evangelical Christians and Baptists.[15] However, unity remained an elusive goal. The Stalinist terror of the 1930s put an end to the quest for unity and indeed to the existence of either body as a distinct denomination.

From the outset there were several differences between the two movements. The Baptists originally had their main strength among poorer people in the Ukraine and in southern Russia, while the Evangelical Christians drew many of their adherents from the higher classes of society in

---

Constitution that eventually emerged can be found in Wallace, "Union" and Sawatsky, *Soviet Evangelicals*, 479–87.

11. Chadwick, *Christian Church*, 52.

12. AUCECB, *Istoriya*, 232. The brief press report is reproduced in *Bratskii vyestnik*, 1945/1, 39.

13. Sawatsky, *Soviet Evangelicals*, 84–86. Mitrokhin comments that in the official AUCECB *Istoriya* the 1944 merger is described "somewhat convulsively and in rapid tones, without any attempt at a serious and conscientious explanation of these events and without any analysis of the basic planning documents" (Mitrokhin, *Baptizm*, 407).

14. AUCECB *Istoriya*, 141–42, 313.

15. Ibid., 193–94, 314.

St. Petersburg and Moscow. With the spread of the two movements these distinctions became less significant, but other differences remained. The Evangelical Christians generally accepted the principle of believer's baptism but they did not see the necessity for the laying on of hands on new church members, as practised among the Baptists. Similarly, unlike the Baptists, the Evangelical Christians did not feel that communion had to be administered by an ordained elder. The tendency among the Evangelical Christians to place little emphasis on what might be interpreted as a "clerical office" reflects the influence of Brethrenism on their origins, as well as being a reaction against the kind of role played by the clergy and hierarchy in the Orthodox Church. Paradoxically perhaps, for their part many Baptists, especially during the 1920s, reacted against what they saw as the patriarchal tendencies of Ivan Prokhanov, the leading representative of the Evangelical Christians. Baptists feared that Prokhanov wanted to absorb them into his own organisation rather than merging the two movements on equal terms.[16] Baptists also reacted against Prokhanov's overtures to the so-called Living Church movement (the "renewers", *obnovlentsy*) that emerged within the Orthodox Church in the 1920s.[17] These factors, combined with Prokhanov's positive attitudes towards socialism and military service, created the impression among Baptists that he was both too broad in his views and too much inclined to impose them on others.[18] This cooling in the relationship between Prokhanov and the Baptists at home is reflected in Prokhanov's absence from among the Vice-Presidents and the other members of the executive elected at the Baptist World Alliance (BWA) congress in Toronto in 1928.[19]

The October 1944 congress that cemented the union of the Evangelical Christians and the Baptists received greetings and good wishes from the world's Baptists in the persons of J. H. Rushbrooke and Walter Lewis.[20] However, both men were soon to express doubts about the degree to

16. Kolarz, *Religion*, 285–86.

17. AUCECB, *Istoriya*, 196, 208–9.

18. Another example of the breadth of Prokhanov's vision is his ordination at the hands of members of the Czech Baptists in Prague, in the presence of members of the Czech Brethren. He wanted to make the point that he saw himself as standing in the spiritual tradition of John Hus (AUCECB, *Istoriya*, 209).

19. Sawatsky, *Soviet Evangelicals*, 45, argues that the BWA was by now deliberately supporting the Baptists as distinct from the Evangelical Christians. At Toronto the Russian Baptists were represented by Pavel Ivanov-Klyshnikov and Nikolai Odintsov (transliterated as "Adinzoff" in the official record of proceedings).

20. Sawatsky, *Soviet Evangelicals*, 85. AUCECB, *Istoriya*, 232, mentions a

which the AUCECB was actually representative of the Baptist churches in the USSR and also misgivings about the extent of the state's involvement in the newly formed union.[21] The problem was that nobody really knew how the people representing either the Evangelical Christians or the Baptists at the time of the 1944 merger had come to occupy the positions that they did. The secrecy that had for long surrounded so many areas of Soviet life, not least in religious affairs, was aggravated by the difficulty of wartime communications. Did October 1944 really represent a merger of two unions given the fact that both unions had virtually ceased to exist during the Stalinist terror of the 1930s? Was the new body not rather a case of *creatio ex nihilo*? If so, who created it? The answer was obvious. Only the Stalinist state, with its emphasis on centralisation and bureaucratisation,[22] was in a position to engineer the creation of an official religious body of this kind. Many of the Russian Baptist leaders that Rushbrooke and Lewis had known before the 1930s (for example, the men with whom Rushbrooke is seen in a photograph dated 1925)[23] were dead or missing. Men such as Alexander Karyev, elected in October 1944 as General Secretary of the AUCECB, and Yakov Zhidkov, elected as its President, were largely unknown outside the USSR. But the AUCECB was there to stay and it was soon accepted by Baptists in the outside world.

In a post-communist publication, the Russian historian Leonid Mitrokhin refers to the 1944 merger as "a marriage Soviet-style" (*brak po-sovyetski*).[24] He comments:

> In my view [the merger] to a significant extent had an artificial character and was imposed by the controlling organs of the Party and the State. However, this did not exclude certain purely "secular" advantages for both sides [Baptists and Evangelical Christians]. The Baptists acquired the status of a legal ("registered") religious organisation and had the opportunity to restore their

---

telegrammed greeting from the BWA "signed by the Alliance's President Dr. Rushbrooke." Walter Lewis is not mentioned here. The text of Rushbrooke's three-line telegram is found in *Bratskii vyestnik*, 1945/1, 39.

21. Sawatsky, *Soviet Evangelicals*, 91–92.

22. These are aspects of Stalin's regime that are particularly emphasized by Volkogonov, who experienced Stalinism at first hand (*Stalin*, 557–66).

23. One of the photographs included in AUCECB, *Istoriya*, between pages 128 and 129.

24. Mitrokhin, *Baptizm*, 11, 399. In 1966 Mitrokhin had published *Baptizm* [The Baptist Movement], which depicted the Baptists in a particularly negative light. In 1997 he published this new study reflecting the spirit of *perestroika*.

ruined denominational structures. The leaders of the Evangelical Christians—a movement which in numbers and concentration of churches was a long way behind the Baptists—noticeably secured leadership roles, as shown by the fact that both the President of the AUCECB (Y. A. Zhidkov) and the General Secretary (A. V. Karyev) were chosen from among their number.[25]

His general conclusion is, "Such major reorganisation could not, of course, have occurred without the recommendation and approval of 'the authorities.'"[26] The eventual inclusion of the Pentecostals and the Mennonites in the AUCECB is for Mitrokhin further evidence of the workings of what he calls the "bureaucratic 'unification' machine."[27]

A note of caution is sounded by another modern Russian (Baptist) historian, Sergii Savinskii. In a study published in 2001 he says:

> The present generation of brothers and sisters, and even those who are older (the first post-war generation) at times interpret the union which occurred in 1944 in a way that is rather crude and uninformed, attributing it exclusively to external influences: the merger, so they claim, was imposed upon the brethren by the authorities, and the AUCECB was the atheists' instrument for the destruction of the Evangelical-Baptist brotherhood. But that raises the question: What was there to destroy if almost everything had already been destroyed?[28]

According to Owen Chadwick, "The war proved to Stalin that he needed the Church. To fight a desperate war he needed to reunite the people and therefore must reconcile himself with the Christians who were so historic a part of the Russian inheritance."[29] That comment leaves another important question: Why did Stalin need the Baptists? Would it not have served his purposes simply to enlist the help of Orthodox believers in the USSR and to ignore (or continue to suppress) the rest? Stalin must somehow have realised the significance of the "dissenting" tradition in Russian and Ukrainian Christianity. This potentially powerful constituency could not be overlooked in the struggle against Nazism. It can hardly be the case that Stalin was launching a more liberal religious policy in order to

---

25. Ibid., 400.
26. Ibid.
27. Ibid., 408.
28. Savinskii, *Istoriya*, 156.
29. Chadwick, *Christian Church*, 93.

secure Western aid to the USSR, or to win the approval of the Western powers and so strengthen his position at the Tehran, Yalta, and Potsdam conferences. What the USSR obtained from the West would have been forthcoming even without the new religious policy, and Stalin had more or less guaranteed himself a free hand in Eastern Europe by the victories of Soviet forces. Experience had taught Stalin and others in the Soviet leadership that attempting to obliterate religion completely was futile; far better to contain and control it and also oppose it through the education of new generations in the spirit of atheism. Eventually, so it was believed, religion would wither and die. The policy of forcible eradication was a waste of state resources, especially as the expanded Soviet empire now included millions more professing believers who had been outside the USSR before the war.

At this point mention should be made of the Law on Religious Associations of 8 April 1929, which remained in force until October 1990.[30] This law limited the rights of religious believers to the performance of religious services in registered buildings, and made almost every other kind of religious activity or witness illegal: the law did not permit evangelism, religious education, literature work, raising money, indeed any activities not specified in the legislation. The 1929 law set in stone the all-important concept of registration, which would have such an impact on Baptist life in the post-war period. In any locality a group of at least twenty adults who wanted to form a religious association were allowed to apply for permission to register as such. They also needed to have a registered building in which to hold meetings. If they failed either to register themselves as a group or to register their building, they could not legally function. As Philip Walters has pointed out, "It is worth noting that these *local* associations were the only religious administrative structures recognised by Soviet law until 1990: no *central* co-ordinating organs had any legal status."[31] In other words, the All-Union Council of Evangelical Christians-Baptists, although established by the Soviet authorities, did not actually have any status in law. In a work published in 1986 Jane Ellis made a similar point about the Orthodox Church:

> As far as legal provisions go, we should remind ourselves that only the parishes have any basis in law . . . The church's other

---

30. The following summary is based mainly on Walters, "Survey," 13–14, and Nikolskaya, *Russkii protestantizm*, 93–95.

31. Walters, "Survey," 14 (italics original).

institutions—the theological schools, monasteries, the Publishing Department of the Moscow Patriarchate and the Patriarchate itself—are nowhere mentioned in any published legislation, and their existence is entirely *de facto*, with, needless to say, the tacit approval of the Soviet government.[32]

POST-WAR DEVELOPMENTS 1945–64

Misgivings about the formation of the AUCECB (whether inside or outside the USSR) did not prevent its growth. Other evangelical groups were brought under its umbrella, as well as the Baptist Unions in the Baltic States, which had been independent before the war but were absorbed into the post-war Soviet Empire. It was not at all certain that the Baptist Council would survive as an officially recognized institution. The immediate post-war period and the beginning of the Cold War seemed to herald a return to the purges of the 1930s and the "GULAG archipelago" once again went into full swing. For three years (1950, 1951, 1952) the official Baptist journal *Bratskii vyestnik* ceased publication, but soon after Stalin's death in March 1953 it reappeared without any explanation of what had happened.[33] The death of Stalin and the advent of what Ilya Ehrenburg labelled "the thaw"[34] brought a measure of relief for believers, and the Khrushchev era (1954–64) saw both an official repudiation of Stalinism and a greater degree of contact between the USSR and the West. However, the latter part of the Khrushchev era was also a period of intense religious persecution (of which more later).

The journal *Bratskii vyestnik* (*Fraternal Messenger*) appeared "not long after"[35] the formation of the Union and began publication early in 1945. Obviously it was not an undertaking that the Baptists could begin on their own initiative, and the non-committal "not long after" of the official history indicates that the publication of a journal was part of the government's plan for Baptist activities. Hence it was no accident that the

---

32. Ellis, *Russian Orthodox Church*, 257.

33. Sawatsky, *Soviet Evangelicals*, 63, 121–22. AUCECB, *Istoriya*, 238, mentions this interruption in the publication of the *Bratskii vyestnik* but offers no explanation. Nor was there any explanation in *Bratskii vyestnik* when it reappeared in 1953.

34. "The thaw" (*ottyepel'*), which was the title of a novel Ilya Ehrenburg wrote in 1954, has become the standard label for the immediate post-Stalin period, although the term is not as famous in the outside world as are *glasnost* and *perestroika*.

35. AUCECB, *Istoriya*, 238.

editorial board announced at the outset that the journal would contain, among other features, "Religious patriotic articles (Evangelical Christians and Baptists and the homeland)."[36] This type of article is actually mentioned at the top of a list that includes topics of a biblical, historical, and biographical nature, and the patriotic note is sounded in one of the very first articles, "The Christian and the Homeland."[37] Emphasizing that Christians cannot fail to love "our native Soviet land" the article extols the many natural resources to be found within her, "treasures of a kind that no other land knows."

> Is it not wonderful that thanks to Soviet power all these treasures have become the property of the nation's masses rather than of a few rich people, which is what we see in other countries. How can we fail to love our homeland which for centuries was a land in a state of slumber but has been transformed into a land of work for all, a great ant-hill of nations, a land which has forgotten the meaning of unemployment?[38]

The article emphasized that, for a Christian, serving one's country entails military service: "Christians who love their country should defend her by bearing arms."[39] In the second issue the journal celebrates Victory Day: "This is the day—a happy and joyful day of victory and peace—the Lord has made (Ps 117[118]:24)." The editors stressed the part played by Christians in the defeat of the enemy and exhorted readers: "As we were in days of war so let us be in days of peace—exemplary citizens of our land. Let us be light and salt for all."[40]

---

36. *Bratskii vyestnik*, 1945/1, 3; Popov, "Evangelical Christians-Baptists," 60. As the phrasing in this issue of the journal indicates, the Council was initially known as the "All-Union Council of Evangelical Christians and Baptists." The "and" was dropped shortly afterwards.

37. I am not sure whether it is best to translate *rodina* as "homeland," "motherland," or "mother-country." The latter two are a bit clumsy, but the Russian word *rodina* is from the same root as "to give birth" and so has a much closer connection to the idea of "motherhood" than "homeland" does.

38. *Bratskii vyestnik*, 1945/1, 6.

39. Ibid., 7. The article cites the examples of the centurion in Matthew 8 and Cornelius in Acts 10.

40. *Bratskii vyestnik*, 1945/2, 4. To commemorate the defeat of Nazi Germany, May 9th was officially declared to be "Victory Day," which it still is in Russia and other former Soviet territories (May 8th elsewhere in Europe). *Bratskii vyestnik*, 1946/3, 5–6, describes how the Moscow Baptist Church celebrated May 9th the following year. The next issue describes the church's "patriotic prayer meeting" held on September 3rd to celebrate the defeat of Japan (*Bratskii vyestnik*, 1946/4, 3). In these reports Soviet

In the spirit of patriotism one writer asserts that ECB believers have "complete freedom not only for worship services but for conducting necessary activity relating to all aspects of our religious life."[41]

> Beyond the borders of the USSR there are people who relate all kinds of fables about religious life in the USSR. But such people are either malicious slanderers or they just don't know what they are talking about. May God judge all these trouble-makers! We, however, will use every opportunity presented to us and will firmly commit ourselves to carrying on our ministry in the name of our dear Saviour and Lord Jesus Christ, giving thanks for everything to our God and Father and our Soviet government, which has given us these glorious and legal opportunities.[42]

The writer is very dismissive of the "many and various foreign missions" that have taken it upon themselves to gather funds for "the work in Russia." Such "help" would only foster conflict and division, and in any case it was unnecessary because AUCECB believers were perfectly capable of providing from their own resources everything necessary for the Lord's work in their land.[43]

Another interesting example of the journal's patriotism is a two-page article on "The Greatness of the Russian Language,"[44] a language that "for its amazing sonority and flexibility knows no equal." The article quotes Lenin's statement "We love our language and our homeland" and also the advice that people should enrich themselves by the knowledge of their language through reading the classics of Russian literature "and also our contemporary Soviet writers."[45] The writer added that it was important also to read the Russian Bible and Christian literature, including *Bratskii vyestnik*, which always strove to set an example of the finest Russian. It is difficult to imagine an article extolling the glories of English appearing

---

forces are depicted as having played the leading role in the defeat of both Germany and Japan.

41. *Bratskii vyestnik*, 1947/1, 16. If my translation sounds clumsy so does the original!

42. Ibid. The neuter gender of the participle that I have translated as a finite verb ("has given") indicates that it is specifically the Soviet government that is the giver.

43. *Bratskii vyestnik*, 1947/1, 17–18.

44. *Bratskii vyestnik*, 1948/4, 3–4.

45. In the article it is not entirely clear whose advice this is. The proximity to a reference to Lenin's article "On the National Pride of the Great Russians" certainly suggests that it was his advice.

in an English-language Christian publication, and such an article might well provoke the question "Which English?" The background is clearly the post-war Soviet drive for greater purity in the use of Russian and particularly the avoidance of "servility towards the West"[46] where language is concerned. The *Bratskii vyestnik* article is not as xenophobic in this respect as some Soviet publications on the subject but it does express concern for the preservation of the purity of Russian, "not ruining the language, not using foreign words incorrectly or unnecessarily." It ends with the clarion call "So let us love our great Russian language!"

As indicated in various reports and letters in *Bratskii vyestnik*, the AUCECB was accepted into the world-wide Baptist family and Soviet Baptists resumed contact with Christians abroad, the kind of contact that was impossible during the 1930s. In a splendid understatement, the official AUCECB *Istoriya evangel'skikh khristian-baptistov v SSSR* (*History of the Evangelical Christians-Baptists in the USSR*) says, "for reasons which did not depend upon our brethren,"[47] Soviet Baptists could not be represented at the BWA congresses in Berlin (1934), Atlanta (1939), Copenhagen (1947) and Cleveland (1950). They were due to be present in Copenhagen, but the conference agenda was felt to be too sensitive politically,[48] and in the USSR by 1950 the Stalinist pressure and the effects of the Cold War were such that the question of their attendance at Cleveland simply did not arise. However, international contacts became an important part of AUCECB life. The "Red Dean" of Canterbury, Hewlett Johnson, visited the Moscow Baptist Church in 1945.[49] According to the

---

46. Ryazanova-Clarke and Wade, *Russian Language*, 34.

47. *po nye zavisyashchim ot brat'yev prichinam* (AUCECB, *Istoriya*, 256). One might think that by 1989 the writers would have felt free to expand a little on those "reasons."

48. Sawatsky, *Soviet Evangelicals*, 121, 361; Popov, "Evangelical Christians-Baptists,"194–95. A letter from Alexander Karyev to Walter Lewis published in 1953 mentions "our decision not to send delegates to the 7th World Congress in Copenhagen, the reason being the hostile attitude of the West towards our country" (*Bratskii vyestnik*, 1953/1, 66). The letter makes no mention of the Cleveland BWA Congress.

49. Popov, "Evangelical Christians-Baptists," 69. *Bratskii vyestnik*, 1946/2, 40, briefly describes Johnson's presence at a "patriotic prayer meeting" in the Moscow Baptist Church, and the journal in 1957/5, 76–80, printed an extract from his book *Christians and Communism*. Adrian Hastings names Hewlett Johnson (1874–1966) among a number of "now mostly forgotten oddities" (*History*, 289). Hastings does not refer to Johnson's contacts with the Russian Baptists in 1945, but mentions his earlier visit to Moscow in the 1930s and comments on Johnson's "wholly uncritical adulation of Soviet Russia" and "his highly simple confidence in the goodness of organized

official AUCECB *Istoriya*, in June 1946 a Soviet Baptist delegation attended a conference of the Swedish Baptist Union.[50] However, according to the report in *Bratskii vyestnik*, by the time they reached Stockholm the conference was over—and they were possibly not helped by the fact that, for some odd reason, it took them five days to get from Moscow to Stockholm.[51] Nevertheless they were able to have some fellowship with Swedish Baptists and then travel on to a Finnish Baptist conference. There, according to the same report, a Finnish Baptist leader

> said that Baptists in Finland very much regretted the misunderstanding which had occurred between Finland and her great neighbour, the Soviet Union, and expressed the hope that this would never again happen in the future, and that Baptists in Finland would work with the aim that the two countries would in future live as good neighbours, in a peaceful relationship with one another.[52]

Not having the original remarks made by the representative of the Finnish Baptists it is impossible to know how much editing or "toning down" took place in the Russian version. Even allowing that the conflict was dwarfed by the scale of Soviet war casualties in 1941–45, "misunderstanding" is an odd way to refer to the winter war of 1939–40, which left some 25,000 Finnish dead and probably many times that number of Soviet fatalities (the Soviets never published any official figures).

There was even some contact with American Baptists. In 1946, Dr. Louie Newton, who was soon to serve as President of the Southern Baptist Convention, visited the USSR and was given an encouraging account of Baptist life there.[53] *Bratskii vyestnik* published a detailed report of his visit[54] during which he apparently reassured Soviet Baptists that their American brethren enjoyed "freedom to serve God" too.[55] According to the report, Alexander Karyev spoke of how Newton's visit had contributed to the development of relationships between Soviet and American Baptists, and he asked Newton "to convey to our brothers and sisters in

---

communism" (Hastings, *History*, 320).
50. AUCECB, *Istoriya*, 255.
51. *Bratskii vyestnik*, 1946/4, 9.
52. Ibid., 11.
53. AUCECB, *Istoriya*, 255; Nikolskaya, *Russkii protestantizm*, 153–54.
54. *Bratskii vyestnik*, 1946/6, 58–64.
55. Ibid., 60.

the USA that Russian Baptists, together with the whole nation, are involved in the great task of the reconstruction of their land."⁵⁶ In the next issue the journal published a "thank you" letter from Newton.⁵⁷ Newton's visit is also mentioned in a letter from a John Cumming, of Portsmouth, Virginia, who had just heard Newton speak at a conference where he displayed a "golden chalice" presented to him in Russia as "a token of greeting and love" from Russian Baptists to Baptists in the USA.⁵⁸ A correspondent (with a Ukrainian name) living in Paraguay informed the journal that they had received a letter from Newton describing his visit: "a very joyful letter in which he tells us that the cause of the Gospel in the Soviet Union is progressing very well."⁵⁹ Correspondence from "brethren overseas" was by now a regular feature. It is interesting to see in particular the number of letters from Baptists in the USA and places as far afield as Brazil and China, written by people with Russian or Ukrainian names and representing communities of Baptists with corresponding ethnic origins—the journal was quite happy to admit, albeit tacitly, the existence of a worldwide Russian and Ukrainian Baptist *diaspora*, many of whom would presumably have fled after the Revolution.

An interesting glimpse of what it was like for foreigners to visit the USSR in the Stalin era was given by a group of English Quakers (four men and three women) who were there for nearly two weeks in July 1951. Among the religious leaders they met was AUCECB President Yakov Zhidkov, "a sincere little man with a neatly trimmed goatee beard," who told them

> that there were over 200 million people in Russia not one of whom was for war, but some Baptists, Congregationalists and Methodists abroad wanted war. Truman and Bevin, he said, were Baptists. "I hope our dear guests will help to draw all sections of the Christian Community into the fight for peace. If you can get the Baptist Truman into that path we will be grateful.⁶⁰

56. Ibid., 84.
57. *Bratskii vyestnik*, 1947/1, 73–74.
58. *Bratskii vyestnik*, 1947/2, 56–57.
59. *Bratskii vyestnik*, 1947/3, 57.
60. Lonsdale, *Quakers*, 19. The comments presumably refer to Ernest Bevin, Britain's Foreign Secretary in the post-war Labour government. A strong supporter of the USA in the early years of the Cold War, he advocated British involvement in the Korean war. As a young man Bevin was baptised in a Baptist Church in Bristol and was involved in Sunday School work and lay preaching, but in later life he became somewhat detached from the Baptist community. Bevin died just three months prior

At a subsequent meeting Zhidkov

> read to us the various peace messages which from time to time they had sent to their brother Baptists in England and elsewhere, including an appeal to the Baptists all over the world to express their categorical protest against "the aggression of the United States in Korea" . . . They complained wistfully, though without bitterness, that they had received little or no response from British and American Baptists.[61]

The Quakers' visit occurred during the three-year period of 1950–52 when no issues of *Bratskii vyestnik* were published. However, a report of the visit appeared when the journal resumed publication in 1953.[62] The report relates specifically to contacts the Quakers had with Russian Baptists and consists mainly of comments made by the Quakers themselves in the publication already quoted. It makes a point of mentioning the Russian Baptist appeal to Baptists everywhere to "express a categorical protest against US aggression in Korea."[63] The very first article in the revived journal was a lengthy one on "The Involvement of the Evangelical-Christians-Baptists of the USSR in the cause of Defending Peace."[64] The article describes how, in 1950,

> Armed forces of the United States of America began their campaign of devastation against North Korea. American planes dropped bombs not only on military objectives but also on non-military: on fields where peasants were peacefully working; on hamlets where innocent children were playing; on factories producing food—in a word, they subjected Korea to total bombardment.

The article describes how world opinion was horrified by "this inhuman destruction of the peaceful population of Korea" and how letters from all over the world were sent to the UN Security Council "condemning this evil in Korea."

> The Council of the Union of Evangelical Christians-Baptists in the USSR also sent a protest to the Security Council. In their

---

to the Quakers' visit and, at his family's request, the funeral service was conducted in Acton Baptist Church, London.

61. Ibid., 27.
62. *Bratskii vyestnik*, 1953/1, 13–15.
63. Ibid., 15.
64. Ibid., 3–8.

> protest the Evangelical Christians-Baptists of the USSR declared: "Thousands of American bombs are falling on towns and settlements where there are defenceless old people, women and children . . . We the Evangelical Christians-Baptists of the USSR express our deep outrage and condemnation of this inhuman destruction of the peaceful population of Korea . . . [and we] unanimously concur with the most noble and most humanitarian demand of the Soviet government that military action in Korea should cease immediately.[65]

In the same issue, an article on women's rights comments on the indignities suffered by women in South Korea where "occupation forces are in control."[66] Condemnation of the "bloodshed in Korea," "the bloodiest of wars," is also found in a letter that Zhidkov had written to Arthur Lewis of Melbourne, Australia, in December 1951, and that now appeared in the revived *Bratskii vyestnik*.[67] By the time the Baptist journal resumed publication in 1953 the Korean War was almost over. Nevertheless, the editors probably had no choice but to regurgitate the type of Cold War rhetoric seen in the Soviet press during the conflict, just as Baptists had probably had to join in the chorus of anti-American protest from the outset of the war.

An indication of the immediate post-Stalin change in government policy, the "Khrushchev thaw," is the attendance of Russian Baptists at an international Quaker conference in July 1953,[68] as is the visit in June–July 1954 of BWA representatives to a number of Soviet cities where they were enthusiastically welcomed by local Baptists. At a farewell breakfast in Leningrad on July 1, Baptist leaders Yakov Zhidkov and Alexander Karyev

> expressed their deep satisfaction that their guests had been able to spend time in the USSR and personally assure themselves of the complete religious freedom which believers enjoy in the USSR, and that now they have the opportunity to tell people in the West the truth about believers in the USSR and about the whole Soviet nation, full of enthusiasm for what they are building and for the struggle in the glorious cause of peace.[69]

65. Ibid., 5.

66. Ibid., 20. The article takes the line that women's rights are violated almost everywhere in the world except the USSR.

67. Ibid., 68–70.

68. AUCECB, *Istoriya*, 255.

69. *Bratskii vyestnik*, 1954/3–4, 100, quoted in Nikolskaya, *Russkii protestantizm*, 155.

The guests were Fred Townley Lord, President of the BWA, Walter O. Lewis, BWA Associate Secretary for Europe, and Ernest Payne, General Secretary of the Baptist Union of Great Britain and Ireland.[70] On their return to London they reported:

> Our Russian brethren assured us that there is now complete freedom of worship in the Soviet territories and that all religious communities enjoy equal rights and opportunities . . . Many young people are applying for baptism and church membership. Before acceptance they have to undergo a prolonged period of testing and probation, their names being made known publicly to the local church.[71]

The names of these young people would no doubt also become known to the authorities. In a further report F. Townley Lord wrote: "We are often asked 'Is there religious liberty in Russia?' I do not think the term 'religious liberty' in the Soviet Union is interpreted in the broad way to which we are accustomed in the West; but from our observation we were left in no doubt that Russia allows a freedom of worship in buildings designated for that purpose."[72]

The establishing of new churches and the designating of buildings for worship was of course totally at the discretion of the communist authorities. Commenting on this trip a few years later Payne wrote:

> For a year or so previously the Baptist Union Council had had a desultory and unsatisfactory correspondence with the All-Soviet [sic] Council of Evangelical Christian [sic] Baptists. The invitation for the British visit came during the easing of tension which followed the death of Stalin. The discovery that there were at least 512,000 Baptist Church members scattered throughout the Soviet Union and enjoying freedom of worship, though not of propaganda, came as a surprise and an encouragement.[73]

At the Jubilee Congress in London, 1955, nine delegates represented the USSR. In his address, the AUCECB President Yakov Zhidkov (who became one of the BWA Vice-Presidents), understandably made no

70. Payne, *Baptist Union*, 255.

71. *The Baptist Times*, 8 July 1954, 1.

72. *The Baptist Times*, 15 July 1954, 9. Lord comments briefly on the visit in his *Baptist World Fellowship*, 168. He says that the visit "received much prominence in the world Press"—a reminder of how isolated the people, and especially the Christians, of the USSR still were. Visits of this kind hit the headlines!

73. Payne, *Baptist Union*, 248.

mention of the reasons why Soviet Baptists had not been present at a BWA congress since 1928. Furthermore, he reassured his hearers: "All our churches enjoy full freedom for preaching the Gospel, and bringing up and educating new members. This liberty, this freedom, is guaranteed by the main laws of our country, and in conducting services we do not encounter any obstacles."[74] Zhidkov's address also reflected the official Soviet policy of being in the vanguard of the World Peace Council:

> Besides the evangelical work which we carry on,[75] the Baptists of the Soviet Union also participate in the cause of the defence of world peace. All Evangelical Christian Baptists in the Soviet Union are advised by Christ's words, "Blessed are the peacemakers," and we understand these words not only as peace in the family, or peace between individuals, but we understand it as peace between countries and nations, and peace for the whole of humanity. We hope that at this Congress, we shall hear the voice of the Baptist World Alliance speaking against cold war [sic], armaments drive, the preparation of a new war, and the production and use of nuclear weapons.[76]

Of course, what Zhidkov could not say was that in his own country anyone, Baptist or otherwise, who dared to criticise Soviet arms spending and production would quickly be "suppressed."

Also in 1955, just after the London Congress, a delegation that included Theodore Adams (BWA President), Arnold Ohrn (BWA General Secretary), and two other prominent (American) Baptists, Joseph Jackson and V. Carney Hargroves, undertook a two-week tour of Baptist churches in Russia, covering over 3000 miles and being warmly received everywhere they went.[77] The Soviet government, anxious to present itself as tolerant of religion and committed to the cause of world peace, saw the propaganda value of fostering these kinds of contacts, and Soviet Baptists were both genuinely patriotic and also anxious to have as many lines of communication open as possible to their government and to their brethren in the West. They also had to keep making the right kind of noises. Zhidkov's lengthy report on the Western visit ends with the comment:

---

74. 1955 BWA Congress Record, 261.
75. About which, incidentally, Zhidkov said practically nothing.
76. 1955 BWA Congress Record, 262.
77. Patterson and Pierard, "Recovery," 123.

> We are sure that the time spent by our dear brethren, our guests from the USA, in the USSR has given them the opportunity to see how our beloved homeland lives a vibrant life, how our Evangelical Christian-Baptist communities live a free and full spiritual life, and how strong is the universal aspiration of our whole nation and of all the believers for peace with all nations including the people of the USA.[78]

Zhidkov (now aged seventy-five) returned to the theme of peace in his address to the tenth BWA congress in Rio de Janeiro, in 1960, where he again highlighted the role of his own government:

> In September, 1959, the Soviet Government submitted to the United Nations a declaration for universal and complete disarmament. As we all know, the declaration found the most favourable response in all countries of the world; and eighty-two countries, members of the United Nations, have approved it unanimously.
>
> This declaration must be dear to the hearts of all Christians, as dear as are the words of the Bible in the book of Isaiah: "And they shall beat their swords into plowshares, and their spears into pruninghooks: nation shall not lift up sword against nation, neither shall they learn war any more."
>
> We are glad to note the words of the Archbishop of Canterbury, Dr. Fisher, said by him in connection with the proposal of the Soviet Government for universal and complete disarmament, "No Christian could have put forward a better program than this". This proposal is a Christian solution of the problem of disarmament.
>
> Dear brethren and friends, it seems to us that now after the declaration has been proclaimed from the rostrum of the United Nations, among Christians there must not be any longer any vagueness concerning what way to choose in order to prevent the new world war and not to permit any local wars. This way lies in the realization of the declaration ...
>
> This most humane declaration can become the only base which will unite all Christian churches for activities in one direction—to beat all swords into plowshares, and all spears into pruninghooks, that is, the destruction of all types of weapons.[79]

---

78. *Bratskii vyestnik*, 1955/5, 37. The report covers pp. 25–37 of this issue and includes a number of interesting photographs. Zhidkov mentions that one of the "Baptists from the USA" had Norwegian origins (Arnold Ohrn).

79. 1960 BWA Congress Record, 202.

Artur Mitskevich (later Assistant General Secretary of the AUCECB), who was elected to the BWA Executive Committee, had on the previous day given a brief report to the Rio congress on Baptist work in the USSR.[80] He too stressed the Soviet Baptists' commitment to the cause of peace and disarmament. In a brief and bland list of statistics he quoted a figure of 500,000 Baptists, "including many young people." Mitskevich reported that every year ten to fifteen thousand people were baptised into membership, adding "They are never younger than eighteen years." Mitskevich was not in a position to say why, according to his report, they were never younger than eighteen, and neither he nor Zhidkov could possibly have said anything about Khrushchev's anti-religious campaign, which was well under way by then.[81] Savinskii comments, "In their meetings with foreign brethren, AUCECB staff always emphasized the necessity of the struggle for peace on earth. This became a kind of incantation [*zaklinaniye*] which could not be omitted."[82]

Near the end of his book, Savinskii concludes:

> When discussing the international contacts between the AUCECB and fellowships in other countries, we cannot but indicate the sad aspects which relate to the question of religious freedom in the USSR. In their meetings with representatives of foreign fellowships the AUCECB leadership, when asked whether in the USSR there were any cases of harassment of believers for religious reason, always answered in the negative, asserting that in the USSR people were not persecuted or put on trial for their faith. And this was when, throughout all the post-war years (with the exception of 1953–1956, the years of the Khrushchev "thaw") persecution and trials of believers did not cease, and in the 1960s actually increased. Such statements by the brethren can be explained, but they cannot be justified. We recall this not in a spirit of condemnation (for God is the judge!), but with deep sorrow.[83]

---

80. Ibid., 186–87.

81. Similarly, the Russian Orthodox Church joined the World Council of Churches in 1961—another example of Soviet image-building. Needless to say, the Russian Orthodox representatives who attended the New Delhi WCC Assembly in 1961 had no comment to make about the renewed and intensified religious persecution in their country.

82. Savinskii, *Istoriya*, 194.

83. Ibid., 256.

KHRUSHCHEV'S POLICIES

As has been mentioned, there was a significant increase in the tempo of persecution against believers in the years 1959–64.[84] This is often overlooked when Nikita Khrushchev's time (1954–64) is portrayed as one of East-West *détente* and of an emphasis on "peaceful co-existence." The anti-religious campaign was very much the initiative of the Soviet premier himself and it marks something of a change from the tense but generally less confrontational tone of Church-State relations in the immediate post-Stalin era. Khrushchev, who was, in Tony Judt's memorable phrase, "reliably unpredictable,"[85] was fired by an almost apocalyptic vision of the collapse of capitalism and the building of socialism and eventually communism, and he and his minions stridently made the point that religion would have no place in this brave, new world. He did not, however, need to enact fresh legislation. The 1929 law simply needed to be applied with all possible rigour, and any uncertainties in the law could easily be interpreted by the authorities to the disfavour of believers. Anti-religious propaganda, it was felt, had to be multiplied and improved, and all possible measures taken to eradicate religious life in "the land of the Soviets."

Savinskii claims that Khrushchev at the beginning of his regime made fairly concessionary noises in the direction of religious believers, while all the time planning a campaign of intensified aggression against the churches, the beginnings of which can be seen in 1957 with the emergence of a more sophisticated "scientific atheism."[86] Such was the intensity of the campaign that "by the end of 1959 the AUCECB was on the verge of dissolution."[87] Although there is ample evidence of damage done to the Orthodox Church, Tatyana Nikolskaya, another post-Soviet Russian Protestant scholar, has argued that the main targets of repression were those who had long been labelled *syektanty*, not only by Soviet society but also by the Orthodox Church. *Syektanty*, roughly translated as "sectarians," is a pejorative umbrella term for non-Orthodox believers such as the Baptists or Pentecostals (and Jehovah's Witnesses), and the

---

84. This is discussed in, for example, Sawatsky, *Soviet Evangelicals*, ch. 5; Chadwick, *Christian Church*, 95–97 ; Hosking, *History*, 438–40; Walters, "Survey," 20–23; Nikolskaya, *Russkii protestantizm*, ch. 5.

85. Judt, *Postwar*, 424.

86. Savinskii, *Istoriya*, 196.

87. Ibid.

word is still widely used today. Baptists and others are not seen as members of true Christian churches but as members of "sects."

Explaining the consequences of this, Nikolskaya writes:

> The distinctiveness of the Khrushchev anti-religion campaign was that, although it was in effect directed against *all* religions and confessions, the ideology of that time bore a clearly expressed anti-sect character. In contrast to the 1930s, when the terms "churchmen" [*tserkovniki*] and "sectarians" [*syektanty*] had an equally pejorative hue, the latter now acquired a particularly negative significance. The Russian Protestants were numbered among the sectarians. A significant proportion of the anti-religious publications of the central and local mass media were directed against them.[88]

As with all persecutions, much depended on local factors and officials, and precise information on variations in severity is not available. But generally speaking, it is very likely that the love-hate relationship with Christianity that Soviet people obviously enjoyed resulted in a greater degree of "hate" being directed against *syektanty* than against the Orthodox. The Orthodox Church was, after all, an integral part of the history of Russia, and the Soviet war effort had made conspicuous use of a type of "holy Russia" discourse, associated with such heroes as Alexander Nevskii, Ivan the Great and Ivan the Terrible, General Kutuzov, and even those who fought in the Russo-Japanese war of living memory.[89] In so many proud moments the Orthodox Church had played a major part, but the *syektanty* were of foreign stock and really had no place in the Russian grand narrative.

Another factor difficult to measure is the dissonance between, on the one hand, the official line as promoted in the anti-religious propaganda, and, on the other, what people on the ground seriously believed about the

---

88. Nikolskaya, *Russkii protestantizm*, 176 (emphasis original).

89. One study of contemporary Russian emphasizes how WWII contributed to significant changes in the language. "Rediscovered archaisms were used in the patriotic discourse of the time," and many of these "archaisms" were associated with Russia's Orthodox heritage. "The war triggered a stylistic change in official discourse. The call to perform one's sacred duty and defend the homeland, the depiction of the immense sacrifices and heroic efforts made by the Russian people during the war called for new heights of expressiveness . . . Stylistic elements, the use of which had been unthinkable in the 1930s, became popular and even approved of in the 1940s; archaic words of Church Slavonic and Old Russian origin made a comeback" (Ryazanova-Clarke and Wade, *Russian Language*, 30–31).

syektanty. Did they really believe them guilty of rituals involving human sacrifice? It is hard to know, since people tended to keep to themselves any doubts they might have had about the veracity of official publications.

Whatever views were held about them by Soviet authorities and society, the Baptist leadership, through the pages of *Bratskii vyestnik*, continued to assure everyone of ECB loyalty to the state and its international policies. A two-page article of 1961 entitled "Christianity and the Cold War" reflects the official line that blame for international tension lies of course with the West. The article commented on "the problem of the relationships between East and West" and lamented "the division of the world into two hostile camps." What makes matters worse is that Christians were being drawn into this conflict, as can be seen (supposedly) from a reading of the Christian press: "Whenever you pick up today's ecclesiastical press, you can't avoid the significant number of articles which are designed to draw Christians into the cold war between East and West and to instil into them the medieval idea of 'the Crusades.'"[90] Where were these articles being published? The writer of the *Bratskii vyestnik* piece does not name names, but obviously no ecclesiastical press existing in the USSR would ever publish material of this kind. The implication is that the Western religious press was being used to encourage a war-mongering spirit among Western Christians. Where else would "the Crusader mentality"[91] take root but in the West? Soviet churches, like the Soviet people in general, were of course not to blame for Cold War tension.

PEACE AND FREEDOM

Twenty-five years after the ECB official publication began life with an article on "The Christian and the Homeland," another (longer) article with the same name was written by Karyev.[92] This article also emphasized the Christian duty to love one's homeland and the special privilege of being a citizen of the USSR with all her proud achievements. Two virtues in particular were highlighted in rapid succession:

> In days when, like the sword of Damocles, the threat of another world war—this time an atomic war—hangs over the human

---

90. *Bratskii vyestnik*, 1961/2, 6.
91. Ibid., 7.
92. *Bratskii vyestnik*, 1970/3, 48–54.

race, our homeland constantly calls all nations of the earth to peace, friendship and mutual co-operation.

We are especially glad that, by God's grace, there are thousands of places in our land where the gospel is being preached and the good news of our Lord Jesus Christ is being proclaimed.[93]

On their visits abroad, in their meetings with visitors to the USSR, in their publications, Soviet Baptists made a point of drawing people's attention to these advantages of the Soviet system. The themes of peace, peaceful co-existence, disarmament, and the dangers of nuclear were a regular feature in *Bratskii vyestnik* articles. A section called "The Voice of Christians in the Defence of Peace" contained a number of items relating to the international peace movement—particularly Soviet contributions to it. Special attention was given to the work of the Christian Peace Conference, which was founded in 1958 in Prague where it continued to have its headquarters. The CPC was criticised by some Western observers for allegedly being a vehicle of communist propaganda. This may not be entirely fair, but it is obvious that the Soviet government regarded this as an organisation that could be endorsed, and that was generally not guilty of going against the wishes of the communist state.

From 1966 onwards we read occasional criticisms of US policy in Vietnam. These criticisms were usually found in reports of international peace conferences or declarations by, for example, the WCC.[94] A report of an interview with Martin Luther King just before his death has King saying that this "unjust war" is "consuming the soul of our nation."[95] A few months later the journal published an obituary for King that mentions in particular his opposition to the Vietnam war and his struggle for justice in his own land.[96] The article that contains the obituary also has a rather strange report of a service held in the Moscow Baptist Church to celebrate King's life. The service was attended by "a group of negro believers from the USA."[97] However, "the leader of the negro group" passed on greetings on behalf of "churches in East Africa and Madagascar" and spoke of the sufferings that "we in Africa" endure.[98] Furthermore, the

---

93. Ibid., 51.
94. *Bratskii vyestnik*, 1967/4, 37.
95. *Bratskii vyestnik*, 1968/1, 8.
96. *Bratskii vyestnik*, 1968/3, 7–10.
97. Ibid., 7.
98. *Bratskii vyestnik*, 1968/3, 8–9.

date of this service is given as April 7.[99] King was assassinated in Memphis in the early evening of April 4—which by Moscow time means the early hours of April 5—and so the speed of preparation for the service must have been breathtaking![100]

Vietnam was the subject of a lengthy article in 1969, "Christians against the Vietnam War,"[101] which reported an address given by Alexander Karyev at an inter-faith conference in Zagorsk. It waxed eloquent on the "horrors" perpetrated by US forces and called upon Christians to follow the example of the Good Samaritan by giving support to the Vietnamese people. The end of the war was noted in a brief article saying how glad the Evangelical Christians-Baptists were when they heard the joyful news: "The ending of the war in Indo-China was the result of the self-sacrificing struggle of the Vietnamese people, the efforts of people of good will, and the fervent prayers of Christians all over the world."[102] At a Sunday service in the Moscow Baptist Church a special prayer of thanksgiving was offered and a collection was made "in aid of the people of Vietnam, ruined by a long and cruel war."[103] Vietnam received another mention a few years later when the journal expressed a protest by ECB believers against the "barbaric aggression" of the Chinese against the people of Vietnam.[104] So what Western commentators dubbed "the new Cold War" (between Moscow and Beijing) did not pass entirely unnoticed.

Although it was not seen as a formal ending to the Cold War, the meeting between President Jimmy Carter and Soviet premier Leonid Brezhnev in Vienna in June 1979, and the signing of the SALT II agreement, seemed to herald an era of better relations between the USSR and the West. *Bratskii vyestnik* published congratulatory telegrams from the AUCECB leadership to Brezhnev and to Carter. The message to the US President acknowledged that the prayers of "your fellow believers, the Baptists of our land" had been answered. Citing the biblical injunction "Choose life" (Deut 30:19) the Russian Baptists said, "We are sincerely grateful to the Lord and to you for this choice of ways that lead to peace

---

99. Ibid., 7.

100. King and his campaign for world peace are also commemorated in *Bratskii vyestnik*, 1968/5, 9–13.

101. *Bratskii vyestnik*, 1969/4, 7–12.

102. *Bratskii vyestnik*, 1973/2, 9.

103. Ibid., 9.

104. *Bratskii vyestnik*, 1979/2, 63–64.

and prosperity."[105] A new chapter in the Cold War was, of course, just about to start, with the Soviet invasion of Afghanistan in December 1979. The ensuing time of tension and name-calling was marked by American absence from the Moscow Olympics in 1980 and Soviet absence from the Los Angeles games in 1984. It was not marked by any noticeable comment in print on the part of Soviet Baptists.

In May 1982, Billy Graham made his long-awaited journey to the USSR. *Bratskii vyestnik* published a report of his meeting with Russian Baptist leaders, which contained the comment:

> From our conversation with him we learned that in the course of his life he had had three points of spiritual rebirth. The first was when the Lord Jesus Christ met with him and named him as His child. The second was when he realised the horrors and the injustice of segregation. And the third was when he understood that Christians have to do everything in their power to prevent a nuclear catastrophe from occurring on earth.[106]

Graham was in Moscow to attend a conference that had the rather cumbersome title: "Religious Activists Working to Save the Sacred Gift of Life from a Nuclear Catastrophe." The conference—attended also by Duke McCall and Denton Lotz—was covered in some detail in the journal,[107] with eight pages devoted to Graham's address on "Christian faith and peace in the nuclear age."[108] Graham was also reported to have commented in conversation that he had "come to the Soviet Union at a time of great tension between our countries."[109] The reports are all rather bland and repetitive, stating the obvious—that nuclear war would be "a bad thing." There was no accusing finger pointed against the USA—there was no Korea or Vietnam to be pressed into service—and in all this material nothing was said about the possibility that Soviet policy in Afghanistan might have contributed to the international tension and the danger of war.

105. *Bratskii vyestnik*, 1979/3, 57.
106. *Bratskii vyestnik*, 1982/4, 22.
107. Ibid., 34–64.
108. Ibid., 51–58.
109. Ibid., 30.

DIVISIONS AMONG THE BAPTISTS

It is impossible in a chapter of this length to do justice to the conflict between the AUCECB and the so-called Council of Churches of the Evangelical Christians-Baptists in Soviet (and post-Soviet) Baptist history.[110] The official *History of the Evangelical Christians-Baptists in the USSR* finds this topic a very painful one and devotes relatively little space to it. Furthermore, it lays the chief blame on the state authorities (it could do this with impunity in 1989!).[111]

The problems began in 1959–1960 and were related to the anti-religious drive of Khrushchev's time. The authorities pressured Baptists into bringing themselves into line with the 1929 laws on religion, which, it was felt, were not being strictly observed. The AUCECB passed a "Statute on the Union of Evangelical Christians-Baptists in the USSR" and issued a "Letter of Instruction to the Senior Presbyters of the AUCECB." These documents imposed severe restrictions on church life, particularly in evangelism and work among children and young people. Opposition to the AUCECB leadership appeared almost at once and was expressed by an Action Group—literally an "Initiative Group," hence the label *initsiativniki*—of twelve people headed by Alexei Prokofiev and Gennadi Kryuchkov. By mid-1962 Prokofiev was under arrest and in August he was sentenced to five years imprisonment followed by five years exile. The Initiative Group was replaced by an Organising Committee (*Orgkomitet*) in which Georgii Vins played a major role. In September 1965, the Organizing Committee changed its name to the Council of Churches of the Evangelical Christians-Baptists (CCECB). Although this was not their original intention, they soon evolved into a rival Baptist Union.[112]

At the AUCECB Conferences in 1966 and 1969 attempts were made to heal the rift and to meet some of the demands of the Council of

---

110. The conflict between the AUCECB and the "Council of Churches" (the CCECB) is described in detail in Bourdeaux, *Religious Ferment*; Sawatsky, *Soviet Evangelicals*, chs. 6–8; Rowe, *Russian Resurrection*, particularly chs. 10 and 11; and Nikolskaya, *Russkii protestantizm*, 201–15. Another recent study by a Russian Baptist is found in Prokhorov, "State," ch. 1. A detailed list of relevant sources is given in Wardin, *Evangelical Sectarianism*, 706–59. There is also a large amount of material in the Keston Archive, now based at Baylor University, which can be accessed online: http://www.baylor.edu/kestoncenter/

111. AUCECB, *Istoriya*, 238–50, with occasional references elsewhere.

112. In English-language publications they are sometimes referred to as "Reform (or Reformed) Baptists."

Churches. Some cautious repentance was expressed for the high-handed way in which the AUCECB leadership had acted in 1960. However, the damage had been done. The Council of Churches considered that the AUCECB leadership had let itself become a tool for state interference in church life and state prohibition of evangelism. The issue of registration became the chief bone of contention. The *initsiativniki* were not necessarily opposed to every type of registration; it was simply that registration in their view imposed impossible conditions on churches. In theory, registration required a church to comply with all the laws on religion; these laws stifled church growth, so it was better to "obey God rather than men'" and remain unregistered. From the outset many of the Unregistered Baptists, as they became known, suffered imprisonment. In 1964 the Council of Prisoners' Relatives was formed to gather data on Baptist prisoners and, as far as possible, disseminate it in the West. Over the next twenty years until the dawn of *glasnost* and *perestroika* much Western concern for the underground church in the USSR was focused on the Council of Churches and on the closely associated Council of Prisoners' Relatives.[113]

As Sawatsky points out, it is impossible to be precise about the relative sizes of the two sides in this split.[114] Furthermore, the picture varied considerably from one region to another and fluctuated over the decades. Sawatsky (whose work was published in 1981) says that "at its height in 1966 the reform movement very likely had around 155,000 supporters."[115] However, he gives the number of Baptists in unregistered congregations as being perhaps 250,000, the implication being that the unregistered Baptists and the reform movement (the *initsiativniki*) were not one and the same thing (which is not surprising since unregistered Baptist churches had been in existence well before the turmoil of the early 1960s). Naturally the AUCECB wanted to play down the size of the split. At one point the official *History of Evangelical Christians-Baptists in the USSR* says: "According to the AUCECB's information, by 1 January 1973 the number of those who had separated was around fifteen thousand."[116]

---

113. Rowe says: "The efforts of the members of the Council of Prisoners' Relatives probably made more impact on ordinary Christians than the work of the Council of Churches" (*Russian Resurrection*, 163). Sawatsky likewise stresses the importance of the CPR: "The CCECB might have been destroyed had it not been for the work of the Council of Prisoners' Relatives" (Sawatsky, *Soviet Evangelicals*, 241).

114. Sawatsky, *Soviet Evangelicals*, 183–84, 193–94.

115. Ibid., 193.

116. AUCECB, *Istoriya*, 250.

The situation was complicated by the difficulty of obtaining precise figures for the AUCECB itself. The official *Istoriya*, published in 1989, admits that it does not have precise statistics and gives a figure of "around 500,000 members of local churches." It then adds, rather confusingly: "Besides registered churches there are unregistered churches and groups of believers."[117] It is not clear whether the figure of 500,000 includes both registered and unregistered Baptists or only the former.

The conflict can be seen as a matter of different interpretations of Acts 5:29 and Romans 13:1–7. The AUCECB argued that any members of unregistered churches who were in prison were there because they violated the law of the land. Representatives of the Council of Churches argued that the law was such that no genuine Christian could comply with it. Western Baptists often found themselves in a difficult position and were sometimes criticised for being duped by the AUCECB leadership. It was difficult for them to know how to respond to the stream of information about religious persecution that was being smuggled out of the USSR from groups such as the Council of Prisoners' Relatives. If they took up the cause of Baptist prisoners in the USSR they risked alienating the AUCECB, who had to repeat the official line that nobody in the Soviet Union would be in prison for purely religious reasons.[118] The Soviet government encouraged official Baptist contacts with brethren abroad as a way of counteracting the information transmitted to the West by the underground church.

The emergence of the underground church presented the government with a new set of problems. Nikolskaya writes:

> Whereas previously they had thought of religious extremes in terms of sectarian exclusivity, rejection of the cinema, theatre, television, etc., now the authorities had to contend with believers on a large scale listening to foreign radio broadcasts, having illegal contact with fellow believers abroad, receiving literature and material help from abroad, sending abroad information about religious persecutions, submitting applications to leave the USSR, rejecting Soviet citizenship.[119]

From the late 1970s on, the authorities started to allow significant numbers of Baptists to leave, which further contributed to the flow of

---

117. Ibid., 291.
118. Russell, "Church/State Relations," 26–27; Sawatsky, *Soviet Evangelicals*, ch. 13.
119. Nikolskaya, *Russkii protestantizm*, 281.

information abroad. The official tendency was to label those who worked on behalf of the underground church agents of Western imperialism. On the other hand they wanted to remain to a certain extent sensitive to Western public opinion, so if a Christian prisoner's case, or an instance of harassment of a local congregation, was known abroad this was often a restraining factor. Controlled emigration was felt to be preferable to an unworkable attempt at total suppression. Nikolskaya argues that Soviet Baptists were generally at a distinct advantage compared with, say, dissident Pentecostals, because of the strength and influence of the Baptist community abroad,[120] and she sees a connection between the start of Baptist emigration from the USSR and the Baptist Jimmy Carter's time as US President (1976–80).

Relationships within the USSR between the All-Union Council and the Council of Churches varied greatly in their local manifestations. There was often a good deal more fellowship and mutual support between members of what were in effect two rival unions than expressed animosity would suggest. Much research remains to be done on the relationships between the AUCECB and the CCECB, with much of the primary source material still in the form of letters, diaries, and personal reminiscences.

Probably the best known of the *initsiativniki* is Georgii Vins (1928–98) who was eventually exiled from the USSR in 1979. He was the subject of a Cold War transaction, being sent to the USA in exchange for captured Soviet spies. In the West he campaigned energetically on behalf of the underground church and sought to advise Western Christians against accepting what was said by the AUCECB leadership. A summary of an interview for *Christianity Today* has Vins saying:

> Did you ever notice that when AUCECB secretary Alexei Bychkov or other leaders of the All-Union Council come to the West they never encourage people to pray for those who are suffering? They don't ask people to pray for the children in Russia or for the work of the gospel. They always say everything is fine. "The government is giving us an opportunity to serve the Lord," they say. But where are the children and the young people?[121]

In the same issue, Denton Lotz offered a different perspective on the churches in the USSR, calling for greater understanding of the situation

---

120. Ibid., 282.

121. "Religion in the USSR: How Much Freedom Is Enough?" *Christianity Today* interviews with Denton Lotz and Georgi Vins. *Christianity Today*, 8 October 1982, 49.

that confronted AUCECB leaders and emphasizing that, in spite of the restrictions, there was a tremendous movement of God's spirit; in particular, "the fact is that the youth are flooding the churches."[122] Thus the complexities of Baptist life in the USSR generated a classic case of conflicting signals.

CONCLUSION

One post-Soviet commentator has written: "The Russian Protestant movement possesses a host of contradictions and conflicts, many of which can be traced back to the structural and ideological reordering of forces during the Soviet era."[123]

The conflicts and contradictions are seen not least in the fine line that the official Baptist leadership in the USSR had to tread in their relationships with the Soviet government and officialdom and also in their contacts with foreigners. For several decades Soviet Baptists lived in a closed society under a regime that was (to varying degrees) hostile towards religion, and in the post-war era the regime was engaged in bouts of tension with the West, particularly the USA. On the one hand they were as entitled to their patriotism as Baptists in any other land or time; on the other hand they were in a situation where open criticism of official policy and ideology invited heavy penalties—something to which patriotic Baptists in Britain or the USA were not exposed. Their extensive championing of peace causes was understandable in a land that suffered the loss of 27 million people killed in the Second World War,[124] and in a world that was threatened by the real possibility of a nuclear holocaust; however, they had to remain silent about their own government's responsibility for international tension and the arms race, about the fate of conscientious objectors, about Soviet dissidents (Christian or otherwise), about Soviet occupation of the Baltic States, Soviet domination of Eastern Europe, Soviet intervention in Hungary, Czechoslovakia, and Afghanistan (and, for that matter, about Stalin's failure to foresee the danger represented by Nazi Germany).

122. Ibid., 46.
123. Shchipov, "Interreligious Relations," 89.
124. This is the figure quoted by Western historians such as Chris Bellamy in his *Absolute War*, 2. Hosking claims that Soviet losses "were probably some forty times those suffered by Britain or some seventy times those suffered by the United States" (Hosking, *History*, 261).

Some Baptists did try to make known a different picture of life in the USSR from what appeared in approved publications. The *samizdat* ("self-published") material of the 1960s and 1970s presented news of the underground church and those in prison for their faith, and a good deal of this material found its way to the West. The Cold War as an international phenomenon did not figure in it, but the illicit publications certainly constituted a prolonged appeal not to believe official Soviet propaganda about freedom of religion. In official Baptist publications as well, the Cold War was marginalised to a greater extent than this paper might suggest—the bulk of the material in *Bratskii vyestnik*, for example, was on biblical, doctrinal, and historical topics.

Reflecting on the significance of the collapse of the Soviet empire, Tony Judt says: "After 1989 nothing—not the future, not the present and above all not the past—would ever be the same."[125] Re-examining the past has become a major industry in the former Soviet lands, and "new history" is one of the many phrases generated by the collapse of communism. The tensions and contradictions that the Soviet era generated have not altogether gone. Russian Baptists have to live with them just as we all have to live with the dark parts of our past, whether individual or corporate. In the Cold War era the Soviet Baptists demonstrated what Tatyana Nikolskaya sees as the "survival capability" that has marked Russian Protestantism throughout its history.[126] Sergei Filatov claims that "Protestantism in Russia is not just growing, it is also becoming more and more Russian."[127] This process of growth will entail not only making the most of opportunities for the future but taking an honest look at the past.

---

125. Judt, *Postwar*, 3.

126. Nikolskaya, *Russkii protestantizm*, 300. The compound word *zhiznyesposobnost* is difficult to translate. Dictionary equivalents such as "vitality" or "viability" are a bit weak. The term means literally "life ability"

127. Filatov, "Protestantism," 102.

Bibliography

BAPTIST NEWSPAPERS

The Baptist Times, 1954.
Bratskii vyestnik, 1945–1982.

OTHER

AUCECB. *Istoriya evangel'skikh khristian-baptistov v SSSR* [*History of Evangelical Christians-Baptists in the USSR*]. Moscow: AUCECB Publications, 1989.
Bellamy, Chris. *Absolute War: Soviet Russia in the Second World War*. London: Pan Macmillan, 2007.
Bourdeaux, Michael. *Religious Ferment in Russia: Protestant Opposition to Soviet Religious Policy*. London: Macmillan, 1968.
Bullock, Alan. *Hitler and Stalin: Parallel Lives*. London: Harper/Collins, 1991.
Chadwick, Owen. *The Christian Church in the Cold War*. London: Penguin, 1993.
Dowling, Maurice. "Baptists in the Twentieth-Century Tsarist Empire and the Soviet Union." In *The Gospel in the World: International Baptist Studies*, edited by D. W. Bebbington, 209-32. Carlisle, UK: Paternoster, 2002.
Ellis, Jane. *The Russian Orthodox Church: A Contemporary History*. London: Croom Helm, 1986.
Filatov, S. "Protestantism in Postsoviet Russia: An Unacknowledged Triumph." *Religion, State and Society* 28 (March 2000) 93-103.
Hastings, Adrian. *A History of English Christianity, 1920–1990*. London: SCM, 1991.
Hosking, Geoffrey. *History of the Soviet Union: 1917–1991*. Final ed. London: Harper/Collins, 1992.
Johnson, Hewlett. *Christians and Communism*. London: Putnam, 1956.
Kolarz, Walter. *Religion in the Soviet Union*. London: Macmillan, 1961.
Judt, Tony. *Postwar: A History of Europe since 1945*. London: Penguin, 2005.
Lonsdale, Kathleen, ed. *Quakers Visit Russia*. London: Friends House, 1952.
Lord, F. Townley. *Baptist World Fellowship: A Short History of the Baptist World Alliance*. Nashville: Broadman, 1955.
Mitrokhin, L. N. *Baptizm:Istoriya i sovremmenost* [*The Baptist Movement: Past and Present*]. Saint Petersburg: Izdatel'stvo Russkogo Khristianskogo Gumanitarnogo Instituta, 1997.
Nikolskaya, Tatyana. *Russkii protestantizm i gosudarstvennaya vlast' v 1905–1991 godakh* [*Russian Protestantism and the State, 1905–1991*]. Saint Petersburg: The European University, 2009.

Patterson, W. M., and R. V. Pierard. "Recovery from the War and the Advance to Maturity." In *Baptists Together in Christ, 1905–2005: A Hundred-Year History of the Baptist World Alliance*, edited by R.V. Pierard, 100–127. Falls Church, VA: Baptist World Alliance, 2005.

Payne, E. F. *The Baptist Union: A Short History*. London: Carey Kingsgate, 1958.

Popov, Alexander. "The Evangelical Christians-Baptists in the Soviet Union as a Hermeneutical Community: Examining the Identity of the All-Union Council of the ECB (AUCECB) through the Way the Bible Was Used in Its Publications." PhD thesis, University of Wales, 2010. Available online: http://www.moscowseminary.info/alexandpopov/alexanderpopovdissertation.zip

Pospielovskii, Dmitri. *Russkaya pravoslavnaya tserkov' v XX-om vyekye* [*The Russian Orthodox Church in the Twentieth Century*] Moscow: Respublika, 1995.

Prokhorov, Constantine. "The State and the Baptist Churches in the USSR (1960–1980)." In *Counter-Cultural Communities: Baptistic Life in Twentieth-Century Europe*, edited by K. G. Jones and I. M. Randall, 1–62. Milton Keynes, UK: Paternoster, 2008.

Rowe, Michael. *Russian Resurrection*. London: Marshall Pickering, 1994.

Russell, D. S. "Church/State Relations in the Soviet Union: Recollections and Reflections on the 'Cold War' Years." *Baptist Quarterly* 36, no. 1 (1995) 21–28.

Ryazanova-Clarke, Larissa, and Terence Wade. *The Russian Language Today*. London: Routledge, 1999.

Savinskii, S. N. *Istoriya evangel'skikh khristian-baptistov Ukrainy, Rossii, Bielorussii, 1917–1967* [*A History of the Evangelical Christians-Baptists in the Ukraine, Russia, and Bielorussia, 1917–1967*]. Saint Petersburg: Bibliya Dlya Vsiekh, 2001.

Sawatsky, W. *Soviet Evangelicals since World War II*. Scottdale, PA: Herald, 1982.

Shchipkov, Aleksandr. "Interreligious Relations in Russia after 1917." In *Proselytism and Orthodoxy in Russia: The New War for Souls*, edited by John Witte Jr. and Michael Bourdeaux, 77–92. Maryknoll, NY: Orbis, 1999.

Underwood, A. C. *A History of the English Baptists*. London: Baptist Union/Kingsgate, 1947.

Volkogonov, Dmitri. *Stalin: Triumph and Tragedy*. Trans. Harold Shukman. London: Weidenfeld & Nicholson, 1991.

Wallace, S. J. "The Union of Evangelical Christians and Baptists in the USSR." *Baptist Quarterly* 21, no. 1 (1965) 37–42.

Walters, Philip. "A Survey of Soviet Religious Policy." In *Religious Policy in the Soviet Union*, edited by S. P. Ramet, 3–30. Cambridge: Cambridge University Press, 1993.

Wardin, Albert W., Jr. *Evangelical Sectarianism in the Russian Empire and the USSR*. Lanham, MD: Scarecrow, 1995.

8

Baptists and the War in Vietnam: Responses to "America's Longest War"[1]

NATHAN A. FINN

IT HAS BEEN CALLED "America's Longest War" and "The War Nobody Won."[2] Despite sometimes acrimonious debates in the last decade over the War on Terror, the Vietnam War remains arguably the most divisive American military campaign since the Civil War. Vietnam both coincided with and contributed to a time of significant cultural upheaval marked by political assassinations, racial violence, student protests, presidential scandal, and the proliferation of sex, drugs, and rock 'n roll. Between 1963 and 1975, the baby-boomers came of age, resulting in heated, frequently generationally-charged debates in living rooms, on college campuses, at political conventions, and at denominational meetings. Many of these localized conflicts centered around the controversial military conflict in Vietnam.

The Indochinese Peninsula seemed to many people to be an unusual place to which to commit American military personnel. Nevertheless, the Kennedy administration viewed it as strategic real estate during some of the most heated days of the Cold War. French Indochina, comprised of present-day Vietnam, Laos, and Cambodia, had been occupied by the French since 1887. From 1946 to 1954, the communist-led Viet Minh

---

1. The research for this paper was made possible with the help of a Lynn E. May Study Grant from the Southern Baptist Historical Library and Archives (SBHLA) in Nashville, Tennessee. I want to express my appreciation to SBHLA director Bill Sumners and archivist Taffey Hall for their assistance. Additional help was provided by my research assistant, Joshua Herring.

2. Herring, *Longest War*; Karnow, *Vietnam*, 2.

engaged in a war of independence against the French. When the communist revolutionaries defeated French forces in 1954, the negotiated peace, called the Geneva Accords, temporarily partitioned Vietnam into northern and southern halves along the 17th parallel. Though free elections were mandated, they were never held, and the region became permanently divided into the communist Democratic Republic of Vietnam in the North and the democratic State of Vietnam in the South.

During the First Indochina War, the Eisenhower administration committed significant American funds to aiding French efforts against the Viet Minh. Eisenhower hoped to prevent communists from establishing a beachhead on the Indochinese Peninsula. For Eisenhower, securing a democratic Vietnam was central to "containment," the foreign policy doctrine that America had applied to communist states since the end of the Second World War.[3] Like Eisenhower, President Kennedy viewed a free and democratic Vietnam as crucial to halting the advance of global communism. After Kennedy's assassination in 1963, President Lyndon Johnson adopted a policy of escalation that included deploying ground forces to defend South Vietnam and conducting strategic aerial bombing campaigns inside North Vietnam. Though Congress never formally declared war on North Vietnam, over 58,000 American troops died in combat, most of them between 1965 and 1973.

Like Americans in general, Baptists in the United States were divided over the Vietnam War. Many Baptists were generally sympathetic to American policy in Vietnam. For example, the Southern Baptist Convention (SBC) mostly supported the war, at least in its denominational public statements. Though he acknowledges a minority of anti-war dissenters in the SBC, David Settje argues:

> The Southern Baptist Convention proclaimed a conservative point of view that both reflected the typical anti-Communist rhetoric of American society and also emerged from actual Baptist experiences within Communist nations. Often articulating a generic fear of communism as evil and atheist, Southern Baptist Convention leaders and members buttressed this anxiety with proof of Communist oppression obtained from missionaries and fellow believers inside Communist countries.[4]

---

3. Containment was first articulated in an anonymous journal article by George Kennan, a staffer in the US State Department during the Truman administration. See Kennan, "Sources." See also Patterson, *Grand Expectations*, 114–15.

4. Settje, *Faith and War*, 33.

Settje claims SBC leadership sided with politically conservative Americans by promoting a broadly pro-war platform within the Convention.[5] Though other scholars argue for a greater range of opinions within the SBC, most agree that Southern Baptists in general supported America's Vietnam policy more than other major denominations, and were at least nervous about those who voiced public opposition to the war.[6] Other theologically conservative Baptists such as the American Baptist Association (ABA) and many independent fundamentalist Baptists also tended to support American military involvement in Southeast Asia.[7]

Some Baptist groups mostly opposed the war. Both the American Baptist Convention (ABC) and Progressive National Baptist Convention (PNBC) embraced a mostly anti-war posture in their denominational pronouncements about the conflict. These two denominations, along with some seminary professors and students in the SBC, "were of the opinion that it was the duty and right of the church to voice prophetic concern over the situation in Vietnam."[8] If most Southern Baptists reflected the position of American conservatives, the ABC, the PNBC, and anti-war dissenters in the SBC reflected broader trends among the so-called New Left, a movement that made opposition to Vietnam a central plank in its cultural agenda.[9] Their position also echoed that of other mainline Protestants, including most of the denominations active in the National Council of Churches.[10] Of course, there were also pro-war minorities in these groups, just as there was an anti-war minority in the SBC.

This chapter will not attempt any sort of comprehensive assessment of Baptists and Vietnam; that deserves a dissertation-length treatment. My aspirations are much more modest. This chapter assumes a diverse range of responses among Baptists—we should expect no less from a tradition that values liberty of conscience and local church autonomy. The chapter is divided into two sections. The first provides an overview of how Southern Baptists, Progressive National Baptists, and American Baptists responded to the war itself. The second section highlights how various Baptist

---

5. Ibid., 68–69.

6. Hall, *Because of Their Faith*, 66; Blevins, "Southern Baptist Attitudes"; Lindley, "Southern Baptists"; Tomlin, "Hawks *and* Doves."

7. Ashcraft, *History*, 339; Rice, *War in Vietnam*.

8. Tomlin, "Hawks *and* Doves," 9.

9. For the New Left's anti-war agenda, see Isserman and Kazin, *America Divided*, 180–86.

10. Hall, *Because of Their Faith*, 51; Settje, *Faith and War*, 62.

individuals and groups responded to three controversial themes or events related to the Vietnam War. Taking the two sections together, we will get a glimpse of Baptist responses to Vietnam at both the macro and micro levels. The chapter focuses most of its attention upon Southern Baptist reactions to Vietnam, though it also demonstrates in broad contours how the other aforementioned Baptist groups responded to the conflict.

BAPTIST HAWKS AND BAPTIST DOVES

In early August 1964, two American naval vessels were allegedly attacked by North Vietnamese torpedo boats while conducting intelligence missions in the Gulf of Tonkin. Though subsequent studies argued that at least one of the attacks never happened, on August 7 Congress passed the Gulf of Tonkin Resolution.[11] The resolution authorized President Johnson to conduct military operations in Southeast Asia without a formal declaration of war. In March 1965, Johnson deployed 3,500 Marines to South Vietnam. By the end of the year, over 200,000 Marines had been deployed to the region. Their mission was originally to defend the South Vietnamese population against the North Vietnamese army and the Viet Cong. The latter was a pro-communist fifth column in South Vietnam that conducted guerilla campaigns south of the 17th parallel.

Scholars agree that most Southern Baptists were in favor of the escalation of military involvement in Southeast Asia. According to Mitchell Hall, Southern Baptists were "the most ardent supporters of military escalation" in Vietnam, along with the Lutheran Church Missouri-Synod, another mostly theologically and culturally conservative denomination.[12] For example, one study found that SBC ministers in Southern California were 82 percent in favor of increasing American military efforts in Vietnam while only 1 percent argued for a cessation of bombing missions in North Vietnam. This was considerably more pro-Vietnam than any other denomination and even the general public; 21 percent of the latter favored halting the American bombing campaign.[13] Southern Baptists in Southern California were possibly more pro-war than their brethren in other states. Darren Dochuk has recently demonstrated that evangelicals in Southern California were significantly more politically conservative in

---

11. Shane, "Vietnam Study."
12. Hall, *Because of Their Faith*, 17.
13. Quinley, "Protestant Clergy."

the 1960s than evangelicals elsewhere, in part because that region was at the epicenter of the post-World War Two military-industrial complex.[14]

Though Southern Baptists in general supported the war, a closer look paints a more nuanced picture. In an article on Southern Baptist responses to Vietnam, Kent Blevins studied denominational resolutions and Baptist state paper editorials from 1965 to 1970. He argues for a subtle evolution in attitudes during the course of the conflict. In 1965, the SBC was characterized by what Blevins called "tacit approval" of American involvement in Vietnam. Between 1966 and 1968, Southern Baptists remained committed to US policy in Vietnam, though there were growing calls for "an honorable and just peace" in Indochina. The years 1969 and 1970 marked a change in tone as a growing number of Southern Baptists expressed hesitation toward and even outright opposition to the war. Yet even during these controversial years, an overwhelming majority of Southern Baptists remained favorable to the war effort.[15]

Gregory Tomlin and Terry Lindley have demonstrated that the annual meetings of the SBC consistently adopted a pro-war posture.[16] Though there was always a minority of "doves" who pushed back against the Convention's support for America's Vietnam policy, the doves never succeeded in persuading the SBC to adopt an even moderately anti-war resolution. Most Southern Baptists supported the Johnson and Nixon administrations throughout the war's duration, and even at the height of the anti-war movement, the Convention was only willing to call for as swift a peace as possible without conceding South Vietnam to the communists. Though undoubtedly pro-war, most Southern Baptists, Tomlin argues, were never uncritical "hawks"; they based their unwillingness to publicly criticize military actions in Southeast Asia on the historic Baptist commitment to the separation of church and state. Simply put, it was not the place of the church to concern itself with military strategy or get involved in the formal peacemaking process.[17]

Many Southern Baptists were especially concerned about any denominational position that could be construed as unsupportive of American soldiers serving in Southeast Asia. In the aftermath of the 1967 Miami Convention, some Baptists interpreted the decisions of the SBC

---

14. Dochuk, *Bible Belt*.
15. Blevins, "Southern Baptist Attitudes."
16. Tomlin, "Hawks *and* Doves"; Lindley, "Southern Baptists."
17. Tomlin, "Hawks *and* Doves," 7–8.

as being disloyal to American military personnel. In Miami, the Convention's Christian Life Commission (CLC) had brought a report that some messengers had thought advocated ending the war in Vietnam. Messengers amended the report to include a statement explicitly supporting continued American military involvement until "an honorable and just peace" was secured. Following the CLC report, Senator Mark Hatfield, an anti-war American Baptist layman from Oregon, delivered what many interpreted as a dovish address.[18] Both the hawkish amendment and the dovish speech were applauded by the Convention, which seemed contradictory to some observers.[19] At least two individuals wrote letters to SBC president Franklin Paschall expressing concerns that the Miami Convention had not appropriately supported American troops. Paschall assured them that the SBC supported American soldiers and agreed that the media had given too much attention to those voicing anti-war sentiments.[20]

Among the most pro-war Southern Baptists were current and former Foreign Mission Board (FMB) missionaries, especially those who had served in South Vietnam. Southern Baptist missionaries in South Vietnam viewed communism as a satanic threat to the gospel and feared that if American forces withdrew from Indochina, it would cripple Baptist witness in that region.[21] Some missionaries even expressed pro-war positions in unlikely places. For example, in a sermon at Crescent Hill Baptist Church in Louisville, Kentucky, former FMB missionary Fred Linkenhoker gave a very positive portrayal of American military personnel in Vietnam. He noted that American soldiers were rebuilding villages, helping place orphans in families, and in some cases even finding opportunities to share their faith with the Vietnamese.[22] Crescent Hill's

---

18. Hatfield was at the time a member of the First Baptist Church of Portland, Oregon, which was an American Baptist congregation. In retirement, Hatfield joined a church affiliated with the Conservative Baptist Association.

19. Lindley, "Southern Baptists," 4–5; *Annual of the Southern Baptist Convention* (1967), 71–72, 292–94.

20. H. Franklin Paschall to Robert L. Dicken, 29 June 1967; H. Franklin Paschall to Mrs. Walter L. Brigman, 20 April 1968; Franklin Paschall Papers, SBHLA, box 14, folder 473.

21. Lindley, "Southern Baptists," 21.

22. Linkenhoker, "Jesus and Vietnam," 8.

pastor, John Claypool, was a leading Convention progressive who was considerably less sanguine about America's Vietnam policy.[23]

Undoubtedly the most famous Southern Baptist during the Vietnam era was evangelist Billy Graham, at that time a member of the First Baptist Church of Dallas, Texas. As a committed anti-communist, Graham was strongly in favor of American involvement in Vietnam and was vocally supportive of Presidents Johnson and Nixon in their prosecution of the war. Graham criticized anti-war protestors and other dovish activists, including his erstwhile friend Martin Luther King, Jr. At President Johnson's request, Graham traveled to South Vietnam during two different Christmas holidays to encourage American troops. During the Nixon administration, Graham continued to support the war, somewhat generally in his public statements but much more specifically in his private correspondence with the President. Graham only backed off in his support of the Vietnam War in the aftermath of the Watergate scandal, an event that chastened Graham's desire to cultivate close personal relationships with politicians.[24]

Despite widespread support for Vietnam, some Southern Baptists dissented from the majority view and expressed hesitancy and even outright opposition to the war. This was especially true of faculty members in denominational colleges and seminaries. As a general rule, their opposition became more strident as the conflict dragged on. In a 1966 article in *The Baptist Program*, New Orleans Seminary theologian William Garman urged Southern Baptists to finance a center for the study of world peace. The proposed center would bring together leading scholars to discuss peace, produce literature promoting peace, and host conferences and symposia for both clergy and laypersons. Garman also suggested Southern Baptists establish a peace library, possibly with regional branches at the six seminaries, and to fund endowed chairs in peace studies at each seminary.[25] Garman's New Orleans colleague, theologian Robert Soileau, summarized biblical teachings on war and peace in a 1967 article in *The Baptist Student*. Though he surveyed both topics, Soileau made little effort to hide his belief that Christian peacemaking efforts are superior to Christian participation in war; he apparently did not see war as a legitimate form of peacemaking.[26]

---

23. Claypool, "Moral Expense."
24. Miller, *Billy Graham*, 93, 96, 108, 138–41; Pierard, "Billy Graham and Vietnam."
25. Garman, "Peace Study Center," 4.
26. Soileau, "War and Peace," 4–5.

Other scholars were less circumspect in their anti-war sentiments. Southern Baptist minister, novelist, and social activist Will Campbell served as the director of the Committee of Southern Churchmen. The organization was devoted to promoting neo-orthodox theology and progressive social ethics among Christians in the South, particularly through its journal *Katallagete: Be Reconciled*. Campbell and his fellow contributors, including Southern Baptist college professors such as Jim Holloway of Berea College, Joseph Hendricks of Mercer University, and G. McLeod Bryan of Wake Forest University, used the pages of *Katallagete* to make a biblical case for progressive ideas, especially racial equality and opposition to the Vietnam War.[27] In 1969, theologian and pacifist James McClendon was terminated from San Francisco University after organizing a group of professors to draft a letter to President Johnson calling for withdrawal from Vietnam. McClendon had been similarly dismissed from the faculty of Golden Gate Seminary in 1966 for encouraging Civil Rights activism among the students.[28]

In a 1968 article in *The Maryland Baptist*, Southern Seminary ethicist Henlee Barnette argued that America should withdraw from Vietnam. He claimed he was not an "absolute pacifist," but argued, "The time is past due for the United States to admit that she has made a mistake by sending troops to Vietnam and withdraw them."[29] Barnette's article appeared alongside a pro-Vietnam piece by *Western Recorder* editor C. R. Daley.[30] Barnette's occupation and family provided him with a unique vantage point on the war. He was an ethicist who had long been interested in peacemaking. He was also the father of two sons; one was a fighter pilot flying missions over North Vietnam, the other a draft resister taking refuge in Sweden. Barnette supported both sons' decisions, citing the historic Baptist emphasis on individual liberty of conscience.[31]

In 1969, Frank Stagg argued that the undeclared war in Vietnam was the immoral product of the American military-industrial complex, and that America should repent of her involvement in Vietnam and halt the war as quickly as possible.[32] The weekend after the article was published,

---

27. Hawkins, *Will Campbell*, 49–53; Miller, "Politics to Reconciliation."
28. Walker, "James McClendon," 101–2; McClendon, "Radical Road."
29. Barnette, "Should? Yes."
30. Daley, "Should? No."
31. Sisk, "Barnette," 89.
32. Stagg, "Christian Conscience and the War in Vietnam," 16.

Stagg expanded his thoughts into a sermon that he preached at Crescent Hill Baptist Church, arguably the most popular church in Louisville among Southern Seminary faculty and students at that time.[33] As hinted earlier, Crescent Hill's pastor John Claypool was opposed to the Vietnam War.

Midwestern Seminary religious education professor Clifford Ingle wrote a strongly anti-war position paper in 1971. Citing reasons both spiritual and political, Ingle claimed he could no longer in good conscience support the Vietnam War. In particular, he bemoaned what he understood to be America's loss of respect among other nations, particularly in Europe. Ingle also outlined eight steps for restoring American credibility, including withdrawing from Vietnam, significantly scaling back the American military, ending the draft, publicly repenting before the United Nations, and adding an emphasis on peace studies to seminary curricula.[34]

Reflecting wider cultural trends, many Southern Baptist students were vocally opposed to the war.[35] Richard Myers, pastor of University Baptist Church in Charlottesville, Virginia, wrote in 1967 on the dilemma the war raised for students. Myers argued that Baptist students will adopt many different views about the war and urged his readers to adopt their respective views with a clear Christian conscience. He also made crystal clear his own opposition to American involvement in Southeast Asia.[36] Many students followed Myers's lead. For example, a Virginia Baptist named Richard McBride, at the time enrolled at Union Theological Seminary in New York, wrote an anti-war letter to the editor of the *Religious Herald* in 1967. McBride argued that the Vietnam War was incompatible with Christian principles and argued for the de-escalation of the conflict. He refused to condemn unequivocally the Viet Cong. He also accused his fellow Virginia Baptists of exalting nationalism over the brotherhood of humanity and urged them to search their consciences

---

33. Stagg, "Christian Conscience and War."

34. Clifford Ingle, untitled paper, 19 April 1971. The original copy of this document is in the Special Collections at Midwestern Baptist Theological Seminary, but a photocopy is available in a folder containing duplicates of Gregory Tomlin's research material for his dissertation, housed in the SBHLA.

35. In an interview with Mark Oppenheimer, former *Home Mission* magazine editor Walker Knight suggested that only about 10 percent of Southern Baptists were opposed to the war, and the majority of that 10 percent were college students. See Oppenheimer, *Knocking*, 176.

36. Myers, "War and Peace."

and oppose the war. McBride's letter provoked harsh criticism from other *Religious Herald* readers.[37]

In a 1970 commencement address at Rice University, graduating senior Jeff Cox argued that most American college students opposed the Vietnam War on moral grounds. Significantly, Cox was president of the Rice Baptist Student Union and spent the summer of 1968 teaching English in Vietnam on a short-term appointment with the Foreign Mission Board.[38] Several students at Belmont University vocally opposed the war between 1969 and 1972. There were at least two vigils held in opposition to the war, though these were quiet affairs that did not disrupt campus activities. Some invited speakers to BSU events were dovish in orientation, including at least one unnamed speaker from the anti-war Fellowship of Reconciliation.[39]

Baptist collegians in the Triangle region of North Carolina were especially anti-war. This area, which includes Raleigh, Durham, and Chapel Hill, is home to several major universities and some of the most socially and theologically progressive churches that were part of the SBC in the 1960s and 1970s. One of these churches, Pullen Memorial Baptist Church in Raleigh, was led at the time by W. W. Finlator, who was arguably the most vocally anti-war pastor in the entire Southern Baptist Convention.[40] Perhaps because of the influence of these progressive churches, the Baptist Student Unions (BSU) at Duke University, the University of North Carolina at Chapel Hill, and North Carolina State University openly advocated leftwing social positions. The state's BSU had been the source of controversy among North Carolina Baptists since the mid-1950s.[41]

Baptist Students Concerned was an organization founded by BSU students in the Triangle in 1968. According to the *Biblical Recorder*, sixteen North Carolinians participated in the efforts of Baptist Students Concerned to dialog about controversial social concerns such as race relations and the Vietnam War with messengers to the 1968 Houston Convention. Their results were mixed; some messengers encouraged

---

37. See McBride, "Christian Responsibility," 3. For the responses, see Causey, "Victory in Vietnam," 12, and Walker, "Another Opinion."

38. Cox, "Silence," 1.

39. Huebner, "Anti-War Movement."

40. See Bryan, *Dissenter*, 11, 18–21, 67, 133–39, 146. Finlator was one of the few Southern Baptists involved in anti-war groups such as the Fellowship of Reconciliation and Clergy and Laity Concerned about Vietnam.

41. Oppenheimer, *Knocking*, 176–78; Finn, "Development,"134.

the collegians, while others urged them to focus on evangelism rather than social issues.[42] Christian Life Commission president Foy Valentine organized a panel discussion with Baptists Students Concerned. Numerous Baptist journalists covered the event, including Baptist Press director W. C. Fields. During the discussion, which was attended by about 250 pastors and leaders, students Ronald Joyner and Terry Nichols argued that many Baptist collegians believed the Vietnam War was fundamentally unjust and immoral.[43] Baptist Students Concerned also attended the 1969 and 1970 Conventions, and though the group did not draw as much press coverage, some messengers were convinced they were a liberal, communist-inspired organization.[44]

Throughout the war, the Christian Life Commission attempted to navigate the differing opinions within the Convention while promoting a generally anti-war policy. CLC staffer Bill Dyal authored a moderately anti-war press release in 1966 titled "The 'Silent Shriek' of Baptists on Vietnam." Dyal called for Southern Baptists to be more vocal in advocating peace in Vietnam, especially in light of the ever-rising body counts in the war-torn country.[45] An undated internal memo written by Dyal in either 1967 or 1968 listed several possible Vietnam-related actions the CLC could take at the 1968 Miami Convention. All of them were meant to promote a swift, just, and peaceful solution to the war. Suggestions included possible resolutions, prospective speakers, potential CLC conferences, and partnering with the seminaries to set up faculty-student dialogs on the topic "Christian Perspectives on War."[46]

In contrast to Southern Baptists, American Baptists and Progressive National Baptists were virtually uniform in their opposition to the Vietnam War. In fact, the latter was one of the first American denominations to go on record officially opposing the war.[47] In addition to formal denominational pronouncements, key leaders in the PNBC agitated against Vietnam. One such leader was leading Civil Rights activist Gardner Taylor, the longtime pastor of the Concord Baptist Church in Brooklyn and

---

42. Druin, "Student Group," 2.
43. Newton, "Concerned Students," 27; Oppenheimer, *Knocking*, 185.
44. Tomlin, "Hawks *and* Doves," 163.
45. Dyal, "Silent Shriek."
46. Dyal, "Memo."
47. Avant, *Social Teachings*, 4.

one of the founders of the PNBC.[48] In his final presidential address before the Convention in 1968, Taylor called for an integrated American society and an end to the Vietnam War.[49]

William A. Jones, also a Brooklyn pastor, was another PNBC leader who was opposed to the war. In October 1965, Jones was one of the speakers at a press conference held by an ecumenical group of Protestant, Catholic, and Jewish clergy. The ministers had signed a declaration defending the right of Americans to protest the government's policy in Vietnam.[50] This declaration helped inspire the formation of Clergy and Laity Concerned about Vietnam (CALCAV), a progressive organization formed in January 1966 that worked closely with the National Council of Churches.[51] In his 1979 book *God in the Ghetto*, Jones argued that militarism was inextricably linked to racism. He noted that President Johnson had declared war on poverty as part of his Great Society while America had never formally declared war on Vietnam. Nevertheless, America spent $2 billion annually on the war on poverty and $3 billion on the conflict in Vietnam.[52]

By far the most significant PNBC critic of the Vietnam War was Martin Luther King, Jr. At the outset of the war, King had been only moderately opposed to the conflict. Though he was calling for a negotiated peace settlement as early as 1965, he initially refused to stage anti-Vietnam rallies along the lines of his marches on Washington DC and Selma, Alabama. King probably refused to take a firm stand against Vietnam because the board of the Southern Christian Leadership Conference, though willing to let King voice his personal opinions about the war, was urging him not to take the focus off of securing full citizenship rights for black Americans.[53] But King was growing increasingly agitated by the war because he feared it was poisoning the popular atmosphere and absorbing funds that he had hoped would finance domestic reform.[54]

---

48. The PNBC was formed in 1961 following Gardner's failed presidential bid in the Northern Baptist Convention against longtime incumbent Joseph Jackson. See Martin, "Formation."

49. Avant, *Social Teachings*, 48.

50. Sibley, "Clergymen," 6.

51. Hall, *Because of Their Faith*, 13–14; Allitt, *Religion*, 101–2.

52. Avant, *Social Teachings*, 62–63.

53. Ling, *Martin Luther King, Jr.*, 258–59.

54. Bartley, *New South*, 363.

Around the same time, King's views on war and peace were in transition. From the beginning he had advocated nonviolent resistance in his desegregation campaigns, but thus far he had not made a wider application of that principle to international affairs. That changed when he received the Nobel Peace Prize in 1964; King viewed this honor as a commission to become a global peace advocate. He moved increasingly toward a more consistently pacifist position, understanding peace as a matter of basic justice. By 1966, he was advocating total withdrawal from the Vietnam War, despite the concerns of other Civil Rights leaders.[55]

On 4 April 1967, King gave a speech titled "Beyond Vietnam" at New York City's Riverside Church. The occasion for the speech was an anti-war rally sponsored by CALCAV, though the event itself was suggested by King and was intended as a national platform for him to come out against Vietnam.[56] Other speakers included Rabbi Abraham Heschel and Amherst College historian Henry Steele Commanger. In his Riverside speech, King called for unilateral withdrawal from the Vietnam War. He claimed the time had come for America to,

> move past indecision to action. We must find new ways to speak for peace in Vietnam and justice throughout the developing world—a world that borders on our doors. If we do not act we shall surely be dragged down the long dark and shameful corridors of time reserved for those who possess power without compassion, might without morality, and strength without sight.[57]

King subsequently became co-chair of CALCAV.[58]

Like the PNBC, the American Baptist Convention frequently and unambiguously adopted an officially anti-war posture. As early as 1965, American Baptists passed a resolution calling for a cease-fire.[59] Later resolutions followed on an annual basis.[60] In protest against the Dow

---

55. Smith, *Ethics*, 126–31.
56. Hall, *Because of Their Faith*, 41–42.
57. King, "Beyond Vietnam."
58. Hall, *Because of Their Faith*, 43.
59. *Annual of the American Baptist Convention* (1965), 73.
60. See *Annual of the American Baptist Convention* (1966), 77–78; *Annual of the American Baptist Convention* (1967), 76–79; *Annual of the American Baptist Convention* (1968), 50, 78, 129–32; *Annual of the American Baptist Convention* (1969), 133–35; *Annual of the American Baptist Convention* (1970), 109–10; *Annual of the American Baptist Convention* (1971), 100–101, 103; *Annual of the American Baptist Convention* (1972), 54–58, 248; *Annual of the American Baptist Convention* (1975), 75–76.

Chemical Company, which produced napalm, the ABC divested itself of its holdings of thousands of shares of Dow stock in 1967.[61] At the 1971 ABC annual meeting, anti-war protestor and ecumenical leader Ruth Rohlfs of Seattle was elected Convention president. Anti-war speakers on the program included future senator John Kerry, then the spokesman for Vietnam Veterans Against the War, and Rev. Jesse Jackson, an ordained minister in the PNBC and a leader in the Southern Christian Leadership Conference.[62] Several American Baptist pastors and denominational employees were also involved in anti-war committees sponsored by the National Council of Churches.[63]

American Baptist scholars periodically spoke out against the war. Two examples will suffice. In the March 1966 issue of the journal *Christianity and Crisis*, the board of editors published a short statement titled "We Protest the National Policy in Vietnam." In the mind of these mainline theologians, American involvement in Vietnam was unjust, ill-conceived, and counterproductive. Among the authors of the statement was Harvey Cox, an American Baptist theologian teaching on the faculty of Harvard Divinity School.[64] In 1968, Prentiss Pemberton, a professor of Christian social ethics and sociology of religion at Colgate-Rochester Divinity School, argued in an article published in *The Christian Century* that Vietnam had become a test of Americans' spiritual integrity. Morally mature Christians understood that anti-poverty initiatives at home were being underfunded due to anti-Communist initiatives in Vietnam. Because it was an election year, Pemberton urged anti-war Americans to take over the Republican and Democratic conventions that were scheduled to meet later that summer.[65]

Because of their shared convictions, anti-war Baptists periodically collaborated. For example, Martin England, a former American Baptist missionary to Burma, and former Southern Seminary New Testament professor Clarence Jordan founded Koinonia Farm in Southwest Georgia in 1942. Koinonia was an intentionally racially integrated community,

61. Hall, *Because of Their Faith*, 132.

62. Rogers, "Peace," 682.

63. See "Notes in Lieu of Minutes." American Baptists Esther Hymes, Grant Gates, Jr., and Kenneth L. Wilson served on this committee. William Dyal of the SBC's Christian Life Commission was also a participant. Baptist Sunday School Board president Clifton Allen was invited to attend, but was not present at the meeting.

64. Editorial Board of *Christianity in Crisis*, "We Protest National Policy."

65. Pemberton and Page, "Translating."

which caused no small amount of trouble in the Deep South during the mid-twentieth century. England used his position with the American Baptist Convention's Ministers and Missionaries Benefit Board to provide aid to Baptist Civil Rights activists such as Martin Luther King, Jr. England, Jordan, and King were not only involved in anti-segregation initiatives, but they were also committed pacifists involved in the ecumenical anti-war organization the Fellowship of Reconciliation. These men and other Baptist progressives were part of a growing interdenominational cadre of Baptist pacifists who argued war was incompatible with biblical Christianity.[66]

EPISODIC BAPTIST RESPONSES TO THE VIETNAM WAR

Like all major events in history, the Vietnam War was the sum of numerous smaller events, many of which provoked reactions from Baptists. This section of the chapter highlights three controversial episodes from the Vietnam War and points to various Baptist responses, especially those from Southern Baptists. It looks at the national moratorium in 1969, the trial of Lt. William Calley in 1970, and the debates over conscientious objection, draft resistance, and granting amnesty to those who dodged the draft.

The National Moratorium

A national moratorium against the Vietnam War was staged at venues across the United States on 15 October 1969. The event was organized by Sam Brown, a Harvard Divinity School student, a former staffer for anti-war Senator Eugene McCarthy's failed presidential bid, and a graduate of the American-Baptist-related University of the Redlands in California. For anti-war activists, the time seemed ripe for peace. In January 1968, the Tet Offensive had soured many Americans toward the war. In 1969, Americans learned that an Army company had massacred women and children in the South Vietnamese village of My Lai in March of the previous year. President Nixon had campaigned with the promise he had a secret plan for ending the war, but by 1969 he implemented a gradual process of "Vietnamization," which included the training of South Vietnamese military forces and the gradual withdrawal of American troops from the region. Several congressmen, including Senator Hatfield, had

---

66. Stricklin, *Genealogy of Dissent*, 54–55, 87–113.

proposed bills calling for an end to the war, though none had yet passed either house of Congress. The idea of a peaceful and respectful national moratorium gained the wide support of liberal religious and university leaders, students, and even politicians.[67]

For the most part, Southern Baptist collegians, seminarians, and professors ignored the moratorium. Most of the fifty-four SBC-related colleges did not observe the moratorium in any formal way. According to Baptist Press (the news service of the Southern Baptist Convention), "Generally, it was the larger Baptist schools on the Eastern Seaboard states that staged moratorium activities which seemed most vocal in opposition to the war, including such schools as University of Richmond in Virginia; Wake Forest University, Meredith and Mars Hill in North Carolina; Stetson University in Florida; and Furman University in South Carolina."[68] At many schools, the moratorium was observed by only a handful of students. For example, at Belmont University a handful of BSU students held a vigil against the war. Foy Valentine of the Christian Life Commission visited the Belmont campus and met with the student protestors.[69]

Two of the six SBC seminaries formally observed the moratorium. According to Baptist Press, at Southern Seminary, "about 300 students and several faculty members declared opposition to the war, wearing black arm bands. The 1,600 seat chapel at the seminary was packed for a showing of a film about war, and discussion afterward lasted so long that about eight professors dismissed their classes." At Golden Gate Seminary, about a third of the 350 students attended a rally where ethicist Arthur Insko spoke on the Christian attitude toward the Vietnam War.[70] Southeastern Seminary did not officially participate in the moratorium, but four students and two faculty members from the school marched in a community-wide observance in downtown Raleigh.[71]

In a speech delivered at Trinity Church in New York City the day following the moratorium, former Johnson Administration staffer and Southwestern Seminary graduate Bill Moyers reflected on the state of the nation at that time. Moyers lamented America's loss of "rectitude in international affairs" and regretted that a generation of young people

---

67. Anderson, *Movement*, 330.
68. Baptist Press, "Baptist Colleges."
69. Huebner, "Anti-War Movement," 9–11.
70. Baptist Press, "Baptist Colleges."
71. Tomlin, "Hawks *and* Doves," 189.

had come of age during an "almost unprecedented period of national disillusionment and self-excoriation." He argued America's "national self-esteem, in fact, is the major domestic casualty of this war." He closed on a somber, but hopeful note: "We seem almost at the point of waking from the long, feverish night of the war with its dreams of violence and despair. And when the awakening comes, if it does not come too late, perhaps then we will begin to understand how near to moral rot we strayed and how near to destruction it brought us."[72]

THE CALLEY AFFAIR

On 16 March 1968 the "Charlie" company of the Army's 11th Infantry Brigade slaughtered as many as five hundred unarmed citizens in the South Vietnamese village of My Lai. The soldiers, under the command of 2nd Lt. William Calley, erroneously believed Viet Cong personnel were hiding in My Lai. Calley and his men massacred the village's inhabitants, even though they found no known enemy combatants. After an initial government cover-up, the American public learned of the My Lai Massacre in 1969. Though all the participants were initially charged, only Calley stood trial. He was court marshaled by a military court and sentenced to life in prison, later changed to three and a half years house arrest. Calley's trial ignited a nationwide debate, in part because Calley claimed he had simply been following orders. Some believed Calley was a cold-blooded murderer, while others claimed he was a hero. Following Calley's court marshal in 1970, Baptists weighed in on the debate in the following months. Most were horrified by Calley's actions and the public's response.

Some used the Calley incident to criticize the American government. Avery Lee, pastor of St. Charles Avenue Baptist Church in New Orleans, argued in an article in his church's newsletter that Calley's conviction was an indictment of "the entire United States government, from the Commander-in-Chief on down."[73] In an editorial in the *Western Recorder*, editor C. R. Daley lamented the fact that Calley was considered a hero in the eyes of many Americans. Daley thought it a shame that soldiers guilty of lesser crimes were in military prison while Calley was simply under house arrest. Daley believed that:

72. Moyers, "Remarks at Trinity Church."
73. Lee, "Lee Lines."

> All other members of the military system share Lt. Calley's guilt to varying extents. This goes from the U.S. president as commander-in-chief . . . all the way down through the Pentagon, every general and other officer giving orders to the troops. Also American society including the one writing these words must also confess its guilt in not finding long ago a way to settle conflicts apart from barbarism characteristic of precivilized man.[74]

As evidenced in Daley's editorial, the events surrounding Calley's trial had led this one-time vocal supporter of the Vietnam War to soften his earlier support of America's war policy.

An editorial in the *Indiana Baptist* took a similar position. The editorial criticized Calley's supporters and critics for emotional reactions to the young officer's trial. The piece argued that the responses to the Calley controversy betray a "national guilt complex" because most Americans had come to believe we were losing a war in which we should probably have never engaged. The editorial closed by hoping the Calley trial had pricked the nation's conscience and would hasten American withdrawal from Vietnam.[75] Southern Baptists who wrote about My Lai and Calley were horrified by the incident and what it said about American culture. They were also convinced that the entire government shared some of the blame, though they fell short of insinuating deliberate malfeasance on the part of the White House or Army Chief of Staff William Westmoreland.

American Baptists also spoke out against the My Lai Massacre. For example, George W. Swank was an American Baptist pastor in Tacoma, Washington, and a chaplain in the United States Naval Reserve. In the wake of Calley's trial, Swank wrote an article for *The American Baptist* titled "Calley, Calvary and the Christian." Swank argued that killing is antithetical to the teachings of Christ and claimed that Calley was only guilty of doing what air bombing campaigns do all the time—murder civilians for military ends. He hoped Calley's conviction would "be seen as a major step forward for civilization" and contribute to a more peaceful future.[76] Swank echoed the concerns of religious progressives, who were convinced that the war itself was immoral and that My Lai pointed to widespread criminal activity the military was perpetrating in Vietnam.[77]

---

74. Daley, "Can Brutality Make a Hero," 4.
75. "Calley and Conscience," 2.
76. Swank, "Calley."
77. Hall, *Because of Their Faith*, 111–12.

Conscientious Objection and Draft Resistance

The twentieth century witnessed considerable diversity in how Baptists approached questions of war and peace, normally depending upon world events at any given time.[78] Because of their commitment to liberty of conscience, Southern Baptists and American Baptists had long recognized the rights of religiously motivated pacifists. Southern Baptists had officially affirmed the right of individuals to serve as conscientious objectors since 1940. Those who wished to receive this status simply needed to fill out a registration card to be kept on file with the SBC's Executive Committee. If necessary, the Convention could then in turn intervene on behalf of the individual with the Selective Service System. The American Baptist Convention formed the American Baptist Volunteer Services to place conscientious objectors in places of alternate service. Placement was coordinated with the approval of the federal government and in cooperation with the Convention's Home and Foreign Mission Societies. During the Vietnam War, both denominations continued to affirm the right of individuals to conscientiously object, though not without controversy within sectors of the SBC.

Following the Tet Offensive in 1968, a growing number of Baptists began to advocate conscientious objection. In April of that year, Wayland University sociology professor Alban Wheeler argued that Christians sometimes have a responsibility to dissent from unjust social and political positions—even when those positions are popular with the general public. He claimed that the right to principled dissent is rooted in the Christian tradition and is intrinsic to American democracy.[79] Later that year, Jay Kaufman, president of the BSU at Johns Hopkins University, wrote a defense of conscientious objection in the same periodical. Kaufman harshly criticized those who insisted it is the patriotic or Christian position to participate in the war. In Kaufman's thinking, objectors, draft-dodgers, and those who burned their draft cards were heroes and martyrs who ought to be honored for their principled stand.[80]

In November of 1969, *The Baptist Student* published an article that explained all the different ways a draft-eligible individual could avoid military service, both legal and illegal. The article explained all the various draft classifications, coached draftees on how to navigate the Selective

---

78. See Hinson, "Baptist Attitudes"; Sehested, "Conformity and Dissent."
79. Wheeler, "Right of Dissent."
80. Kaufman, "Refuse of the World," 3.

Service System's bureaucracy, and included extensive information about the qualifications for conscientious objectors and the expectations placed upon them for civilian service in aid of the American cause. The editors also reprinted the 1940 SBC resolution on conscientious objection.[81] By all appearances, the editors of *The Baptist Student* were at least implicitly encouraging conscientious objection.

That same year, Fred Miller, the minister of youth at First Baptist Church of Austin, Texas, wrote an article for *Home Missions* magazine titled "Why I Am a Conscientious Objector." In the article, Miller recounted the bureaucratic hoops he had to jump through to file as a conscientious objector and some of the social ostracism he had faced from family and friends for taking this step.[82] In 1970, Paul Simmons wrote a dissertation at Southern Seminary advocating selective conscientious objection. Simmons was subsequently appointed to a permanent faculty position teaching ethics at Southern.[83] That same year, William Deneke wrote a ThM thesis at Southern describing the experiences of Southern Baptist draft resisters who had fled to other countries.[84]

State conventions periodically debated conscientious objection and related issues. For example, at the 1968 annual meeting of the Baptist State Convention of North Carolina (BSCNC), Southeastern Seminary student Terry Nichols proposed a resolution affirming conscientious objection. Nichols was a recent graduate of North Carolina State University and was the founder of Baptist Students Concerned. Nichols had previously indicated his own conscientious objection to the war during the panel discussion Foy Valentine had hosted with Baptist Students Concerned during the 1968 Houston Convention.[85] After intense debate, Nichols's resolution was referred to the Convention's Council on Christian Life and Public Affairs, which was to report back the following year.[86] In response to Nichols's resolution, the council published a brochure affirming conscientious objection in 1969, an action that was approved by messengers to that year's BSCNC annual meeting. Sensing a possible opportunity, W. W. Finlator proposed a resolution affirming the right to draft resistance,

81. Phillips, "The Draft."
82. Miller, "Why I Am a Conscientious Objector," 22–24.
83. Simmons, "Selective Conscientious Objection."
84. Deneke, "War Resistance."
85. Audio Reel of Baptist Students Concerned News Conference, 1968 SBC Annual Meeting, available in the SBHLA.
86. *Annual of the Baptist State Convention of North Carolina* (1968), 58–59, 79–81.

a far more controversial topic. Finlator's resolution was subsequently referred to the Council on Christian Life and Public Affairs, where it was ignored.[87] As Terry Lindley notes, "while the messengers accepted the publication of a pamphlet on conscientious objection, it [sic] drew a hard and fast line at amnesty for draft dodgers."[88]

Controversy over conscientious objection spilled over at the 1972 SBC annual meeting in Philadelphia. A resolution was proposed that simply restated the Convention's position on conscientious objection, which had first been affirmed in 1940. The resolution ignited heated debate, with several messengers arguing that conscientious objection was an insult to American troops in Southeast Asia. One messenger argued that conscientious objection and the right to engage in war cannot both be right, since that would imply Scripture was contradictory in allowing for both views. The resolution ultimately failed, actually reversing the SBC's previous position endorsing the right of conscientious objection. The resolution likely failed because it followed on the heels of another unsuccessful resolution proposing that the SBC support amnesty for draft resisters.[89]

If conscientious objection was a hot discussion, the debate over amnesty was nuclear. An overwhelming majority of Southern Baptists were firmly opposed to granting amnesty to those who had burned their draft cards or fled to other countries to avoid service in Vietnam. But as Gregory Tomlin notes, "The draft was perceived by a small but growing number of Southern Baptists as an enemy to liberty of conscience."[90] This included many draft-age students, a handful of professors, and progressive pastors such as Finlator. The most notable scholar to argue for amnesty was Henlee Barnette. In an article in *The Christian Century*, Barnette argued for amnesty for draft resisters, a group that included his son. He contended that amnesty honored the individual conscience of those who opposed the war and hoped that amnesty would bring about national reconciliation in a nation divided over the late war.[91] Though most Southern Baptists did not share Barnette's view, ironically enough it was a Southern Baptist layman, President Jimmy Carter, who granted amnesty to draft-resisters on his first day in office in 1977.

87. *Annual of the Baptist State Convention of North Carolina* (1969), 68–70, 84, 165–66.
88. Lindley, "Southern Baptists," 17.
89. Ibid., 24–25.
90. Tomlin, "Hawks *and* Doves," 243.
91. Barnette, "Agony and Amnesty," 1133–34.

Not surprisingly, American Baptists were far more favorable to both conscientious objection and draft resistance. The ABC passed several resolutions affirming the right of individuals to dissent from the war and publicly endorsed amnesty for draft dodgers. For example, in 1969 the ABC adopted a statement that argued:

> Just as we respect the convictions of those young men who have felt that it was their duty to comply with the draft laws of our country by entering military service, so we also respect those young men who, during recent years, have resisted the draft because of their sincere conviction that participating in the Vietnamese war would constitute a violation of their consciences . . . [W]e call upon the President of the U.S. to grant amnesty upon the cessation of hostilities or upon the major reduction of American forces for all persons who are either in jail or outside the country due to their acts of conscience against the war in Vietnam and the Selective Service system.[92]

In 1975, the ABC reaffirmed their position on amnesty, arguing that it was necessary to forgive draft resisters in the interests of national reconciliation.[93]

Many individual American Baptists publicly advocated amnesty. For example, in an article in *The American Baptist*, peace activist Malcolm Broome argued that Christians should support amnesty for draft resisters. Broome put forth three lines of argument. First, amnesty reflects the best of the Judeo-Christian tradition upon which the church has been built and upon which America was founded. Second, amnesty recognizes the importance of liberty of conscience, a principle rooted in the Judeo-Christian tradition and uniquely emphasized by Baptists. Third, draft dodgers and deserters actually took the moral high ground, since American involvement in Southeast Asia was very possibly immoral. Broome concluded by noting that granting unconditional amnesty to draft resisters would not cure America's war disease but it could be a first step in the right direction.[94]

---

92. *Annual of the American Baptist Convention* (1969), 133.
93. *Annual of the American Baptist Convention* (1975), 75–76.
94. Broome, "Church and Amnesty," 28–29.

CONCLUSION

It has been said that where two or three Baptists are gathered together, one finds at least a half dozen opinions. Though it is a tired cliché, to be sure, this old saw proves true when it comes to the Vietnam War. Some Baptists, especially within the SBC and among other theologically conservative groups, supported the war effort, viewing it as strategic in America's Cold War against communism. Other Baptists, including some denominations such as the American Baptist Convention and Progressive National Baptist Convention, voiced significant opposition to the conflict. Virtually all Baptists desired to see peace in Southeast Asia and elsewhere, though they disagreed over the best means to bring about that peace. In other words, when it came to Vietnam, Baptists were very much like Americans in general.

One final observation about Southern Baptists in particular: during the Vietnam era, one's position on the war was something of an indicator where he or she would stand on the inerrancy controversy that engulfed the Convention during the final two decades of the twentieth century. Many of the progressives who dissented against the Convention's mostly pro-war stance opposed the resurgent conservatives who captured the denomination's key leadership positions in the 1980s and 1990s. The same conservative grassroots that supported American intervention in South Vietnam mobilized in support of inerrantist presidential candidates in the SBC. Similar trends were also evident in how both groups responded to the Reagan Revolution that captured the Republican Party and controlled the White House during the 1980s. When it came to Southern Baptists, response to "America's Longest War" was a prelude to various responses during the Convention's Longest War, though in the case of the inerrancy controversy, it was a war that somebody actually won.

Bibliography

Primary Sources

Newspaper and Magazine Articles

Barnette, Henlee. "Agony and Amnesty." *Christian Century*, September 29, 1971, 1133-34.

———. "Should the United States Get Out of Vietnam? Yes." *The Maryland Baptist*, 6 September 1968, 8.

Broome, Malcolm L. "The Church and Amnesty." *The American Baptist* (January 1974) 28-29.

"Calley and Conscience." *Indiana Baptist*, 14 April 1971, 2.

Causey, L. E., Jr. "Victory in Vietnam." *Religious Herald*, 9 February 1967, 12.

Cox, Jeff. "You Cannot Silence a Generation." *The Rice Thresher*, 3 September 1970, 1.

Daley, C. R. "Can Brutality Make a Hero?" *Western Recorder*, 17 April 1971, 4.

———. "Should the United States Get Out of Vietnam? No." *The Maryland Baptist*, 6 September 1968, 3, 8.

Druin, Toby. "Student Group of 16 Small but Makes Impression on SBC." *Biblical Recorder*, 15 June 1968, 2.

Editorial Board of *Christianity in Crisis*. "We Protest the National Policy in Vietnam." *Christianity in Crisis* 26 no. 3, 7 March 1966, 33-34.

Garman, William S. "A Peace Study Center for Southern Baptists?" *The Baptist Program*, October 1966, 4.

Kaufman, Jay. "The Refuse of the World: Students Speak Out." *The Baptist Student*, October 1968, 3.

McBride, Richard. "Christian Responsibility and Government Policy." *Religious Herald*, 12 January 1967, 3.

Miller, Fred. "Why I Am a Conscientious Objector." *Home Missions*, May 1969, 22-24.

Myers, Richard. "War and Peace: Our Present Dilemma." *The Baptist Student*, April 1967, 11-15.

Newton, Jim. "Concerned Students Urge Pastors to Face Issues." *Biblical Recorder*, 15 June 1968, 27.

Pemberton, Prentiss, and Homer Page. "Translating Anti-war Protest into Political Power." *The Christian Century*, 3 January 1968, 11-14.

Phillips, David. "The Draft." *The Baptist Student*, November 1969, 24-27, 49.

Quinley, Harold E. "The Protestant Clergy and the War in Vietnam." *Public Opinion Quarterly* 34 (Spring 1970) 43-52.

Rogers, Cornish. "Peace Breaks Out at ABC Convention." *Christian Century*, 2 June 1971, 682.

Sibley, John. "Clergymen Defend Right to Protest Vietnam Policy." *New York Times*, October 26, 1965, 6.
Soileau, Robert R. "War and Peace: A Biblical Look." *The Baptist Student*, April 1967, 4–5.
Stagg, Frank "Christian Conscience and the War in Vietnam." *Arkansas Baptist*, 17 April 1969, 16.
Swank, George W. "Calley, Calvary and the Christian." *The American Baptist*, July-August 1971, 24–26.
Walker, Wilbur. "Another Opinion about Vietnam." *Religious Herald*, 9 February 1967, 12–13.
Wheeler, Alban L. "The Right of Dissent." *The Baptist Student*, April 1968, 11–14.

SBHLA = Southern Baptist Historical Library and Archive Materials

CLC/ERLC = Christian Life Commission/Ethics and Religious Liberty Commission
Claypool, John R. "The Moral Expense of War." Crescent Hill Sermons 2.5, 6 February 1966, 1–6. CLC/ERLC Papers, SBHLA, Box 24, folder 20.
Dyal, William M., Jr. Interoffice Memo to Foy Valentine and Ross Coggins, undated. CLC/ERLC Papers, SBHLA, box 141, folder 13.
———. "The 'Silent Shriek' of Baptists on Vietnam." Christian Life Commission press release, 13 December 13, 1971, CLC/ERLC Papers, SBHLA, box 24, folder 8.
King, Martin Luther, Jr. "Beyond Vietnam." Speech given at Riverside Church, New York City, 4 April 1967. CLC/ERLC Papers, SBHLA, box 24, no. 2.
Lee, G. Avery. "Lee Lines." *The Tower*, St. Charles Avenue Baptist Church, 18.14, 4 April 1971, no pages, CLC/ERLC Papers, SBHLA, box 24, folder 11.
Lindley, Terry. "The Southern Baptists and the Vietnam War: A Diversity of Opinion." Undated. SBHLA.
Linkenhoker, Fred D. "The Man Jesus and Vietnam." Crescent Hill Sermons 4.25, 10 December 1967, 1–8. John Claypool Papers, SBHLA, box 1, folder 8.
Moyers, Bill. "Remarks at Trinity Church, New York, October 16, 1969." CLC Papers, SBHLA, box 24, folder 10.
"Notes in Lieu of Minutes, Reporting the Ad Hoc Meeting on Vietnam Action." 7 January 1967, CLC/ERLC Papers, SBHLA box 24, folder 9.
Stagg, Frank. "Christian Conscience and War." Sermon preached at Crescent Hill Baptist Church Louisville, Kentucky, 20 April 1969. Manuscript in CLC/ERLC Papers, SBHLA, Box 24, folder 21.

Other Primary Sources

Annual of the American Baptist Convention, 1965–1975.
Annual of the Baptist State Convention of North Carolina, 1968, 1969.
Annual of the Southern Baptist Convention, 1967.
Baptist Press (news service). "Baptist Colleges, Seminaries Support, Ignore Moratorium." 17 October 1969, 2–4. Online: http://media.sbhla.org.s3.amazonaws.com/2871,17-Oct-1969.pdf.

Deneke, William Thomas. "War Resistance and Emigration: A Study of American Exiles Who Have Refused to Participate in the War in Vietnam." ThM thesis, The Southern Baptist Theological Seminary, 1970.

Rice, John R. *War in Vietnam: Should Christians Fight?* Murfreesboro, TN: Sword of the Lord, 1966.

Simmons, Paul D. "Selective Conscientious Objection as an Approach to Christian Participation in Warfare." PhD diss., The Southern Baptist Theological Seminary, 1970.

Secondary Sources

Allitt, Patrick. *Religion in American since 1945: A History.* New York: Columbia University Press, 2003.

Anderson, Terry H. *The Movement and the Sixties: Protest in America from Greensboro to Wounded Knee.* New York: Oxford University Press, 1995.

Ashcraft, Robert, ed. *History of the American Baptist Association: Commemorating the Seventy-Fifth Meeting, June 20-22, 2000.* Texarkana, TX: Baptist Sunday School Committee of the American Baptist Association, 2000.

Avant, Albert A., Jr. *The Social Teachings of the Progressive National Baptist Convention, Inc., since 1961: A Critical Analysis of the Least, the Lost, and the Left-out.* New York: Routledge, 2003.

Bartley, Numan V. *A History of the South.* Vol. 11, *The New South, 1945–1980: The Story of the South's Modernization.* Baton Rouge, LA: LSU Press, 1995.

Blevins, Kent B. "Southern Baptist Attitudes toward the Vietnam War in the Years 1965-1970." *Foundations* 23, no. 3 (1980) 231–44.

Bryan, G. McLeod. *Dissenter in the Baptist Southland: Fifty Years in the Career of William Wallace Finlator.* Macon, GA: Mercer University Press, 1985.

Dochuk, Darren. *From Bible Belt to Sunbelt: Plain-folk Religion, Grassroots Politics, and the Rise of Evangelical Conservatism.* New York: Norton, 2010.

Finn, Nathan A. "The Development of Baptist Fundamentalism in the South, 1940–1980." PhD diss., Southeastern Baptist Theological Seminary, 2007.

Hall, Mitchell K. *Because of Their Faith: CALCAV and Religious Opposition to the Vietnam War.* New York: Columbia University Press, 1990.

Hawkins, Merrill M., Jr. *Will Campbell: Radical Prophet of the South.* Macon, GA: Mercer University Press, 1997.

Herring, George C. *America's Longest War: The United States and Vietnam, 1950–1975.* 4th ed. Columbus, OH: McGraw-Hill, 2001.

Hinson, E. Glenn. "Baptist Attitudes toward War and Peace since 1914." *Baptist History and Heritage* 39 no. 1 (Winter 2004) 98–116.

Huebner, David E. "The Anti-War Movement at Belmont in the Late 1960's and Early 1970's: An Oral Documentation and History of the Debate on the Vietnam War on the Belmont Campus." Paper submitted for the Belmont Remembers: The Belmont Oral History Project, Belmont University, 7 December 2004.

Isserman, Maurice, and Michael Kazin. *America Divided: The Civil War of the 1960s.* New York: Oxford University Press, 2000.

Karnow, Stanley. *Vietnam: A History.* 2nd ed. New York: Penguin, 1997.

Kennan, George. "The Sources of Soviet Conduct." *Foreign Affairs* 25 (July 1947) 566–82.
Ling, Peter J. *Martin Luther King, Jr.* Routledge Historical Biographies. London: Routledge, 2002.
Martin, Sandy Dwayne. "The Formation of the Progressive National Baptist Convention: Gardner Calvin Taylor and the PNBC in Historical Context." *Baptist History and Heritage* 46 no. 1 (Spring 2011) 18–27.
McClendon, James William, Jr. "The Radical Road One Baptist Took." *Mennonite Quarterly Review* 74 (2000) 503–10.
Miller, Steven P. *Billy Graham and the Rise of the Republican South*. Philadelphia: University of Pennsylvania Press, 2009.
———. "From Politics to Reconciliation: *Katallagete*, Biblicism, and Southern Liberalism." *Journal of Southern Religion* 7 (2004). No pages. Online: http://jsr.fsu.edu/Volume7/Millerarticle.htm.
Oppenheimer, Mark. *Knocking on Heaven's Door: American Religion in the Age of Counter-Culture*. New Haven: Yale University Press, 2003.
Patterson, James T. *Grand Expectations: The United States, 1945–1974*. The Oxford History of the United States. New York: Oxford University Press, 1996.
Pierard, Richard V. "Billy Graham and Vietnam: From Cold Warrior to Peacemaker." *Christian Scholars Review* 10 (September 1980) 37–51.
Sehested, Ken. "Conformity and Dissent: Southern Baptists on War and Peace." *Baptist History and Heritage* 28 no. 2 (April 1993) 3–18.
Settje, David E. *Faith and War: How Christians Debated the Cold and Vietnam Wars*. New York: New York University Press, 2011.
Shane, Scott. "Vietnam Study, Casting Doubts, Remains Secret." *The New York Times*, October 31, 2005. Online: http://www.nytimes.com/2005/10/31/politics/31war.html.
Sisk, Ronald D. "Henlee Hulix Barnette (1911–2004): Principlist in the Southern Seminary Tradition." In *Twentieth-Century Shapers of Baptist Social Ethics*, edited by Larry L. McSwain, 81–98. Macon GA: Mercer University Press, 2008.
Smith, Ervin. *The Ethics of Martin Luther King, Jr.* Studies in American Religion 2. New York: Edwin Mellen, 1981.
Stricklin, David. *Genealogy of Dissent: Southern Baptist Protest in the Twentieth Century*. Lexington, KY: University Press of Kentucky, 1999.
Tomlin, Gregory D. "Hawks *and* Doves: Southern Baptist Responses to Military Intervention in Southeast Asia, 1965–1973." PhD diss., Southwestern Baptist Theological Seminary, 2003.
Walker, Graham B. "James McClendon (1924–2000): Theologian of the Ethical Stance." In *Twentieth-Century Shapers of Baptist Social Ethics*, edited by Larry L. McSwain, 99–119. Macon GA: Mercer University Press, 2008.

Author Index

Adams, Doug, 115
Allen, Richard, 143
Barnette, Henlee, 210
Barrett, John, 156–57
Berger, Carl, 106
Blevins Kent, 207
Brewster, Paul, L, Sr., 32
Chadwick, Owen, 175
Cox, Harvey, 216
Cross, Anthony, 1
Dekar, Paul, 2
Dochuk, Darren, 206
Dowling, Maurice, 169
Ehrenburg, Ilya, 177
Ellis, Jane, 176
Finn, Nathan A., 203
Fuller, Andrew, 32, 34, 37–43
Garman, William, 209
George, Timothy, 2, 7, 9, 11
Heath, Gordon L., 98
Helwys, Thomas, 4, 7, 8, 9, 13, 14, 16
   Declaration of Faith, 12
   An Advertisement or Admonition, 12; his death, 15
Ingle, Clifford, 211
Linder, Robert D., 150
Lindley, Terry, 207, 223
Lorkin, H.F., 1, 3, 24–25
Marpeck, Pilgram, 6, 7
McBride, Richard, 211

McClendon, James, 210
McGregor, J.F., 21
Myers, Richard, 211
Nikolskaya, Tatyana, 189, 197–98
Orr, J. Edwin, 151
Page, Robert, 99
Pemberton, Prentiss, 216
Porter, Andrew, 109
Price, Richard, 143
Riedemann, Peter, 5
Robertson, James Tyler, 58
Samson, Jane, 109
Savinskii, Sergii, 175, 188–89
Settje, David, 204–5
Simmons, Menno, 6
Smith, Wheaton, 105
Smyth, John, 4, 7, 8, 9, 13, 14
   Defense of de Ries' Confession, 10
   Short Confession of Faith in XX Articles by John Smyth, 10
   his death, 11
   Propositions and Conclusions, 11
Soileau, Robert, 209
Stacey, C.P., 99
Stagg, Frank, 210–11
Stanley, Brian, 106
Tarr, Leslie, 119
Tomlin, Gregory, 207
Walters, Philip, 176
White, Barrie, 22, 24

Subject Index

Anabaptists, 4, 5, 7, 8
  The Schleitheim Confession, 5

Bagust, Gwendolyn, Driver, 156
Baldwin, Cyril, 156
Baptist, All-Union Council of
  Evangelical Christians-Baptists,
  170, 176, 179–81, 195, 198
  American Baptist, 59, 60, 63, 68, 72,
  74, 77, 88, 89, 93, 94, 181, 183,
  215–16, 220–21, 224
  American Baptist Association, 205,
  213
  American Baptist Convention,
  224–25
  American Baptist Volunteer
  Services, 221
  Australian Baptists, official church
  membership, 152, Hobart
  Baptist Tabernacle, 153–54
Baptist Students Concerned, 212–
  13, 222
Baptist World Alliance, 162
Bratskii vyestnik, 177, 179–81, 183–
  84, 191–94, 200
Canadian Baptist, 98, 111, 143–45
Connections to Britain, 103
Council of Churches of the
  Evangelical Christians-Baptists,
  195, 198
Council of the Union of Evangelical
  Christians-Baptists, *protest to the
  Security Council*, 183–84
Christian Life Commission, 208,
  213
*The Faith and Practise of Thirty
  Congregations*, 17

Particular Baptist First London
  Confession, 16–17
Progressive National Baptist
  Convention, 205, 213–15
Southern Baptists, 205, 207, 209,
  213–14, 217–18, 221, *in favor
  of increasing American military
  efforts*, 206
Southern Baptist Convention, 204–
  5, 207, 212, 223, 225
Unregistered Baptists, 196–97
Barnes, William, 154
Barnette, Henlee, 223
Brezhnev, Leonid, 193
Broome, Malcolm, 224
Bychkov, Alexei, 198

Calley, William, 217, 219–20
Carter, Jimmy, 1, 193, 198, 223
Chamberlain, J.C., 162
Clergy and Laity Concerned about
  Vietnam (CALCAV), 214
Council of Prisoners' Relatives, 196–97

Denck, Hans, 7
De Ries, Hans, 4; Waterlander
  confession of faith, 9

English Puritanism, 4

Filatov, Sergei, 170, 200
Fifth Monarchy, 19, 20, 23
Finlator, W.W., 212, 222–23
Forward Movement, Check earlier, 139,
  143

Glasnost, 196

Subject Index

Graham, Billy, 194, 209
Gulf of Tonkin Resolution, 206

Hancox, Phil, 156, 163–65
Hobbs, Flora, Sergeant, 156
Holloway, W.H., 162
Holmes, Elkanah, 64
Hubmaier, Balthasar, 7

Initsiativniki, 195–96, 198

Just war, 13, 15, 38, 53, 60–61, 78, 162

Karyev, Alexander, 184, 191, 193
Khrushchev, Nikita, 189
    Khruschev Thaw, 184, 188
    Anti-religion campaign, 190, 195
Kiffen, William, 21, 22
Korea, bombing, 183–84
Kryuchkov, Gennadi, 195

Law on Religious Associations, 176
Lewis, Arthur, 184
Lockie, Gladys, Sergeant, 155
Luther, Martin, Peasant's Revolt, 7

Mahdi, 110
Martin Luther King, Jr., 1, 24, 192, 209, 214, 217
Mennonites, *Waterlander Mennonites*, 4, 7, 13, 14, 15
Miami Convention, 1967, 207–8
Mitskevich, Artur, 188
Münster, 6
    John of Leiden, 6
    Münsterites, 7
Murton, John, 15
My Lai, 217, 219–220

Napoleon, 32–57
National Council of Churches, 205, 214
Newton, Louie, 181–82
Nile Expedition, 98–115

Orgkomitet, 195
Passive resistance, 20
Patterson, Margaret, Sergeant, 155
Perestroika, 196
Pietism, 4
Popov, Alexander, 170–75
Prokofiev, Alexei, 195

Quinn, John Wyndham, 156

Rippon, John, 36

SALT II, 193
Second Gulf War, 2
Separatism, 4
Shields, Rev. T.T., 115, 147,
Shute, Betty, Sergeant, 155
Stewart, Ailsa, 155
Stillman, Samuel, 91
Swank, George W., 220
Syektanty, 189–91

Taylor, Gardner, 213
Tookey, Elias, 15, 16
Tserkovniki, 190

Viet Cong, 206, 211, 219
Viet Minh, 203–4
Vietnam War, 2, 192, 203–4, 206, 209–15, 217–18, 220–21, 225
    "Christians against the Vietnam War", 193
Vins, Georgii, 195, 198

Wannan, Elsie, 156
War of 1812, 58–97
West, Gwendolyn, 156
Wilson, J.B., 162
World War One, 115–49
World War Two, 159–68
Wright, Gilbert, 162, 164–65

Zhidkov, Yakov, 182–87
Zwingli, Huldrych, 7